THE BATTLE FOR GERMANY

H. Essame

SAPERE
BOOKS

THE BATTLE FOR GERMANY

Published by Sapere Books.
24 Trafalgar Road, Ilkley, LS29 8HH
United Kingdom

saperebooks.com

ISBN: 978-0-85495-169-7.

TABLE OF CONTENTS

INTRODUCTION

The history of the invasion of North-West Europe in 1944 up to the end of the Battle of Arnhem is a well-charted sea. Less has been written concerning the Battle for Germany which began in late September and ended on Luneburg Heath and at Rheims in the first days of May 1945. And yet it is one of the most illuminating and ominous phases of World War Two. It witnessed the astonishing revival of the German Army in the West after a defeat which any other nation would have regarded as final. It demonstrated the immense strength of the well-conducted defence even in an age of highly mechanised war. It showed that the Allied command of the air was only a decisive factor when combined with the operations of the land armies. It emphasised the peculiar difficulties of winter warfare, not least in the maintenance of troop morale. It also illustrated many of the difficulties which inevitably arise in the command of an Allied Force, especially one whose components are open to democratic criticism in the press and on the radio. Finally it culminated, during the fatal months of April and May, in political misjudgement by the Western Allies with regard to the USSR, for which the penalty is still being paid a quarter of a century later.

My aim in writing this book has been to meet the need, felt by those who themselves took part in the Battle for Germany or who lived through the period, for a simple account of what happened, why it happened in the way it did and what the consequences were both for the day and for the future. I have been further stimulated to write by the embarrassing questions raised by two of my grandsons nearing the age of 12, after they had rummaged among my books and papers in search for skeletons in the cupboard of their ancestors.

My approach to the subject is frankly influenced by the late Field-Marshal Wavell's remarks at the end of three lectures delivered in 1938 to an undergraduate audience at Trinity College, Cambridge. Summing up he said:

> What I have tried to show you is that military history is a flesh and blood affair, not a matter of diagrams and formulas or of rules; not a conflict of machines but of men. In the lecture hall of a French infantry school which I once attended was written from Ardent du Picq: 'The man is the first weapon of battle, for it is he who brings reality to it. Only the study of the past can give us a sense of reality and show us how the soldier will fight in the future.'
>
> When you study military history don't read outlines on strategy or the principles of war. Read biographies, memoirs, historical novels.... Get at the flesh and blood of it, not the skeleton. To learn that Napoleon won the campaign of 1796 by manoeuvre on interior lines or some such phrase is of little value. If you can discover how a young unknown man inspired a ragged, mutinous, half-starved army and made it fight, how he gave it the energy to march and fight as it did, then you will have learnt something.

In committing my reflections to paper a quarter of a century after the event I am conscious of my own limitations and prejudices. They are those to be expected from a professional soldier who spent nearly four years of his life with the infantry in operations against the Germans in North-West Europe. I had the good fortune as an infantry subaltern to survive the battles of the Somme, Arras, Passchendaele, the German Offensive of March 1918 and the final advance. In the Second War, I commanded an infantry brigade from Normandy to the

Baltic. My sympathies are therefore with the majors, the captains, the subalterns and the warrant and non-commissioned officers in the front line rather than with the denizens of the higher headquarters and corridors of power. This bias the reader must discount for himself.

In both wars it seemed to me that the overriding problem at the front was the maintenance of morale. In this respect, in the First War almost every possible mistake was made. In the Second War, Alexander, Montgomery and Slim handled this fundamental problem with an imaginative efficiency which approached genius. How it came about that the British Army emerged from the Battle for Germany with its morale higher that at any time in its long history is the main theme of this book.

H.E.

CHRONOLOGY

SEPTEMBER
3: Fall of Brussels
4: Fall of Antwerp
26: End of Battle of Arnhem

OCTOBER
2: Start of Battle of Scheldt estuary
18: Brussels Conference

NOVEMBER
8: End of Battle of Scheldt estuary
16: Bradley's offensive on Roer and in Hürtgen forest
28: Antwerp open

DECEMBER
7: Maastricht Conference
16: Start of Ardennes campaign

JANUARY
12: Russian winter offensive
25: Capture of Roermond triangle completed

FEBRUARY
4-10: Yalta Conference
8: Start of Battle of Rhineland ('Veritable', 'Grenade', and 'Blockbuster')

MARCH

7: Remagen Bridge captured
10: End of Battle of Rhineland
22/23: Patton crosses Rhine at Oppenheim
23/24: Montgomery's Rhine crossing

APRIL

1: Ruhr encircled
12: Death of Roosevelt. Bradley reaches Magdeburg
18: All resistance in Ruhr ceases
25: Patton reaches Czechoslovak border
30: Hitler dead

MAY

2: Berlin falls to Russians
4: German surrender to Montgomery
7: German surrender to Eisenhower at Rheims. Russians enter Prague

1: THE STRANDED WHALE

If I had been in the Commander-in-Chief's shoes, I would
have marched straight away on Berlin.
Marshal Suvorov on Saltykov's victory over Frederick the Great at
Kunersdorf, 1759

Dawn on 26 September 1944 broke over the dark swirling
waters on the Neder Rijn near the village of Driel, wet and
grey. German machine-gunners on the far bank crept down
amongst the reeds and skimmed the waters of the river. Little
fountains marked the points where mortar bombs and shells
from the high ground of the Westerbouwing bluff struck the
water. The debris of many boats and men struggling in the
water marked the hits. The guns of XXX Corps in the suburbs
of Nijmegen opened up and built up a thin fog of smoke over
the river. The Engineers of 1st Canadian Army and 43rd
Wessex Division had struggled all night to rescue what
remained of 1st Airborne Division. As the darkness faded each
trip became more hazardous. So strong was the current of the
Neder Rijn that most of the canvas assault boats had long since
swirled downstream. Only the Canadian storm boats could
take it. There were still about 100 men on the far bank. A
young Canadian officer took over a load of life belts and left
them there. He made two final trips: on each he brought back
a boatload of exhausted men. On the first he had five
casualties; on the second, hardly a man got across unhit; many
were dead. The Engineers had done all they could. Any further
attempt would merely result in useless sacrifice of life. Under
heavy shell fire from Arnhem they fell back from the bank,

taking with them the few boats they had been able to recover from the river to such of their lorries as the Germans had not put to flames.

Montgomery's desperate eleventh-hour endeavour to canalise the drift of the Anglo-American advance after the Battle of Normandy had failed. His last chance of getting a bridgehead over the Rhine in 1944 had gone.

On the Eastern front, the Russian summer offensive, launched at the time of the Normandy landing, had reached the borders of East Prussia in the north. In the centre the Russians were now outside Warsaw but still 300 miles from Berlin; in the south they had driven into Rumania and secured the Ploesti oilfields. For the time being, however, they too had shot their bolt. Until the winter frost hardened the vast and bottomless plains of Poland, no further Russian advance could be expected. Meanwhile, on the Italian front, Alexander's Army Group faced the formidable defences of the Gothic Line. If the four battle-experienced American divisions and the French mountain divisions had not been withdrawn from him for the landing in the South of France he might well have broken through. Now, with the approach of winter, he faced stalemate.

In the West, Eisenhower had recreated a situation closely resembling the Old Front Line of World War One; his forces were strung out on a 600-mile front, like some gigantic Leviathan marooned in the shallows by the receding tide. Montgomery's 21st Army Group stretched all the way from near Zeebrugge to the Dutch eastern frontier. The Germans still held the seaward approaches to Antwerp and were still in a position to bombard London with long-range rockets. Bradley's 12th Army Group, with the 1st United States Army around Aachen and the 3rd Army between the Ardennes and

Verdun, had been halted at the Western Wall. Here, with petrol supplies exhausted, all hope of breaking through the concrete fortifications had gone. To the south, the 6th Army Group sprawled from Nancy to Belfort. In the rear, the 9th US Army, as yet unblooded and full of the valour of ignorance, was moving up from Brittany. This was dispersion of effort with a vengeance. Although Eisenhower had some 56 full-strength divisions on the Continent, eight of them could not be moved for want of transport. For every 10 miles of front he could only deploy less than a division. With his forces still dependent for their sustenance on the Normandy beach-head, he now faced an administrative collapse. By the end of September it was slowly becoming apparent to all that, until the port of Antwerp could be opened, there was no further prospect of continuing the advance into Germany.

Ever since the days of Hannibal it had been a platitude that the climax of any battle should be an annihilating pursuit. This had not followed the overwhelming defeat of the 7th and 15th German Armies in Normandy. Instead, since 1 September, when Eisenhower officially assumed direct command of the Allied Land Forces, they had advanced not on a broad front but on several uncoordinated fronts. Discussion of the Broad versus Narrow Front controversy properly belongs to the Battle for Normandy. There is no point in delving deeply into its complex issues here. It will suffice to say that for Montgomery's concept of concentration on a narrow front to have succeeded, the decision would have had to be taken towards the end of August, when he first put the proposal forward, to enable Eisenhower's vast logistic staff to provide adequate backing. The last chance of its success, if implemented, would have come on 4 September when the British 11th Armoured Division captured Antwerp and could, if pressure had been applied and support given, have cleared the approaches as well. There were then two feasible courses open to Eisenhower. The first was the Montgomery plan for a concentrated drive across the Rhine backed by all the Allied administrative resources. This plan, in view of the chaos behind the German lines at the time, might at least have secured a bridgehead over the Rhine in September. The other course was to leave the enemy garrisons still holding out in the Channel ports to the care of the vast Allied air forces and, masking them with the minimum troops, concentrate immediately the whole of Montgomery's Army Group and 1st US Army on opening up Antwerp. If Eisenhower had done either of these things, his armies would at least have been spared the frustration to which they were now condemned. The Arnhem effort was too ambitious and too late.

Injustice to Eisenhower, the problem which faced him was by no means as simple as Montgomery claimed. As an American, he could hardly be expected to allow the laurels of the final defeat of the Germans to fall to the British — despite the fact that they had stood alone in 1940 and that the United States had only entered the war 18 months later when forced to do so by the Japanese. In fact, the Anglo-American Alliance had ceased to be one between equals. The Americans were now the predominant partner and conscious of the fact. Moreover, United States public opinion would never have tolerated the idol of the press, the flamboyant Patton, being arrested in full cry. A reverse would probably have resulted in the downfall of Roosevelt in the presidential election due in November and the relegation of Eisenhower himself to the retired list. His own generals, Bradley, Patton and Hodges, would have resented serving under Montgomery, firstly because he was British and secondly because he was

Montgomery. Patton was six years senior in the Army to Eisenhower and had behind him a record of front-line service in World War One and in North Africa and Sicily which his Supreme Commander lacked. Finally, Eisenhower had received no indication from his government of the postwar settlement in Europe the United States wished to achieve. So far as he was concerned, the Soviet Union was an ally. Lacking a political aim and the political guidance he was entitled to expect, he conceived it to be his duty to defeat the Germans in accordance with the plan approved by his master, Marshall, the United States Chief of Staff, and leave it to the politicians to sort the mess out afterwards.

As a result of this uncertainty he failed to take a firm grip of his command and seize the fleeting opportunity of striking the single concentrated blow which in the opinion of von Rundstedt, who reassumed the command of the German forces in the West on 4 September, 'would have torn the German front to pieces'. Instead, for what he considered good reasons at the time, his inaction had the effect of condemning the Allies and the people of Germany to endure another winter of war and punished the governments of the United States and Great Britain for their failure to educate their commanders in time of peace and properly to brief them in war. For the atmosphere of the American Army before 1939 had not been calculated to develop commanders with the qualities of Marlborough; nor had that of the British Army been likely to foster leaders combining both political sense and battlefield expertise. Sandhurst and West Point had their virtues: neither, however, before 1939 could be described as a hotbed of intellectuals.

Both Eisenhower and Montgomery were slow to realise the serious nature of the situation. When the operations at Arnhem closed down, Montgomery, with Eisenhower's approval, turned to a project for a thrust by 2nd Army south and south-east from Nijmegen between the Rhine and the Maas to link up with 12th US Army Group's intended advance towards Cologne, as a preliminary to crossing the Rhine. At the same time 1st Canadian Army with its existing resources was to concentrate on clearing the approaches to Antwerp. It soon became apparent, however, that the large German forces on the flanks of the 'Market Garden' salient would have to be pushed back across the Maas before 2nd Army's advance could be contemplated and that 1st Canadian Army would need additional help in clearing the approaches to Antwerp. On 8 October he therefore put into cold storage for the moment the thrust towards the Ruhr and ordered all effort to be concentrated on Antwerp operations, with 'complete priority without any qualifications whatsoever', and on clearing up the large enemy bridgehead west of the Maas. On the same day Eisenhower suddenly reached the conclusion that the Canadians were unlikely to clear the 60-mile estuary of the Scheldt before November. Stung to unequivocal action at last, he warned Montgomery that unless Antwerp was put in a workable condition by the middle of November, Allied operations would come to a standstill. Montgomery was thus finally left in no doubt of the importance Eisenhower attached to the opening of the Scheldt with all speed. 'Of all our operations from Switzerland to the Channel', wrote Eisenhower, 'I consider Antwerp of first importance and I believe that the operations designed to clear up the entrance require your personal attention.' He went on to deal with the subject of command, making it plain that he proposed to continue in the dual role of Supreme Commander and Commander of the Allied Land Forces and that, if

Montgomery after receiving his views still classed them as unsatisfactory, 'an issue would exist which would have to be settled by higher authority'. The threat of the sack was clear. Montgomery must knuckle under or go in the interests of Allied accord. Like a bank manager Eisenhower reminded the British that they were living on an overdraft and that they could only continue to do so on the bank's terms.

In principle, so far as the command situation was concerned, Montgomery knew he was in the right. The dangers of continuing two distinct roles were self-evident. He had no intention, however, of becoming a martyr in a cause temporarily lost. At least the two were of one mind with regard to the importance of opening Antwerp. Mindful perhaps of the maxim of the Duke of Wellington that the best test of a great general is to know when to retreat and to do it, he dutifully replied:

> You will hear no more on the subject of command from me.... I have given you my views and you have given your answer. I and all of us will weigh in one hundred per cent to do what you want and we will pull it through without a doubt. I have given Antwerp top priority in all operations in 21 Army Group and all energies and efforts will now be devoted towards opening up the place. Your very devoted and loyal subordinate.

The wildly optimistic hopes of September extending from the British Cabinet right down to the front line, that the war would be over by Christmas thus finally vanished as the days shortened and the weather worsened. With them also vanished for ever British claims to an equal voice in the decisions of the Alliance. From now onwards, the Americans, providing most of the logistic backing of the campaign and with already twice as many troops in the theatre as the British, would call the tune. There is, therefore, in the strategic controversies of the rest of the war in Europe an air of unreality. Whatever policy the British urged, the American view was bound to prevail.

In the actual strategic situation there was an element of the ludicrous. The Western Allies, with twice as many men as the Germans, two and a half times as many tanks, and air forces 23 times the size of the Luftwaffe, backed by the inexhaustible resources of the United States in money, men and material, must (provided they were directed from above with a minimum of elementary common sense) eventually swamp the Germans with the inevitability of an avalanche. Meanwhile, however, the unpalatable truth had to be faced that the initiative had been temporarily lost, that the German Army was still prepared to fight with the skill and tenacity it had shown since 1939 in country which discounted the great Allied preponderance in armour and motor transport, and that the long winter months lay ahead. The infantry soldier — British, Canadian and American — must gain the victory which air and armoured might in the halcyon days of September had failed to achieve.

On 26 February 1944 Bernard Shaw had met Montgomery in Augustus John's studio where he was having his portrait painted in case he did not survive the war. That night he wrote to Augustus John:

> Take that old petrol rag that wiped out so many portraits of me (all masterpieces) and rub out this one till the canvas is blank. Then paint a small figure looking at you straight from above as he looked at me from the dais. Paint him at full length (some foreground in front of him leaning forward with his knees bent back gripping the edge of his camp stool), and his expression one of piercing scrutiny, the eyes unforgettable.

The background: the vast totality of desert Africa. What a nose. And what eyes.... Fancy a soldier being intelligent enough to want to be painted by you and to talk to me.

Bernard Shaw, who in his plays had never missed a chance of pouring contempt on the profession of arms, had nonetheless sensed the essential steel-like strength of the man. Churchill's epithet 'that Cromwellian figure' hit the mark: in another age he might well have stepped into the shoes of the great Lord Protector.

In any attempt to assess the character of Montgomery account must be taken of three major influences — firstly of his father who, in his son's eyes, had many of the qualities of a saint; secondly of the traditions of his regiment and the Army; and finally of his front-line experience in World War One. He had been severely wounded in action, had lived through the muddle of 1914 and 1915, and in 1916 and 1917 had witnessed the wanton waste of attacks delivered without surprise and adequate support, the almost insane persistence in battles long since lost, the treatment of men as if they were expendable material. Haunted and perhaps embittered by his experience, he had emerged with the profound conviction that morale is the most important factor in war, that a commander carries a responsibility both to God and to his country for ensuring that human life is expended as wisely and economically as possible compatible with success, and that professional incompetence is not only the ultimate military sin but morally unforgivable as well.

To him, a man's duty to his country came before everything. Amusement was only justifiable as the means of increasing capacity for further work in the cause of duty. Physical fitness was an obsession heightened by the loss of a lung in the thirties. The Seven Deadly Sins were deadly: they took a man's mind away from his duty. With this faith went the conviction that he had been personally selected by the Almighty to lead the fight against the hosts of Satan, of which Hitler was the embodiment. Total abstinence from drink and tobacco further enhanced his conviction of moral superiority over his contemporaries (with the exception of Alanbrooke). For him there were moral and military principles on which no compromise was possible. Simplicity should be the keynote of life and war. It is unfortunate that he never met Mahatma Gandhi. The two, stimulated no doubt by glasses of orange juice, would have found much in common: agreement on ultimate aims and morals and profound divergence of view on the means.

There were two sides to Montgomery's military make-up: the academic and the practical. Instances of commanders excelling in both are very rare. Like Frederick the Great, Montgomery had devoted his youth and life before 1939 to military study and reflection. He has said that most of his conceptions were based on the practice of Napoleon: the Chief of Staff system, the small Advanced Headquarters and the liaison officers, the need for meticulous planning, the importance of the delegation of authority, the fitting of the right man to the job and above all the importance of morale. As a Staff College instructor and later as a commander, he had proved himself a brilliant lecturer, at home with a large map, blackboard and pointer. He could describe a complex situation with amazing lucidity and sum up a long exercise without the use of a single note. He looked straight into the eyes of the audience when he spoke. He had a remarkable flair for picking out the essence of a problem, and for indicating its solution with startling clarity. It was almost impossible to misunderstand his meaning, however unpalatable it might be. In argument he was formidable and ruthless: quick as a ferret to detect faulty reasoning or half-truths (some said 'and about as lovable') and to see through bluff. At the High Level Exercises held at Camberley in the winter of 1940-41 only Alanbrooke could shut him up.

At no time in his career had there ever been any doubt on the part of his subordinates as to who was in command. As Polybius said of Hannibal: 'One man and one mind directed all.' Like Wellington, whom he much resembled, every plan he ever made had been thought out to the last detail: it had to be. Unlike the Americans in North-West Europe, he commanded Britain's last army and had to pinch and scrape. All his plans seemed simple: in fact from Alamein onwards they always embodied an element of subtle deception, calculated to catch his opponent off balance. Despite his insistence on making his own plans, he could nonetheless delegate authority. Within the sphere of the tasks allotted to them, he allowed his subordinates considerable latitude. Once they were selected, he gave them his trust and backed them up through thick and thin so long as they were successful. They were well-chosen, at least for his purpose. A few were brilliant, especially his Chief of Staff de Guingand.

Underpaid and ill-equipped by the Government between the wars, the Army before 1939 still tended to regard itself partly as an instrument of war and partly as a social institution. Some officers rose to high rank by virtue of their social charm and private means as much as by military merit. Montgomery had neither the means nor the inclination to waste his time with the trivialities of the social round. He reserved such charm as he possessed for the young and unimportant. To them he could be very kind. Had there been no World War Two, it is doubtful whether he would have risen above the rank of brigadier. At Sandhurst he had not endeared himself to higher authority. His report speaks of a 'troublesome and erratic figure', 'far too self-opinionated and grievously lacking in the polished manner one would like to see in a Sandhurst Cadet'.

His rise to high rank had been characterised only too frequently by bitter opposition both from above and from below. He had made few friends among his contemporaries and some enemies — equally ambitious men. Some unfortunately were now on Eisenhower's staff. After his victories in the Western Desert and in Normandy he now stood out as the most successful British commander since Wellington. He was obviously aware of the fact — an attitude not likely to appeal to the equally career-orientated American commanders, men from an equally narrow cultural background, with whom he had to cooperate. Sociability and the will to compromise are seldom the mark of dedicated men. They would have unanimously summed Montgomery up as the reverse of the Rotary ideal — the good mixer, who off duty could swap stories and play cards over a bottle of whisky. Equally irritating was the fact that he obviously did not care whether he was liked or not. He was as God made him and saw no reason for presuming to improve on His handiwork. Later Eisenhower went on to become head of a great political party and President of the United States. It is impossible to imagine Montgomery in a similar role. In his make-up there were none of the qualities which make a successful politician: this may well be one of the main reasons why his soldiers trusted him.

The British have a deep sympathy for the man who, however eccentric, has the courage to be himself. From the dark days of 1940 this austere man had captured the imagination and inspired the trust of the men in the ranks. From the start he had taken all under his command irrespective of rank into his confidence, stated frankly what he intended to do and how he was going to do it, convinced them that his plans were good, that they had the tools for the job and that success under his leadership was certain if they played their part. He had an almost uncanny ability to reach right down to the troops and to see beyond them to the homes from which they came. These men's lives were in his care; behind every one of them was a woman; their lives must not be thrown unnecessarily away. He and they together would see the business through.

With the collapse of the German armies in Normandy had come high hopes that the war was near its end. In the early days of October Montgomery's soldiers suddenly realised that it must now drag on through the winter. At home the civil population had suffered 130,000 casualties in air raids, more than half of them women and children. Since D-Day 5,000 flying bombs had descended on London. Now the bombardment by long-range rockets from Holland had started. Letters arrived from home telling men that their families had been destroyed. For the men who received them the light went out of life. A conscript army is a reflection of the nation as a whole. Many of the troops had been separated from their families for over four years. No people in World War Two except the Russians made a greater demand on its women than the British. Meagre rations, war strain, family bereavement and matrimonial disaster were now the theme of the soldiers' mail from home. The arrival of the American and Canadian troops in England had been welcomed with gratitude and such scanty hospitality as could be offered. Their presence however had an evil side. Better-paid and with material resources such as silk stockings and canned food at their disposal — luxuries long beyond most people's reach — and with the bogus glamour of Hollywood heroes, some had not been slow to take advantage of the weakness of women separated from their husbands. German propaganda was quick to exploit this chink in the British armour. In early October, leaflet shells began to descend within the British lines containing indecent pictures depicting the alleged activities of American troops in England. 'Why get maimed or killed and make your family suffer when you could easily desert and stay safe as a prisoner of war?' The wording and the pictures were crude, but the point often went home. To be effective propaganda should contain an element of truth, and this the pictures did.

With 12 millions out of her employable population of 22 millions either serving in the Armed Forces or on war production, Britain had stretched herself to the limit. To continue the war to 1945, the Services needed 225,000 more men. The Ministry of Labour could promise only 140,000; the bottom of the manpower bucket had been scraped. At the end of the Normandy battle, Montgomery had had to break up the 59th Division and divert considerable numbers of anti-aircraft gunners to fill the depleted ranks of the infantry. All the British divisions had lost more than 50 per cent of the men who had landed on D-Day and afterwards. In the 15th Scottish, 43rd Wessex and the 2nd and 3rd Canadian Divisions the losses had been considerably higher. The casualties in company commanders, subalterns, warrant officers and NCOs, the junior leaders who really close with the enemy, had been disproportionately heavy. The 50th Northumbrian, 51st Highland and 7th Armoured Divisions had come all the way from Alamein and were understandably tired. Henceforward, to keep the Army in the field, battles must be fought with as little as possible expenditure of human life consistent with success.

The outlook for the men in the ranks of the British Army was black. The drift of Allied strategy since early September had landed their armies against the concrete defences of the Western Wall and in the flat, featureless, low-lying country of Holland, intersected every 100 yards or so by dykes and canals, traversed by roads only a foot or so above bottomless reclaimed marshes — country in which the enormous Allied preponderance in armour and mechanical equipment was virtually useless and in which the air arm could only deliver bludgeon blows remote from the battlefield. Higher direction, determined to some extent by men with little or no experience of war at the cutting edge, had lowered the contest to the level of a soldier's war in which the will and courage of the captain, subaltern and soldier to get to grips with the enemy must be the deciding factor in conditions not unlike those of World War One.

Realising all this, understandably resentful of his own downgrading to the command of an Army Group on a level with Bradley and Devers, disillusioned about Eisenhower's ability as a Supreme Commander, outraged at the violation of what he considered to be fundamental principles, uncertain of the support of his own countrymen on Eisenhower's staff, Montgomery turned grimly to the task of opening up the Scheldt and moved his tactical headquarters to the vicinity of Antwerp. He had ordered the clearing-up of the estuary; he would now see that it was done efficiently, economically and as humanely as possible within the limits of his power.

2: THE GERMANS RALLY

A Conqueror, like a cannon ball, must go on. If he rebounds, his career is over.

Wellington

In World War One the Intelligence summaries emanating from the Higher Command were known to the front-line men as 'Comic Cuts', a pink paper with a wide circulation amongst schoolboys and workers. In misappreciation of the actual situation at the end of August and the first half of September, the Allied Intelligence staffs sank to a level only reached by Brigadier-General Chatteris, Haig's Chief Intelligence Officer at the time of the Passchendaele battles in 1917. During the last days of August the Intelligence summaries, both British and American, were almost unanimous: the Germans had been knocked right out of the ring. The end of the war was in sight. Eisenhower's own Intelligence staff in the summary for the week ending *2* September declared that the German Army was 'no longer a cohesive force but a number of battle groups, disorganised and even demoralised, short of equipment and arms'. On 8 September, the Combined Chiefs of Staff Joint Intelligence Committee in Washington concluded that the German armies would surrender piecemeal and that 'it was improbable that any organised resistance under German High Command could continue beyond 1 December 1944 ... it might end even earlier'. Even Major-General Sir John Kennedy, the normally sober Director of Military Operations at the War Office, recorded in a note made on 6 September: 'If we go at the same pace as of late, we should be in Berlin by the

28th. The Germans have only ten to twenty divisions to man their frontier, as against a requirement of seventy or eighty. We should therefore go into Germany quickly. Then we may be faced with guerilla fights.' This overweening optimism infected even the unemotional, dependable Commander of United States 1st Army, Lieutenant-General Courtney H. Hodges. On crossing the German border on 16 September, he ordered a reconnaissance in force of the Western Wall about Aachen. On the 15th he hoped for an enemy collapse in the Rhineland and the 'enormous' strategic advantage of seizing the Rhine bridges intact. As late as the last week of September, he believed that, given two weeks of good weather, Allied air and ground forces could 'bring the enemy to their knees'.

Almost alone, Churchill refused to believe in an early German collapse. On the *Queen Mary* on his way to his meeting with Roosevelt at Quebec, he warned the British Chiefs of Staff against exaggerated optimism, reminding them of the German onslaught in March 1918. As early as 11 September, according to Major-General Kennedy, Montgomery too had begun to take 'a gloomy view of the situation' and to think that his operations 'will now have to be slowed up and the war prolonged'. Even Eisenhower was sceptical. The wild, unthinking optimism of the press correspondents, ignorant of the true facts of the Allied logistic situation, horrified him.

For the troops themselves, suddenly released from the tension of close combat, sober judgment in the heady atmosphere of liberated France and Belgium was impossible. The foul stink of German occupation had suddenly vanished with the wind. The populace abandoned all restraint. The sun shone and the fruit was ripe. All — and more — that the Germans had acquired by force was freely offered and freely taken. A letter to his family in Canada sent at the time by an officer who drove through Rouen and on to the north on 2 September vividly evokes the scene.

> I cannot possibly convey the cumulative effect of passing for hours through liberated countryside, with the wreckage of the beaten enemy — his tanks and vehicles, his dead horses and the graves of his dead men — littering the roadside ditches and the population free once more, welcoming the oncoming troops with smiles and flowers and the V sign …
>
> The scene in a liberated town is quite extraordinary. The place, of course, is festooned with flags. They always have plenty of tricolours but the Union Jack and the Stars and Stripes are in short supply and had to be home-made for the occasion. (I even saw some versions of the Canadian Red Ensign, which would scarcely have pleased the College of Heralds but must have pleased a good many Canadians.) Everyone seems to be in the street, and no one ever seems to tire of waving back (particularly at the female population). The young people wave and laugh and shout; the children yell and wave flags; the mothers hold up their babies to see the troops, and wave their little paws too; the old people stand by the roadside and look happy; and the Army rolls through ….

Even the Guards, who from long practice have developed a capacity for understatement and for never showing emotion in any circumstance, were slightly shaken by their reception in Brussels on the evening of 3 September.

> Everyone was crazy in a delirium of happiness that knew no bounds. Effigies of Hitler were burning round which they danced.… the usual gifts of food and wine, the display of flags and bunting and the cheers were not only more overwhelming than ever before but the normal handshakes of gratitude were more often than not amplified with embraces. Most frequently it was the children who were held up to be

kissed, but young ladies and old ladies, some pretty and some not at all, and even on occasions gentlemen, some of whom had beards, all competed to welcome their liberators with embraces in which one felt were pent-up all the sufferings and emotions of the past four years. It was as un-English a scene as can be imagined and yet so natural and touching did it seem that scarcely one of us could feel shy or embarrassed or even flinch, other than perhaps mentally, at the enforced attentions of the bearded old gentlemen.

In the Palais de Justice, the Gestapo had left behind a vast store of excellent wine. 'What could be more right and proper', say the normally reticent historians of the Guards Armoured Division,

> than that we should share some of this looted store with the people of Brussels and toast victory in it together? This was what they thought and we were in no mood to disagree, as case after case was deposited on the pavements in the lurid glare that came from the burning buildings. It is a curious fact and a pertinent one that demands study by prohibitionists that, though an enormous amount must have been consumed, no case of drunkenness was recorded, nor did any man fail in his duty either during the course of that night or of the following morning.

Meanwhile, unknown to the victors, some sort of order was beginning to emerge from the confusion behind the German lines. The 20 July plot had convinced Hitler that he could trust none of the senior hierarchy of the Army — the men with an orthodox military background and handles to their names. For the command of his disintegrating Armies in France he sought a man like himself who would obey his orders without question and fight to the bitter end. He found him in Field-Marshal Walter Model, commanding Army Group Ukraine in

30

Galicia, who on 20 July had been the first to reaffirm his loyalty to the regime. He had arrived at the headquarters of Army Group B at La Roche-Guyon to relieve von Kluge on 17 August at the moment when the Allied jaws were closing on the Falaise gap and the Americans were bursting over the Seine at Mantes. In this man there was — despite his Nazi convictions — an element of brute strength and determination which commands respect. In August 1943 he had withdrawn from the Orel salient in defiance of Hitler's order to stand fast. He had already displayed technical military skill of a high order. His personal courage was undoubted: wherever the situation was critical, there was to be found Model. Foul-mouthed and apparently always in a vile temper, he drove his officers with threat and insult. Nonetheless, he inspired the troops themselves with his own brutal determination to fight on. Thanks to him considerable numbers, including especially tank crews, succeeded in escaping over the Seine near Rouen.

In one respect the German Army outclassed all its opponents — in the flexibility and simplicity of its organisation and in the professional skill of its battle-experienced corps and divisional commanders and their staffs. In the debacle German respect for organisation and discipline had preserved the machinery of command virtually intact. Although, in the first week of September, 7th and 15th Armies had been reduced to skeletons, the army and corps staffs still functioned. Each of the two Armies had at least 10 divisional staffs capable of rounding up the fugitives and reasserting a measure of control. When Antwerp fell on 4 September Hitler rushed to the Netherlands the headquarters of the 1st Parachute Army to fill the gap between the 7th and 15th Armies. Under their direction, military police and Waffen SS detachments sifted the fugitives and despatched them to reorganisation centres whence they quickly emerged as units capable at least of defensive action. On the same day Model was able to report that he could hold the line running from Antwerp via the Albert Canal and the Maas to the Siegfried Line provided he was given reinforcements. Within Germany, 10 Panzer Brigades, each built around a Panzer battalion with about 40 Panther tanks, were either on their way to the front or in process of being formed. At the same time, 80 'Fortress' battalions consisting of men of the older military classes were released to man the Siegfried Line.

In the first days of September, Hitler reinstated von Rundstedt, aged 68, in his old command, Commander-in-Chief West. In a personal briefing, he ordered him to hang on to the V1 and V2 sites in the Netherlands aimed at London, to defend every inch of German soil, to prevent the Allies using the port of Antwerp by holding the mouth of the Scheldt, and to keep the Allied air bases as far as possible from the heart of Germany. On 5 September von Rundstedt, accompanied by his Chief of Staff Westphal, formally assumed command at Koblenz, Model reverting to the command of Army Group B — 15th, 7th and Parachute Armies in the north. Blaskowitz continued to command Army Group G in the south.

Von Rundstedt's moral disintegration was now complete. After the 20 July plot he had accepted the presidency of the 'Court of Honour' which tried and condemned 55 of his brother-officers, including Field-Marshal von Witzleben and nine generals who had been involved. During the battle of Normandy, before his dismissal, he had been content to pass on the orders issued by Hitler and Jodl. He now resumed his former role — postmaster for the passing-on of orders from the Führer's headquarters. Nonetheless, his return to command in the West gave once more an air of respectability sufficient to satisfy any scruples his subordinate officers may have had in continuing to fight on. Up to this moment Model, endeavouring to stop the rot in the north, had given scant attention to the situation on the Western front as a whole. With von Rundstedt back once more in the chair, his staff soon brought the overall situation under control.

For months past every major military decision in the German High Command had been made by Hitler himself (not only in principle but also in considerable detail) in the *Wolfschanze*, the Wolf's Lair in a forest near Rastenburg in East Prussia. Here, in the safety of concrete shelters and closely guarded by the SS, he endeavoured to exercise direct command over his armies. Jodl and Keitel and occasionally Warlimont were the only members of his immediate staff who had access to him. Jodl, a general without battlefield experience, seems to have been the most closely associated with him. Whenever Hitler conceived a new plan, it was with Jodl that he discussed it and Jodl who obtained the information necessary to transmute it into intelligible orders and saw to their execution. The bunker in which Hitler spent all his time was a heavily sealed concrete box with no window, kept at a high temperature and lit for 24 hours a day by electricity. The fusty smell of half-dried concrete was all-pervading.

Hitler did not get up out of bed until after 11 a.m.; his 'briefing' conference was held in the afternoon; at 5 p.m. he took a siesta; then began an interminable evening session which left his staff exhausted. At midnight there came an evening briefing conference, followed by tea and a spasmodic talk. Eventually, after a dose of castor oil, Hitler would go to bed in the small hours. It is not surprising therefore that the decisions taken in this atmosphere and emanating from the

Führer's bunker bore little relation to the facts of the military situation.

Viewed from this remote headquarters, the overall German position was not one of unrelieved gloom. Despite the loss of over three million men since the outbreak of war, from a population of 80 millions, the Wehrmacht could still muster 10 million officers and men on its strength on 1 September. On paper at any rate the Army had 327 divisions and brigades of which 31 divisions and 13 brigades were armoured. Admittedly many were under-strength. Surprisingly, however, even after five years of war German manpower resources had not been fully exploited. The hospitals could be relied on to provide a constant flow of replacements. Physical standards for frontline service could be reduced. On the British front there appeared a 'stomach' battalion, composed of men with gastric complaints, who had to be fed on a special diet. There was also an 'eye' battalion of men with sight defects and an 'ear' battalion of deaf men. The age limit of the annual call-up could be lowered and men up to the age of 60 were called to the colours. The Navy and Air Force were carrying on their strength large numbers of men in excess of their needs. Furthermore there existed a reserve of over four million civil servants and individuals who had had their military service deferred. There were many able-bodied men in the factories who could be combed out and replaced from the seven million foreign workers and prisoners of war. Unlike Britain, the reserves of woman power had scarcely been touched.

A new mobilisation plan on these lines had in fact already been announced by Reichsminister Joseph Goebbels with all the rabble-rousing cant in which he excelled. The 'back-area swine' to use the Führer's own felicitous phrase, were to be driven out of their funk holes. Schools and theatres were closed down. A 60-hour week was introduced and holidays abolished. Small shops were ordered to close; civil administration was cut to the core. Himmler, now commanding the Home Army in addition to his responsibilities as Minister of the Interior, Chief of Police and Head of the SS, put his full weight behind the drive. As a result, by early September the programmes were in full swing.

Rather than bring back to full strength those units which had been bled white in battle, Hitler preferred to create new units and formations. There already existed in the Army 18 divisions of a new type — the Volksgrenadier Divisions (the people's grenadiers). On 2 September he decreed a further 25 to become available in the West between 1 October and 1 December. Into these poured the men discharged from hospital, the prunings from the Navy and the Air Force, the men combed out from the factories and the offices and the youths just reaching military age. Early in 1944 the strength of the normal infantry division had been reduced from 17,000 to 12,500. By cutting each of the three infantry regiments from three to two regiments, the Volksgrenadier Divisions were brought down to 10,000. To supplement their artillery Hitler at the same time ordered the formation of 12 motorised artillery brigades (about 1,000 guns), 10 Werfer brigades, 10 assault-gun battalions and 12 machine-gun battalions.

However, the best of the manpower now becoming available was diverted by Himmler to the Waffen SS, the regime's private army of men fanatically loyal to the Führer. Although this constituted less than five per cent of the Army, one third of the Panzer Divisions and one fourth of the Panzer Grenadier Divisions belonged to this force. These divisions were larger and better equipped than those of the Regular Army. Their great strength lay in their young officers, selected for physical fitness, racial purity and Nazi convictions rather than for education, social background and emotional stability. These coarse, ruthless and arrogant young men from the SS cadet schools set a low value on human life, including their own. By this time hundreds had risen to the command of battalions. From them Hitler planned to produce a new generation of leaders to give him the victories the officers of the Regular Army had failed to achieve.

Although it is not the weapon that has the last word but the quality of the man behind it, the armoury of the German Army compared by no means unfavourably with that of the Allies. Their close-range anti-tank weapon, the Panzerfaust, was as effective as its Allied counterparts: the American Bazooka and the British Piat. The 'Burp' sub-machine-gun with its peculiar emetic sound and the 88-mm., high-velocity, dual-purpose, anti-aircraft and anti-tank piece particularly impressed the Allied soldier. Moreover, in the Nebelwerfer, a multi-barrel, 150-mm. mortar, the Germans possessed a weapon superior in its class to anything the Allies could produce at this stage of the war. The British, against whom the majority of these weapons had been used south of Caen, had learnt to hate the curious whining screech and violent blast of the 'moaning minnie'. Easy to conceal and quick to move, it had presented a baffling problem to Allied artillery.

The light and medium artillery of both sides were roughly comparable. In the matter of tanks the advantage in performance, though not in numbers, was definitely with the Germans. The Tiger, the Panther and the medium Mark IV outgunned the majority of the Allied Shermans, the majority of which still mounted the 75-mm. and had wider tracks and thicker armour. Now that the Army was back virtually on the prewar German frontier within easy reach of the factories in the Ruhr, supply presented no problem.

In one sector alone did the Allies have the advantage — assault equipment. The British equipment was grouped in 79th Armoured Division under Major-General Hobart — Flails to force a track through minefields; dd tanks which swam; cdl armoured searchlights, to provide artificial moonlight; Crocodiles which belched flame up to 120 yards; Buffalo troop carriers, which could transport across rivers; and AVREs (assault vehicles, Royal Engineers) for crossing gaps, which could fire a 25-lb. bomb known as the Flying Dustbin. Lastly there were the Arks, which lowered a platform fore and aft so that a fighting tank could climb over them.

Of all the delusions under which the Allies laboured in this climacteric month of September none was greater than that of the effect of the operations of the vast fleets of Bomber Command and the US 8th Air Force on German war industry. In fact the output from the factories, thanks to Reichsminister Albert Speer's efforts, with the major exceptions of the oil and aircraft industries, had reached its peak. An average of 1,500 tanks and assault guns and 9,000 vehicles were rolling off the assembly lines every 30 days. Ball-bearing production, the top priority target of the Allied war effort during the summer, was virtually unaffected. The production of single-engined fighters had risen from 1,016 in February to 3,031 in September. There was no justification for the widely held Allied assumption that on economic grounds alone Germany would collapse before the end of 1944. Oil and ammunition production alone showed a decline. Speer assured Hitler that war stocks could be expected to last for another year. The excellent railway and canal system was still functioning at maximum capacity and with almost prewar efficiency.

In 1938 the Todt organisation had used one third of Germany's total production of cement and the labour of half a million men to construct the fortified barrier of the Western Wall. This ran along the western frontier of Germany from Cleve on the Dutch border to Lorrach near Basle on the Swiss frontier. More than 3,000 concrete pill-boxes, bunkers and observation posts were constructed. The strongest parts of the line, often supplemented by 'dragon's teeth' five rows deep, were on the Saar river and at the Aachen gap, which the US 1st Army had now reached. From Geilenkirchen, about 15 miles north of Aachen, to Cleve it was unfinished, consisting only of a single belt covered by natural obstacles. The myth of its impregnability — a myth fostered by Hitler's propaganda — had undoubtedly contributed to his success in bluffing Chamberlain and Daladier at Munich and was in part responsible for the supine attitude adopted by the Allied High Command in 1939, when the bulk of the German Armies were committed to Poland. On the fall of France in 1940 all work on it had been abandoned. When the Armies fell back they found a five-year-old derelict. The embrasures had been constructed to accommodate weapons now obsolete. There was a shortage of artillery. There were no mines and no barbed wire. A last-minute attempt by Himmler to modernise the defences with civilian labour had merely resulted in confusion. Nonetheless, despite the fact that its strength had been widely exaggerated by propaganda, it still provided a formidable barrier behind which the German armies could be reconstituted and fresh reserves found. Time had camouflaged the works and Allied Intelligence concerning them was scanty. More important, in Hitler's mind as well as in that of the German people and of the rank and file of the Army, it was still impregnable.

It is a biological fact that, when the territory of an animal or bird is threatened, it will fight to the death, regardless of the odds; so it is with man. In 1940, when driven back into their island, the British had good, sane reasons to accept an accommodation with the Germans, which Hitler, many believe, was eager to offer. The British, illogically in the circumstances of the time, chose to fight on. Now that the sacred soil of the Fatherland itself was menaced, this deep-seated animal instinct took possession of the German people too. A German doctor captured in Holland about this time, on being asked, 'Why, when you have so obviously lost this war, do you continue to inflict this suffering on your people?', indignantly replied, 'I'm fighting for my country the same as you!' Vast areas of devastation, where the Allied bombers had struck, disfigured most of the larger German cities west of the Elbe. In the raid on Hamburg in July 1943 the dead numbered 40,000. Nonetheless the lesson of London was being repeated: the civilian will to resist was positively hardened rather than weakened by the continuous blows from the air. The Allied demand for unconditional surrender and the Morgenthau plan announced at this time to eliminate the industries of the Ruhr and Saar and convert Germany into a primarily agricultural and pastoral country convinced many not in sympathy with the Nazis that it was better to go down fighting under Hitler than to accept a Carthaginian peace. Despite the 20 July plot the bulk of the people still cherished the belief that, with his secret weapons or in some other vague and mysterious way, the Führer would emerge triumphant in the end.

Swamped by the mass of statistics beyond his capacity to analyse intelligently, and still shaken by the 20 July attempt on his life, Hitler lived in a world of fantasy. His favourite reading was military history, particularly as interpreted by Carlyle. From it he would select whatever precedent he thought justified his intention at the moment. Behind his desk hung the portrait of his hero, Frederick the Great, who, when apparently hopelessly outnumbered and surrounded by the converging armies of the French, Austrians, Russians and Swedes, had defeated them one by one and saved Prussia from extinction. Throughout all the disasters of August, in long meandering tirades, he had insisted that the final decision must come in the West and that, if necessary, other fronts must suffer so that a concentrated major blow could be struck there. In circumstances far more desperate Frederick had not abandoned hope. Neither would Hitler, his spiritual heir, do so now. Behind the ramparts of the Western Wall, the Army stood firm. Reinforcements were surging towards the front. The tanks and guns were rolling off the assembly lines. The British and Americans had stretched their communications to the limit: without the use of the port of Antwerp, they were hamstrung for lack of supplies. The autumn rains had slowed down the Russians' advance. In Italy, Kesselring's Armies astride the Apennines held the immensely strong barrier of the Gothic Line. The hearts of the great German people and their soldiers were still sound. Two hundred Mark XXI submarines, soon due to be launched and capable of cruising at 16 knots and remaining submerged at great depths for long periods, would wrest command of the seas from the Allied fleets. The V2 bombardment of London, started on 8 September, would finally crack the morale of the British. A thousand Messerschmitt 262s, the first jets, against which the Allies had no defence, would soon be in service. Even at this late hour they could be thrown back into the sea in a second Dunkirk.

On Saturday 16 September a conference of the inner circle assembled in the Wolf's Lair. Apart from Hitler, Jodl, Keitel and Kreipe, Göring's Chief of Staff, alone were present. Jodl opened the proceedings with a broad survey of the situation in his usual quiet voice using words designed to soften the impact of bad news. The Western Allies had some 96 divisions at or near the front; 10 more were on their way; the Allied Airborne Army was still in England. The forces in the South of France were withdrawing according to plan. Suddenly Hitler cut him short and, pointing to the map unrolled on the desk before him, rasped out: 'I have just made a momentous decision. I shall go over to the counter-attack, that is to say, here, out of the Ardennes with the objective — Antwerp!'

3: ANTWERP — THE THIEF OF TIME

I may lose a battle, but I will never lose a minute.

Napoleon

Of the Canadian Army which fought in Europe in World War One only 50 per cent were Canadian-born: in World War Two 80 per cent of the Field Force were Canadian by birth. This marked change was immediately apparent when, in December 1939, General McNaughton arrived in Aldershot with the 1st Division. Between the wars Canada had risen from Dominion to national status and General McNaughton and his officers were not slow in making clear to the British that they expected to be treated as allies and not as just another component of the British Army. Their Army to them was a living symbol of their country's position in the world. At the outbreak of war in 1939, it consisted only of some 4,500 professional soldiers and a non-permanent active militia destitute of equipment. By the spring of 1943 it reached its final form in Europe of an army headquarters, two corps headquarters, two armoured and three infantry divisions and two independent armoured brigades, making a total of over 250,000 men — all volunteers, backed by a highly efficient and expanding war industry.

For the first years of the war — fortunately, as it turned out in the long run — they took almost no active part in operations, although their potential contribution to the defence of Great Britain did much to sustain the British will to fight on in their greatest hour of need. Aldershot was an unfortunate choice for their first location. On leaving Canada, they had been saluted as heroes. The welcome of the population of

Aldershot, hardened by over 100 years of close propinquity with soldiers and cherishing no illusions concerning their habits, seemed cold; cold too were the unheated barracks. They found to their surprise that softness was no part of the British tradition: the soldiers if they felt cold could always go out of doors and take exercise or visit the large number of public houses, Aldershot's main attraction, to keep warm. Many Canadians chose the latter alternative. Understanding between the two races did not develop until after the Battle of Britain and the bombing of London and the cathedral towns. Moved away from Aldershot to Sussex, they received a more cordial welcome, which helped at least to mitigate the boredom of protracted waiting — made all the more galling by the fact that the British Army was fighting in Africa and South-East Asia. It is remarkable that the will to fight of these good-natured extroverts, essentially civilian and transatlantic in outlook, should have survived the dreary months of 'shadow boxing' on exercises and the off-duty company of a population who, to their way of thinking, were obsessed by obsolete class distinctions.

The move to Sussex brought them within the domain of General Montgomery in the flush of his campaign to remove what he called the 'dead wood' in the British Army — 'the old retired officers called up from the reserve and inefficient regular officers from major upwards who had never seen a shot fired in action and didn't want to'. Many senior territorial officers, who had gained their rank for other than purely military reasons, were also being diverted by him to tasks more suited to their talents than active command. To this end, he designed exercises embodying all the discomforts and exasperations of war without the risk. In these exercises the Canadians took part. Assembled afterwards in a cinema, forbidden to smoke or cough, the senior Canadian officers were left in no doubt as to his opinion of their capacity — that a decoration acquired on Vimy Ridge in 1917 and 20 years' militia service were unlikely to count for much in the coming contest with the most professional and toughest soldiers in the world, and that their magnificent physique did not necessarily imply equivalent mental capacity. Montgomery's ability to hit hard verbally as well as in battle did nothing to mitigate the sting of his criticism. That his comments were resented, no Englishman visiting the bar of many Sussex public houses frequented by Canadian officers during the frustrating and monotonous period of waiting could ignore. When he left England in mid-1942 to smash Rommel at Alamein he had no illusions about the Canadians: their soldiers were, potentially, as good as any in the world but their senior officers had more to learn than they realised. To many of them he seemed the epitome of everything they found unattractive in the people of Southern England. The fact that he was efficient, and a teetotaller as well, in no way tempered their disapproval.

Although the 2nd Canadian Division landed on D-Day, closely followed by the 3rd, the Headquarters of 1st Canadian Army under General Crerar did not start to function until 23 July, when it took over responsibility for the thrust down the Falaise road. Its title was a gesture to Canada's great contribution to the war effort rather than an actuality: throughout the campaign more than half the troops involved were British or Polish, a fact which the press frequently chose to ignore. In Normandy, the individual Canadian soldier in close-quarter fighting showed himself to be second to none on either side. The same cannot be said of the professional skill of his commanders and staffs. The final breakout in particular on 14 August, called 'Tractable', was frustratingly costly, slow and confused. 4th Canadian Armoured Division at the crucial moment became disorganised: as a result many Germans escaped from the Falaise pocket. The large number of changes in command in August, from divisions down to battalions, told its own tale. It is impossible to avoid the conclusion that, if more attention had been paid to Montgomery's criticisms and more effort put into weeding out unsuitable officers, the costly muddles on the Falaise road might have been avoided.

On 26 August Montgomery ordered 2nd Army to force the Seine with all speed and, regardless of the situation on its flanks, to drive ahead on Antwerp with the ultimate aim of isolating the Ruhr. At the same time, 1st Canadian Army was to clear up the coastal belt as far north as Bruges. Dieppe, Le Havre and Boulogne were to be secured in the process. That the pursuit was on and that it called for an all-out effort by everyone to the limits of their endurance was explained with all the incisive and unequivocal stress characteristic of Montgomery. And yet, on 2 September, when XXX Corps was on the point of entering Brussels, it was difficult to detect in General Crerar's orders any feeling of urgency. The Polish Armoured Division, lagging some 100 miles behind the spearheads of XXX Corps, was to cross the Somme and advance in the general direction of Ypres; the 3rd Canadian Division was to clear up the area around the mouth of the Somme; the 4th Canadian Armoured Division was to halt and reorganise east of Abbeville and the 2nd Canadian Division to do likewise at Dieppe, which had fallen without a shot fired. That, at a time when every minute counted, General Crerar should have granted two of his divisions, one of them armoured, a period of repose failed to impress Montgomery. As was expected, the backlash came in the form of a signal:

Personal for Army Commander C-in-C.... Second Army now positioned near Belgian frontier and will go through towards Brussels tomorrow. It is very necessary that your two Armoured Divisions should push forward with all speed towards St Omer and beyond, not repeat not consider this the time for any division to halt for maintenance. Push on quickly.

The situation was changing from hour to hour. Coordination of the movements of the three northern Armies was urgent and vital.

On the same day, therefore, Montgomery called a conference at his tactical headquarters for 1 p.m. on the following day, to be attended by Crerar, Dempsey and Hodges, commanding 1st US Army. Crerar found the time inconvenient, as he had arranged to attend a religious service at Dieppe being held by 2nd Canadian Division to commemorate their comrades who had fallen in the raid of 1942. He therefore asked by signal that the time of the conference should be postponed to 5 p.m. Next morning, having received no reply, he decided to go to the service as planned. It does not seem to have occurred to him to send his Chief of Staff or Lieutenant-General Simonds, the Commander of the 11 Canadian Corps, to the conference in his place. After he had left, a message from 21st Army Group Headquarters stating that the conference could not be postponed arrived at 10.20 a.m. in Crerar's signals office. What happened gives a poor impression of the efficiency of Crerar's staff and signals: it did not reach him until over four hours later, when the march-past at Dieppe was about to start. Crerar completed his part of the ceremonial parade and then flew to 2nd Army Headquarters to find that the conference was long since over. He then drove on to Montgomery's tactical headquarters, two miles away. The meeting in Montgomery's caravan, as might have been expected, was the reverse of cordial, Montgomery making it clear that he had given an order which had not been complied with, Crerar asserting that he had a responsibility to Canada as well as to Montgomery.

The two parted on what not even a Whitehall press secretary could call the best of terms. Montgomery's feelings were reflected in a signal to the CIGS sent on this day stating that 1st Canadian Army's operations since crossing the Seine had been 'badly handled and very slow'. What passed between Crerar and his government and Montgomery and Alanbrooke is not known. The delay in handling the message informing Crerar that the conference could not be postponed was investigated to the apparent satisfaction of all concerned with the exception, it is to be hoped, of the staff and signal officers responsible for the delay. A few days later Crerar received a conciliatory note from Montgomery saying he was 'sorry he was a bit rude the other day and somewhat outspoken. I was annoyed that no one came to a very important conference. But forget about it and let us get on with the war. It was my fault.' Thus ended the only unpleasant clash between Montgomery and Crerar for the rest of the war. On purely military grounds Montgomery would appear to have had every justification for annoyance. If Bradley and Hodges, who were not under his command, could manage to attend the conference, so could Crerar who was. Canada had long since attained undisputed national status; whether this was an appropriate moment for Crerar to remind Montgomery of the fact only a Canadian can decide.

That the operations of the 1st Canadian Army during September were slower than they need have been is an unavoidable conclusion. Le Havre did not fall to 1 British Corps until 12 September; Boulogne held out till the 22nd; the

Calais area was not cleared until the end of the month; Dunkirk remained in enemy hands; on 1 October the Germans still held a lengthy stretch of the south bank of the Scheldt, the northern suburbs of Antwerp, Walcheren Island and the approaches to the South Beveland peninsula.

Von Zangen, now responsible for the defence of South-West Holland, with the resilience and professional competence of his caste, had not wasted his time. Ordered by Hitler himself to hold Walcheren as a 'fortress' — that is, to the last man and the last round — and to maintain a permanent bridgehead on the south bank of the Scheldt, he had found a task congenial to his talents and one which offered him almost every advantage for the conduct of a defensive battle. Most of the area immediately south of the Scheldt lay below sea level and was a maze of canals and rivers. The roads were built on narrow embankments, bordered by trees commanding a good view of the surrounding country and thus easily defended. Once off these roads the ground was soft as butter and tanks and vehicles of all kinds quickly became bogged down. To flood the polders and thus create an obstacle was merely a matter of breaching the nearest dyke. The autumn rains were rapidly converting the whole area into one vast bog.

Antwerp itself lies some 50 miles from the sea. For the first dozen miles below the city, the Scheldt is narrow; it then turns westward and widens out. On the northern side of this estuary lies the long, low peninsula of South Beveland, which is joined to the mainland by a road and a railway. Downstream of South Beveland is the island of Walcheren, connected to South Beveland by a single causeway. This causeway was heavily fortified. Heavy coastal batteries at Breskens and Cadzand covered the approaches to the estuary and on Walcheren there were a further 25 which could engage shipping in the Scheldt.

The southern bank of the estuary is mainland. Here, in the mouth of the Scheldt opposite Walcheren, there existed an almost ideal site for the permanent bridgehead which von Zangen had been ordered to maintain south of the river — the 'Breskens pocket', 25 miles long and 10 miles deep, extending from the Braakman inlet to Zeebrugge and protected by the Leopold Canal. For more than a dozen miles from the sea this canal ran parallel with the Canal de Dérivation de Lys, the two separated only by a narrow dyke. The remainder of the front was further protected by extensive inundations.

This section, known to the Germans as 'Scheldt Fortress South', von Zangen entrusted to the 64th Division, over 10,000 strong and commanded by Major-General Eberding. This division included a high proportion of men with battle experience in Russia as well as Normandy. It was well provided with machine-guns, mortars and artillery, and its morale was high.

Von Zangen gave the task of holding the approaches to the South Beveland peninsula north of Antwerp and of Walcheren Island to Lieutenant-General Wilhelm Daser's 70th Division, about 8,000 strong. The composition of this division was peculiar to say the least. It consisted of men suffering from stomach troubles and because of their special diet it bore the nickname of the 'White Bread Division'. Presumably to compensate for this handicap, the division was unusually well provided with artillery — 170 pieces including 67 naval guns.

As the 64th and 70th Divisions were considered to be holding a fortress, they came under the direct command of von Zangen. North of Antwerp he entrusted the defence of his left flank to LXVII Corps under General Sponheimer.

He left his troops in no doubt as to the vital character of their task, declaring in an order of the day: 'The defence of the approaches to Antwerp represents a task which is decisive for the further conduct of the war...' After overrunning the Scheldt fortifications, the English would finally be in a position to land great masses of material in a large and completely protected harbour. With this material they might deliver a death blow at the North German plateau and at Berlin before the onset of winter.... 'The German people are watching us .... each additional day you deny the port of Antwerp to the enemy and the resources he has at his disposal will be vital.' Reorganised and reanimated with the will to fight by an able and ruthless commander, the Germans faced the coming struggle with grim determination. An operation of the utmost complexity and difficulty in the face of rapidly deteriorating weather thus faced the 1st Canadian Army.

The major burden of planning and preparation starting in mid-September fell on the shoulders of Lieutenant-General G. G. Simonds, Commander of the II Canadian Corps. The son of a Regular Lieutenant-Colonel, Royal Artillery, and born in Great Britain, he had been educated in Canada and had joined the Royal Canadian Horse Artillery from the Royal Military College, Kingston, in 1925. In the 1930s as a student on the two-year course at the Staff College, Camberley, he had impressed the directing staff and his fellow-students, many of whom were themselves to rise to high rank in the British Army, with his abilities. Thus, unlike many of his contemporaries in the Canadian Army, he could talk the same language as his British counterparts, in particular Montgomery. Arriving in England in December 1939 as a major on the staff of the 1st Canadian Division, his rise had been meteoric. In Sicily and Italy in 1943 he had commanded both the 1st Canadian Division and the 5th Canadian Armoured Division with considerable skill and to Montgomery's satisfaction. He was the obvious choice as Commander of 11 Canadian Corps for the invasion of Normandy. His plans for the thrusts down the Falaise road in August had shown him to be a commander of unusual originality. That they were not as immediately effective as they might have been was not his fault. Given more intelligent support by Bomber Command and his own subordinate commanders, there is every reason to believe that the Falaise gap might have been closed much earlier than it in fact was. On 26 September, General Crerar, who had been suffering from persistent dysentery for some time, was obliged to go sick and to return to England for treatment. In his place he nominated Simonds to command 1st Canadian Army.

The problems which now faced Crerar's replacement would have shaken the confidence of any commander, no matter how experienced and determined, in any war. The first enthusiasm of his troops, full of the valour of ignorance when they first landed in Normandy, had now evaporated. Their casualties had been heavy, particularly in the infantry divisions. Between D-Day and 1 October, 2nd Canadian Division lost 8,211 and 3rd Canadian Division 9,263 men. These were the highest casualty rates of all the divisions in Montgomery's Army Group. Inevitably, these figures included a considerable proportion of the best leaders in the forefront of the battle. The gaps in the ranks were now being filled by reinforcements, many of whom were untrained. Furthermore the source of supply of volunteers from Canada was drying up. Although compulsory military service had been instituted, it did not apply to service overseas. If further heavy losses were sustained and the Army kept up to strength, a political crisis in Canada itself was inevitable. In the circumstances, therefore, Simonds was compelled to design his operations on lines calculated to ensure the greatest possible economy in the expenditure of Canadian manpower.

The Breskens pocket, protected by water-barriers and virtually tank-proof, was primarily a task for the infantry — and a tough one at that. Walcheren Island, strongly fortified and connected with the South Beveland peninsula by only a single causeway, presented a far more complex problem. An attack from the sea would have to overcome the coastal batteries strongly established in the concrete. To reach the causeway, troops would have to fight their way through the bottleneck at Woensdrecht and along the narrow isthmus which connects South Beveland with the mainland. A further hazard was a wide canal at the eastern end running from north to south. Clearly, therefore, the more help the attackers could get from airborne and amphibious troops, the easier their task would be. As for the island itself, Simonds proposed to unloose the vast destructive power of Bomber Command to break its dykes and completely flood it. Those parts of the island which remained above water would then be destroyed by further heavy bombardment, day and night. Finally, when the morale of the survivors of the garrison had been thoroughly shattered, airborne and waterborne troops would land and deliver the *coup de grâce*. Simonds fully realised that flooding Walcheren in this way would subject the Dutch civil population to great hardship: the inrushing sea would swamp their crops and their homes and the rich farmlands would be ruined for years to come. It would, however, not only enable Antwerp to be opened up with the minimum delay and thus shorten the war, but also save many Canadian and British soldiers' lives. Simonds therefore asked for maximum possible support by the Strategic Air Forces for this plan. Neither Montgomery nor Eisenhower could see any alternative to his drastic proposal, although the latter's final approval was not given until 1 October.

In his demand for airborne troops, Simonds was less fortunate. Two tasks eminently suitable for airborne troops presented themselves — a drop designed to seize the causeway connecting Walcheren Island with South Beveland and another to capture a bridgehead at the small port of Hoedekenskerke on South Beveland through which waterborne troops could be sent into battle. On this point Simonds met uncompromising opposition from Lieutenant-General H. Brereton, Commander of 1st Airborne Army, backed by Air Chief Marshal Leigh-Mallory, the Air Commander-in-Chief. The 17th United States Airborne Division, although admittedly an inexperienced formation, was available while the British 6th Airborne Division, which had fought right through the Normandy battle, was expected to be ready again for operations by the beginning of October. A deadlock having been reached, the matter was referred to Eisenhower. Brereton and Leigh-Mallory apparently considered that the intense anti-aircraft fire on Walcheren, the difficult terrain and the inevitable loss by drowning ruled out any prospect of success. Faced by this opposition from the Commander of the Allied Air Forces and the Airborne Army, Eisenhower gave way. As a result of the decision at the Quebec conference in mid-September that in future the strategic bombers would operate under the direct control of the Combined Chiefs of Staff, he was no longer in a position, as he had been in Normandy, to order them to carry out specific tasks. He did, however, promise to demand complete saturation of the targets selected by Simonds. To what extent the Army's requirements were actually met will be seen later.

In marked contrast to the airmen, Admiral Ramsey, when brought into the planning, unequivocally offered all the forces at his disposal. The Royal Navy, when asked to cooperate, traditionally understate what they are prepared to do and then exceed their promises. They were to be true to their tradition. Captain Pugsley RN got to work at once on the planning with 11 Canadian Corps without fuss or equivocation.

Despite all delays and frustrations, Simonds' plan reached its final form by the end of September. In simple terms there were to be separate operations north and south of the Scheldt: the 3rd Canadian Division would wipe out the Breskens pocket; XII British Corps with 2nd Canadian Division under command was to thrust northwards from Antwerp, seize and hold the Woensdrecht defile and thence drive forward along the isthmus to occupy South Beveland.

By 1 October, the stage was set.

4: PER ARDUA AD ASTRA

The moral qualities of a commander are exceedingly important. Honour and truthfulness are inseparable features, and modesty adorns a man.

Marshal Malinovsky

Walcheren Island resembles a large flan of the type used by pastrycooks to hold jam or fruit salad. However, to describe it in September 1944 as appetising would be an overstatement. The outer crust was composed of high sand-dunes and the interior of flat land lying below sea level. The Westkapelle dyke at the north-west corner, one of the largest, oldest and most solid in Holland, was about 300 feet wide and stood 30 feet above low water-mark. Its sides were flat. By no means the least of the objections to bombing it which Simonds had to face came from his own Chief Engineer who, after studying the problem, reported that it would not be practicable to flood the island by breaching this dyke. Simonds was undeterred by this high-level specialist advice. Strengthened by his promotion to command of the Army, he called a conference on 29 September and by sheer force of personality finally overcame the reluctance of the Royal Air Force officers present to make the attempt. Air Commodore L. W. Dickens of Bomber Command departed acquiescent but unenthusiastic, emphasising 'that it was not possible to guarantee that the attempt to breach the dykes would be successful'.

On the early afternoon of 3 October, 247 Lancasters and Mosquitoes of Bomber Command attacked from 6,000 feet, dropping their bombs with, in the words of Montgomery, 'truly magnificent accuracy' at places where the dyke was thickest; they soon created a breach 75 yards wide. Through this surged the full weight of the North Sea. Only moderate anti-aircraft fire greeted the attacking bombers. During the raid Wing Commander J. B. Tait arrived over the target at the head of 617 Squadron carrying 12,000-lb. 'Tallboy' bombs. When he saw that the sea had already reached the streets of Westkapelle he decided that to drop these heavy bombs, of which only a few had been manufactured, would be wasteful. It does not seem to have occurred to him to release them instead on any of the concrete gun emplacements which studded the western coast of the island. So he took them back to England to be dumped, in all probability, on some housing estate in Germany.

All got back to England safe and sound in time for tea. Nor were there any losses on 7 October when the dykes at Flushing were attacked. Five further assaults on the 11th at Flushing and Veere were also successful. Thus, in the event, Simonds showed himself to have a better grasp of the bombers' capabilities than his expert advisers, his own Chief Engineer and the Air Staff officers whose lukewarm objections he had had to overcome. Nonetheless, although the whole of the middle of the island was flooded, the rim in which the batteries were sited in concrete remained intact and the batteries alive and active.

The Battle of the Scheldt may be said to have started on 2 October when 2nd Canadian Division, taking off from their positions immediately north or north-east of Antwerp, began the 13-mile advance to seal the South Beveland peninsula at the bottleneck at Woensdrecht. On their right at this time 1 British Corps were already committed to a strong thrust in the general direction of Tilburg and 's-Hertogenbosch on a wide front.

The country immediately north of Antwerp is typically Belgian — low-lying fields and market gardens interspersed with mean and haphazardly built villages — the results of hundreds of years of uncontrolled private enterprise on a small scale and the national desire not to spend more than could be avoided on paint, housing and public buildings. Within Belgium, despite sporadic tough resistance, progress was fairly rapid. On 5 October, the troops crossed the border and entered Holland, where in sharp contrast to Belgium, all seemed as neat and tidy as an exclusive residential estate. The Dutch villages of Ossendrecht and Santvliet fell on the 6th: with Woensdrecht only three miles away the Canadians were almost within sight of their first objective.

The threat was not lost on von Zangen. He had ready at hand a commander and a force in every way capable of dealing with it — the Battle Group Chill, commanded by Lieutenant-General Kurt Chill. This formation contained the remainder of three infantry divisions, part of the Hermann Göring Replacement Training Regiment and — most formidable of all — the 6th Parachute Regiment. When 2nd Canadian Division resumed their advance on the 7th, they soon found themselves brought to an abrupt halt.

In front of the village of Woensdrecht is another village — Hoogerheide. Against the latter the Canadians launched the Black Watch, with orders to take it and push on to Korteven, a mile to the north on the road to Bergen-op Zoom. A violent battle flared up around Hoogerheide at the end of which the Black Watch found themselves back where they started. Dutch civilians reported large numbers of guns and tanks near Korteven. During that night a violent counter-attack developed, to be followed by another next day. Some of the Canadians had to be withdrawn. For the moment, there was no escaping the fact that the young paratroops of Battle Group Chill were prepared to fight to the bitter end to hold Woensdrecht and the vital isthmus. Their right flank resting on a flooded area, and their left providing good going and concealment for their reserves and armour, the Germans' position was immensely strong. An attempt to turn their open flank on the 8th came to nothing, partly owing to the fog.

The Canadians faced stalemate. On the 10th, a bold thrust by the Royal Regiment of Canada across the wet polderland south and west of Woensdrecht reached the near side of the embankment carrying the railway across the isthmus at its narrowest point, almost closing it but not quite. In the face of a fierce counter-attack they stubbornly held their ground. On the 13th the Black Watch, put in here to break the deadlock, fared no better. Faced by dense mortar, airburst and small-arms fire they ended the day's fighting back where they started having lost 145 men. The 2nd Division's final effort to break the deadlock came on 16 October. At 3.30 a.m. the Royal Hamilton Light Infantry, covered by a heavy barrage and supported by tanks, finally fought their way into the straggling village of Woensdrecht, and on to the low ridge above it. It was close, hand-to-hand fighting — the enemy not giving up in the way he had in the past. Persistent counter-attacks and heavy casualties failed to dislodge them. Despite this success, the enemy still barred the way into South Beveland. Ominously, the floods at the eastern end of South Beveland were rising. Rifle companies were down to one officer and 45 men. An uneasy calm descended on the blood-soaked battleground around the ruins of Woensdrecht.

Meanwhile, in the Breskens pocket, the 3rd Canadian Division had encountered equally fierce resistance. As has been explained, the western end of the front held by the German 64th Division was covered by the double obstacles of two canals: the eastern half was flooded throughout its length apart from a heavily fortified gap at the eastern end at the Isabella Polder. There did however exist in the centre, at a point where the two canals diverged, a narrow, dry strip of land a few hundred yards wide. Major-General Spry, the Divisional Commander, therefore planned to force a crossing here with his 7th Brigade and, embarking his 9th Brigade in amphibious vehicles at Terneuzen two days later, to land them in the north-east corner of the pocket in the enemy's rear. He then proposed to pass his remaining brigade, the 8th, through the 7th's bridgehead and thus secure the eastern end of the pocket as a base for the final liquidation of the 64th Division.

At about 5.30 a.m. on 7 October, 27 Wasp flame-throwers opened up across the canal along the front of the 7th Brigade. The assaulting companies picked up their boats, struck out for the far bank and, taking advantage of the initial demoralisation of the enemy, soon established two separate narrow bridgeheads. 64th Division's reaction came with surprising speed and violence. Mortar, machine-gun and small-arms fire battered the tiny bridgeheads. Fighting of the closest and fiercest character flared up. Nonetheless, the Canadians hung on. After dark the engineers succeeded in getting two Kapok bridges across the canal: a further battalion was moved into the bridgeheads. Here the Canadians fought on in almost unspeakable conditions under continuous fire. 'The ground was water-logged; slit trenches rapidly filled with water...' The whole area was pounded with fire, including heavy shells from the 26 guns of 75 mm. or over of the coastal batteries on

Walcheren. The gap between the two minute bridgeheads was not closed until three days later. For seven days the Canadians and the 64th Division fought a soldiers' battle. At last, on the 12th, the 7th Brigade broke the deadlock and carried the outskirts of the village of Eede, about a mile beyond the canal.

The tense and precarious situation of the 7th Brigade, hanging on almost by their eyelids in the bridgehead on the Leopold Canal, made the amphibious operation by the 9th Brigade all the more urgent. This brigade was therefore embarked in Ghent on the evening of 7 October in Buffaloes manned by the 5th Assault Regiment Royal Engineers. It had been hoped to land them in the rear of 64th Division east of Hoofdplaat early the following morning. The passage of the locks at Sas van Ghent, however, caused unexpected delay, and the landing had to be postponed until the early hours of 9 October. Soon after midnight, the flotilla of Buffaloes led by Lieutenant-Commander R. D. Franks RN emerged from the mouth of the canal at Temeuzen and sailed westward in two columns.

About 2 a.m. the leading craft touched down on beaches marked by coloured shells fired a few minutes before by the artillery. There was no opposition: the enemy had been completely taken off guard. By dawn, the Buffaloes had turned round to fetch the remainder of the brigade and by 9.30 a.m. despite enemy shell fire, its third battalion was ashore. Now thoroughly alerted, 64th Division reacted with the violence to which the Canadians had become accustomed. Nonetheless, by nightfall the bridgehead was two to three miles deep. Reinforcing success, Major-General Spry moved the 8th Brigade into the bridgehead. Thus by 12 October he was ready to open up a land entry into the pocket via the Isabella Polder and finally break the still-stubborn resistance of 64th Division.

The final advance, brilliantly supported by Typhoons of the Tactical Air Force and a heavy air strike on the Flushing batteries, began in clear weather on 21 October. The little port of Breskens fell, but it was not until 3 November that the last traces of German resistance were finally wiped out. General Eberding, game to the last, was finally rounded up at Het Zoute. He and his men fought a gallant fight — in the opinion of the 3rd Canadian Division, 'they were the best infantry we have met'. They certainly paid a heavy price: so did the 3rd Canadian Division with over 2,000 casualties. An entry in the operations log of Headquarters 3rd Canadian Division timed 9.50 a.m. on 3 November read 'Operation Switchback now complete'. Somebody wrote beside it 'Thank God'. Despite excellent artillery support, it had been essentially a battle in which the staunch courage of the individual soldier fighting without the aid of tanks, rather than tactical subtlety, had been the decisive factor.

Whilst the 2nd and 3rd Canadian Divisions were engaged in this sordid struggle on the Leopold Canal and at Woensdrecht in the first fortnight of October, differences of opinion between Eisenhower and Montgomery reached a climax. Who was to undertake the task of capturing the Ruhr? Montgomery's Army Group or Bradley's? Was it sound for Eisenhower to attempt to fill the role of Supreme Commander and Commander of the Land Forces as well? There was no denying the fact that the machinery of command was creaking badly. On purely military grounds Montgomery's arguments were not easy to refute: on personal and political grounds, there was nothing to be said for them that would convince the Americans. The stalemate at Woensdrecht brought the issue to a head. The conquest of South Beveland was clearly out of the question until the country north of Woensdrecht and the shores of the East Scheldt could be cleared of the enemy. The whole weight of Montgomery's Army Group would have to be concentrated to this end and with all speed. His orders issued on 16 October were simple, realistic and in the event decisive. The 2nd Army would take over the eastern end of the Canadian front and launch a drive to sweep the south bank of the Maas whilst the Canadian Army, their line thus shortened, would, using 1 British Corps, push their right wing forward at and immediately east of Woensdrecht to Bergen-op Zoom and Breda. To assist them Montgomery allocated reinforcements in the shape of the 104th United States Division and 52nd Lowland Division.

In Lieutenant-General Sir John Crocker, Simonds had a corps commander in every way equal to the task. A man of few words with his feet on the ground, modest, straightforward and imperturbable, his obvious ability inspired confidence. Starting in the rain of 20 October, his corps advanced on a front of four divisions. The 4th Canadian Armoured Division attacked on the left. Next came the 49th (West Riding) Division directed on Roosendaal. On their right 104th (Timber Wolf) United States Division was directed on Zundert and Moerdijk. Finally came the 1st Polish Armoured Division — destination Breda. Simultaneously, Montgomery initiated a drive by 2nd Army on Tilburg and 's-Hertogenbosch.

The 104th United States Division were fresh from home and this was to be their first action. Nonetheless they brought to the operations an enthusiasm and skill in night movement which surprised the Germans. On 26 October Bergen-op Zoom fell to 4th Canadian Armoured Division and 49th Division were approaching Roosendaal. Thus relieved of anxiety with regard to their eastern flank, the 2nd Canadian Division were able on 24 October to begin their advance across the isthmus into South Beveland. Fighting their way forward along the flooded strip of land, where armour was impotent, they forged ahead through the mud for about five miles. It was a hard fight, for the Germans now had on the peninsula four battalions of infantry, two battalions of fortress troops and 10 battalions of artillery. Seven miles further on lay the flooded banks of the Beveland Canal. The men were now, according to the war diary 'very tired as a result of constant fighting and movement in the past 48 hours over difficult country'.

The 52nd Lowland Division had originally trained as a mountain division. In the Arnhem operation they had been allotted an airborne role which did not materialise. Simonds now called upon them to adopt an amphibious role — to cross the Scheldt, land in the rear of the Beveland Canal and thus, catching the enemy between two fires, ease the way ahead for 2nd Canadian Division on the isthmus. In the early hours of 26 October a strange fleet — Buffaloes, small naval assault craft and DD Tanks with the 156th Brigade tightly packed on board — led by Lieutenant-Commander Franks RN set sail from the little port of Terneuzen. Tracer shells fired from the south bank aided them in keeping on course: at 4.30 a.m. all the guns of II Canadian Corps opened up on the beaches at Hoedekenskerke. Twenty minutes later, only five minutes behind schedule, the leading craft touched down. There was little opposition. When day dawned, the Lowlanders found themselves amidst green fields, isolated farm houses, windmills and church towers. During the day the Allies rapidly expanded the bridgehead.

Thus outflanked, General Daser of the 70th Division had no alternative but to abandon the canal line and to evacuate the peninsula, fighting all the way for a last-ditch stand on the island. 2nd Canadian Division resumed the advance and on 29 October, linking up with 52nd Division's bridgehead, pushed on to Goes, the capital of the island, to receive a delirious welcome. 'The men had to kiss babies and sign autographs all the way through the town.' By the morning of 31 October they had reached the eastern end of the causeway leading to Walcheren Island. At long last, South Beveland was clear of the enemy and the stage was set for the final operations against Walcheren itself.

Planning for this final assault had been going on ever since the last week of September. Pressure on Simonds both from the Navy and the Army Higher Headquarters now reached an intensity equalled only by that of the German resistance. In brief, Simonds planned to use 4th Commando Brigade under Brigadier Leicester to carry out the assault using his three Royal Marine Commandos against Westkapelle and 4th Army Commando against Flushing supported by the Royal Navy's Force T commanded by Captain Pugsley. Because of the strength of the defences, a strong force of 25 close support craft under Commander K. A. Sellar was included to shoot the Commandos in — LCGs (landing craft guns), LCFs (landing craft for anti-aircraft use), LCTs (landing craft tanks) and LCT(R) (landing craft tank rocket). These were to be backed by a bombarding force of a battleship (*Warspite*) and two Monitors mounting between them 10 15-inch guns, and the Typhoons of 89th Group RAF. Once ashore, the Commando Brigade would come under the command of 52nd Lowland Division, whose task it would be to complete the reduction of the island. The fact that the tidal conditions only permitted landings in the period 1-4 November and 14-17 November made a decision highly urgent. On 31 October the weather began to deteriorate. Some of the batteries around Westkapelle were still very active, despite the bombing. A decision had to be taken at once. Simonds took it: the Commando Brigade would put to sea. If Brigadier Leicester and Captain Pugsley, on arrival off Westkapelle, found weather conditions impossible, they could postpone the assault and return to port.

At 3.45 a.m. the force sailed from Ostend. The weather was thick and getting worse. At 7 a.m. the lighthouse tower at Westkapelle hove in sight. The sky was overcast but the sea was calm. Leicester and Pugsley decided to go in. At once 'pinpoints of light sparkled from the south batteries'. Every German gun came into action. *Warspite* opened up with her 15-inch guns firing blind — her spotting aircraft were still fogbound in England. Sellar did not hesitate. The age-old tradition of the Royal Navy is that an escort must be prepared to sacrifice itself for its convoy. At all costs the commandos must be put ashore. He would close in and engage the batteries at close range, bringing their fire on to his own ships to enable the commandos to land. The action lasted from 9.20 a.m. to 11.15 a.m., as bitter and bloody as any in the long history of the Royal Navy. Thus shielded from the murderous fire of the German batteries, 41st Commando landed on the northern side of the gap in the dyke and fought their way into the streets of Westkapelle. South of the breach 48th Commando forced their way ashore and closed with the German defences. 47th Commando then passed through. At 12.30 p.m., his task accomplished, Sellar withdrew what remained of his squadron, carrying with them 126 badly wounded officers and ratings and those of their 172 dead not already at the bottom of the sea. Out of 25 ships only seven were still fit for action. The rest had been shot to bits or sunk.

The landing four hours earlier at Flushing had a less bloody reception. With the full weight of the support of over 300 guns from the south bank of the Scheldt behind them, 155th Brigade and 52nd Lowland Division, preceded by 4th Army Commando, were soon ashore. By nightfall, fighting from house to house and street to street, they had cleared the greater part of the town.

Meanwhile, the 5th Canadian Infantry Brigade fought a costly and abortive action on the causeway of South Beveland. It was 1,200 yards long and only 40 yards wide. Just west of the centre the Germans had blown a series of craters which made it impassable to tanks or vehicles. The Brigadier could see no alternative to frontal assault: there was not enough water on either side to take amphibious vehicles. The mud flats presented an impossible obstacle to vehicles. A gallant attack on the afternoon of 31 October by the Canadian Black Watch got as far as the eastern end but could get no further in the face of fierce artillery, mortar and machine-gun fire. Armour-piercing shells ricocheted down the causeway. An attack by the Calgary Highlanders next day made some headway in establishing a bridgehead at the far end but was driven back. At 4 a.m. on 2 November the Régiment de Maisonneuve made a last and final attempt with little success.

Direct assault across the causeway thus being shown to be futile, other means of overcoming the obstinate German defence at the far end had to be found. 52nd Lowland Division now took over responsibility here. The Slooe channel to the south of the causeway is about 300 yards wide at high tide: at low tide it shrinks to half this size leaving a grey stretch of glutinous mud not unlike the Essex marshes. The Germans deemed it impassable. However, on the nights of 1/2 and 2/3 November, Lieutenant Turner and Sergeant Humphrey of the Divisional Engineers found a way across the marshes which would carry men on foot; here in the early hours of 3

November, 6th Cameronians using infantry assault boats to cross the water, succeeded in establishing a bridgehead almost unobserved. By dawn, in the face of considerable resistance, they had linked up with the troops on the causeway.

With the 4th Special Service Brigade firmly ashore at Westkapelle and rapidly fighting their way north and south, 155th Brigade in possession of Flushing, and an effective bridgehead established at the causeway, the position of the Germans at Walcheren had become untenable.

On 6 November, a Dutch surgeon, Dr E. L. Nauta, set out in a small boat from Middelburg across the floods to the headquarters of 52nd Lowland Division to convey the message that the Germans were ready to surrender. A company of the Royal Scots was thereupon despatched across the waters to accept the surrender of General Daser and some 2,000 men.

Mine-sweeping of the Scheldt had already started: altogether some 267 mines had to be removed before the channel could admit the long-awaited convoys of storeships vitally needed to sustain Eisenhower's Armies. The work was not completed until 28 November. Appropriately the first ship to reach Antwerp was Canadian — the *Fort Cataraqui* — built in a Canadian yard and Canadian-registered.

Of the 13,000 total casualties sustained in the battle to open the Scheldt approximately half were Canadian. That the operations at times lacked 'finesse' is legitimate criticism if made by those with experience of front-line action against the Germans. Coming from others without that advantage, it lacks weight. The truth of the matter is that so far as the actual battle was concerned, there was no alternative to a head-on confrontation with the Germans. The indirect approach so widely advocated as the solution to all strategic and tactical problems is by no means infallible. The German divisional, regimental and battalion commanders were adept at their job; their experience was greater than that of their opponents; on the whole their men were well-trained, prepared to fight and, if necessary, to die. The sodden polders, innumerable waterways and floods gave them advantages in the defensive battle which they were quick to exploit. It says much for the moral stamina of the Canadian soldier that he should have been as willing to attack at the end of the battle as he was at the start.

Montgomery frankly admitted a bad mistake on his part: 'I underestimated the difficulties of opening up the approaches to Antwerp so that we could get the free use of the port. I reckoned that the Canadian Army could do it while we were going on to the Ruhr. I was wrong.' Injustice to him it must be pointed out however, that it was not until 9 October that Eisenhower named the free use of Antwerp as having priority over all other missions. In consequence, 1st Canadian Army did not receive the support it needed until the third week of October. If Eisenhower had made available to Montgomery and Simonds one of the two uncommitted airborne divisions early in the month, the pace of operations could undoubtedly have been accelerated.

Montgomery had been assured by Eisenhower on 20 September that although he could not have the use of the airborne divisions, a priority demand would be made on Bomber Command and 8th Air Force for the complete saturation of the targets he selected. This promise had not been kept. In fact these strategic air forces were no longer under Eisenhower's orders as they had been in Normandy, but those of the Allied Chiefs of Staff The airmen were wedded to the conviction that their vast destructive effort should be concentrated on industrial targets in the heart of Germany as the best means of bringing Hitler quickly to his knees. How utterly out of sympathy they were with the Army's needs at this time has since been revealed by Marshal of the Royal Air Force, Lord Tedder, the so-called Deputy Supreme Commander at the time. In October, Portal, Chief of the Air Staff wrote a letter to Tedder.

> I believe that the constant application of heavy bomber power to the land battle, when it is not essential and when its only purpose is to save casualties, must eventually lead to the demoralisation of the Army. If one division captures an objective with strong heavy bomber support and loses only a few men, other divisions will naturally be reluctant to attack without similar support, and we shall sooner or later reach a stage when almost the whole of the bomber effort has to be frittered away in small packets if the army is to attack at all.

Tedder, now able to attend the campaign almost on a commuter basis, replied on 25 October, at the height of 2nd Canadian Division's struggle to break out in the swamps of Woensdrecht and at a time when the 3rd Canadian Division, exposed to the fire of the Walcheren batteries, were at death grips with the 64th Division in the Breskens pocket.

> As you are aware the British Army have for months now been allowed to feel that they can, at any time, call on heavy bomber effort, and it will be laid on without question.
>   We are now, I am afraid, beginning to see the results in precisely that demoralisation of which you speak. The repeated calls by the Canadian Army for heavy bomber effort to deal with a part-worn battery on Walcheren, and the evacuation of Breskens because of intermittent harassing fire from this battery is in my opinion only too clear an example. It is going to be extremely difficult to get things back on to a proper footing. You can see the argument, i.e. Antwerp is vital, Antwerp cannot be used without Walcheren, Walcheren

is vital, every possible effort must be directed towards Walcheren, therefore Bomber Command should continue to pour bombs into the mud. I am doing my best to get things straight, but I am sure you will realise that, the army having been drugged with bombs, it is going to be a difficult process to cure the drug-addicts — particularly since the troops are undoubtedly getting pretty tired.

That two Air Marshals living hundreds of miles behind the front as far removed from the stark realities of the land battle as Hitler in his concrete bunker in East Prussia should have considered themselves competent to judge the state of morale of the Army is remarkable. The suggestion that demoralisation had set in in the Army was as offensive as it was untrue. The batteries on Walcheren showed themselves to be by no means part-worn when the attack went in on 1 November. No record can be traced of a visit by Tedder to the forward troops throughout the campaign. Half an hour in the Breskens pocket or at Woensdrecht in mid-October would at least have given a lesson of the need, even in war, for humility, humanity and a sense of proportion. The air bombardment of Germany, on which the Chiefs of Bomber Command had set their hearts, could have been suspended for a few days to enable the Walcheren forts to be adequately dealt with without any appreciable lengthening of the war. The secret of success in war is concentration at the decisive time and place. In this instance the decisive time was October 1944 and the place the Walcheren coastal defences. On D-Day in their attack on the concrete defences along the beaches, Bomber Command had shown what they could do. Without their aid, the landing might well have ended in failure.

Instead of dealing direct with Air Chief Marshal Harris, the Commander-in-Chief of Bomber Command, Simonds throughout the battle had to negotiate with Headquarters of 84th Group RAF of the Tactical Air Force. A purely RAF staff at the headquarters of this group of the Tactical Air Force, the air staff at Eisenhower's own headquarters and the Deputy Supreme Commander, himself an airman, were thus interposed to explain, modify and dilute Simonds' demands for support before they reached the explosive Commander-in-Chief of Bomber Command. If Simonds had been able to talk to Marshal of the RAF Sir Arthur Harris direct there would have been much plain speaking on both sides. That once he understood the Army's need the assistance of the C-in-C Bomber Command, a fighter if ever there was one, would have been generous and effective there is little doubt. Military bureaucracy is an infallible device for keeping two commanders apart. In this respect it succeeded.

The operational record of Bomber Command in October is sufficient evidence of the RAF High Command's lack of comprehension of the Army's needs and of their failure to give it the support which was within their power. In all the attacks on Walcheren during October, including those against the dykes, Bomber Command lost six aircraft. Four were lost in a single attack, that on Flushing on 23 October. In the days immediately preceding the landing on Walcheren the record is particularly illuminating. On 28 October, when between 200 and 300 bombers attacked Walcheren, 734 hit Cologne in a day attack. On the night of 30/31 October 984 aircraft dropped 4,142 tons on Cologne but none on Walcheren. On the night of 31 October/1 November, when 4th Commando Brigade set sail for Walcheren, 493 aircraft of Bomber Command dropped 2,703 tons on Cologne, none on Walcheren — apparently because the weather precluded operations in Holland. During the whole of October, Bomber Command made 21,930 sorties against factories and city areas in Germany, dropping some 56,612 tons of bombs; 'Army support and tactical targets' got only 1,616 sorties and 9,728 tons — in other words, Bomber Command's effort against targets remote from the battlefield was six times greater than the support it gave 1st Canadian Army at the time of its greatest need. As a result it was left to Sellar and his gallant little squadron to draw the fire of the batteries on Walcheren upon themselves at a cost of three-quarters of their strength, to enable the commandos to get ashore.

As a result of this experience it is not surprising that Canada after the war should have been the first of the Western powers fully to integrate the three services in the hope of breeding airmen capable of appreciating the needs of the soldiers on the ground.

The extent to which demoralisation as a result of drugging by bombs had infected the rest of the Army as alleged by the Chief of the Air Staff and the Deputy Supreme Commander is examined in the next chapter.

5: 'S-HERTOGENBOSCH

I see you stand like greyhounds in the slips, Straining upon the start. The game's afoot!

Henry V

It will be recollected that when Montgomery on 16 October ordered 1st Canadian Army to break the deadlock at Woensdrecht by striking north towards Bergen-op Zoom, Roosendaal and Breda he relieved them of responsibility for the eastern end of their front. Here he directed 2nd Army to break out westwards from the 'Market Garden' salient south-west of the great bridge over the Maas at Grave, to cut the supply escape routes of the German 15th Army south of the Maas and to force them back across it. Faced by this new threat, German resistance to the Canadians must inevitably weaken: the line of the Maas also offered Montgomery a shorter and more easily defended front. Accordingly on 22 October XII Corps, with 53rd Welsh Division directed on 's-Hertogenbosch, 51st Highland Division on Vught, and 15th Scottish on Tilburg, took off from the 'Market Garden' salient between Grave and Eindhoven.

Three enemy divisions, shortly to be reinforced by a fourth, barred the way, all in fairly good shape judged by the standards of the time. Some 16 miles of difficult country separated the 53rd Welsh and 15th Scottish Divisions from their objectives — Tilburg and 's-Hertogenbosch. The northern part consisted mainly of thick woods, alternating with large stretches of pine-covered sand-dunes up to within three miles of 's-Hertogenbosch. To the south it was slightly more cultivated with woods and fields dropping imperceptibly into polder, heavily cultivated fields of silt or clay, each surrounded by a dyke and often lined with trees. The roads were few and liable to collapse under the weight of armoured vehicles and heavy traffic. Dykes of an average width of four yards, some four feet deep and with an average depth of water about three feet, criss-crossed the whole area. The large canals and lakes, the embanked railways and roads and the boggy nature of the ground made it impossible for tanks and indeed any trucked vehicle to operate off the roads. Except along the roads there was almost no way of approaching 's-Hertogenbosch. The country was dead flat: finding an observation post presented the gunner with almost insoluble problems. All the odds were with the defender: the 712th German Division, charged with the defence of 's-Hertogenbosch, had exploited their advantages to the full, strewing and wiring all likely approaches with mines and siting their forward defended localities with considerable skill.

's-Hertogenbosch itself, an ancient city of some 70,000 inhabitants, stands on a sandy island at the point where the Dommel and the Aa rivers unite to form the canalised Dieze river. The older part of the city is solidly built, lying roughly within the arms of two waterways, one running from south-east to north-west and the other from south-west to north-east: embanked railways flank the northern and western sides. The southern edge is protected by a *bund*, or embankment. At the north edge outside the limits of the old city was a large housing estate. The country around was open polderland intersected by innumerable dykes. In October 1944, therefore, the city had all the ingredients for a successful Stalingrad-type defence. This task the 712th Division had allotted to four battalions, nine companies of which were located within the bounds of the city: the remainder were disposed in the defences in the open country to the east and south-east. All had orders to hold the town at all costs.

It is only in the despatches of commanders anxious to draw attention to their own military genius or the writing of military historians lacking personal contact with the enemy in action that battles proceed exactly according to plan. 53rd Welsh Division's attack at 's-Hertogenbosch certainly did not. Battles in fact are chaotic affairs in which personalities and the element of chance play a considerable part. Victory goes to the commander who can first create some sort of order out of the terror and confusion.

Major-General Ross's plan for the capture of 's-Hertogenbosch is easily understood. One brigade would advance on the north side of the railway which runs from Oss to 's-Hertogenbosch: another on the south side. On reaching an intermediate objective about six miles east of the town, the reserve brigade, the 158th, spearheaded by elements of the Reconnaissance Regiment, B Squadron 5th Inniskilling Dragoon Guards and the 1st East Lancashire Regiment in Kangaroos would pass through the enemy defences along a second-class road and capture the bridges over the canals leading into the town. In order to ensure sufficient daylight for the capture and consolidation of the bridge area it was prescribed that this breakout should start no later than 1 p.m. on 22 October. It is the fortunes of this force which will now be followed.

The Kangaroos were a novelty to the 1st East Lancashire Regiment: indeed, when 39 turned up in their lines in the little village of Berghem two miles east of Oss in the early morning of 21 October none of the troops had ever set eyes on them before. They were in fact Sherman tanks with the turret and the gun removed: each carried nine men — nine Kangaroos to a rifle company. In August the Canadians and the 51st Highland Division had used them with some success in a night attack on the Falaise road; but in the waterlogged country of Brabant, with dykes intervening almost every 50 yards, an attack was likely to end in most of the Kangaroos soon becoming bogged down. The prospect of an attack in column down a single road seemed equally unpromising.

In terms of vehicles, the force now under Lieutenant-Colonel Burden's command was by no means small. In addition to his battalion he had the tanks of the 5th Royal Inniskilling Dragoon Guards with a detachment of Flails, a troop of assault engineers, the Wasp sections (flame-throwers) of the 7th RWF and the 1st/5th Welch Regiment and a section of 202nd Field Ambulance, in Kangaroos — a total of in vehicles. The column, spaced out at 20-yard intervals, was one and a half miles long.

Throughout the morning of 22 October, the East Lancashire Regiment in Kangaroos waited in Berghem for the order to advance. News of the progress of the two leading brigades slowly filtered through. The advance of the brigade north of the railway was apparently going well: on the left, however, the other brigade, unsupported by armour, had struck trouble. The vital hour of 1 p.m. at last arrived: exactly on time came the order to advance — not by the route originally intended, but by a much worse one south of the railway line. If the Reconnaissance Regiment got held up, they were to push through with their tanks. All ranks leaped into the vehicles and the column roared out of Berghem. A few miles ahead in the village of Geffen, the column halted for a few minutes to enable the tanks to take the lead. Here a small boy climbed on to the CO's Kangaroo and presented him with a tie-clip trophy; it was accepted gratefully as a good omen.

At Geffen the route ordered by the Brigadier took a turn for the worse: there were many twists and turns. The tracked vehicles soon ripped it to bits. There were many checks. Soon the column was moving forward at little more than a walking pace. Ahead, the Reconnaissance Regiment had struck mines and was in action with a party of the enemy with bazookas near the village of Kruisstraat. At 3.45 p.m. they reported that they could make no further advance. Lieutenant-Colonel Burden, mindful of his Brigadier's order 'to push through somehow', decided to pass through the Reconnaissance Regiment and the minefield. The Tank Squadron Commander, fearing the certain loss of his leading tanks, viewed the prospect without enthusiasm. Lieutenant-Colonel Burden made it clear that they could neither retreat, nor stay where they were, that it would soon be dark and that they must therefore push on. So on went the leading troop of tanks followed by D Company of the East Lancashires, still in their Kangaroos; Kruisstraat was reached, but just beyond the crossroads, what the Squadron Commander had feared happened. The leading tank struck a mine; another tank jammed a traversing gear leaving only one tank to continue the advance. D Company therefore dismounted from their Kangaroos, deployed and, driving the enemy before them, forged on a further 1,200 yards to the outskirts of the next village, Bruggen. Meanwhile the Flails cleared a passage through the minefield. About 5 p.m. considerable numbers of the enemy advanced to attack the company, but a quick call for artillery support brought fire which soon drove them to the ground. It was now quite dark: to continue the advance with the armoured column clearly offered no prospect of success.

Lieutenant-Colonel Burden therefore disposed his battalion in an all-round defensive position at Kruisstraat. The armoured thrust on 's-Hertogenbosch thus ended four miles from the objective.

Hardly were the defensive arrangements for holding Kruisstraat complete when at 8 p.m. the East Lancashires were ordered over the air to push on to Bruggen with the least possible delay. The night was black as pitch. All that could be done was to call down the fire of the Divisional Artillery on to the village and advance against it with an ample reserve to meet the unforeseen. The attack got going at 9.45 p.m. in the face of sporadic bursts of machine-gun and mortar fire. Soon, as a result of the artillery bombardment, the village was in flames which brilliantly lit up the way ahead. The East Lancashires therefore did not enter the village but took up positions east and west of it. Dawn came at about 7 a.m. and soon afterwards the 2nd Monmouths arrived to continue the advance for a further 1,000 yards to the Molen Stra, a road running due south from the railway embankment and about one and three quarter miles from 's-Hertogenbosch.

Meanwhile, on the left of the East Lancashires, the 71st Brigade had slowly worked forward and, by the afternoon, Major-General Ross was in a position to give orders for the final assault on 's-Hertogenbosch. During the night of 23/24 October the 5th Welch on the right and the 1st East Lancashires on the left were to advance along the railway, get into the northern outskirts and then clear the town. On their left the Royal Welch Fusiliers were to seize the village of Hintham: the 7th Royal Welch Fusiliers would then advance to seize the bridges at the south-east corner of the town. The attack by the 1st East Lancashires would start at 2 a.m., an hour in advance of the 5th Welch, and would be provided with movement light by a searchlight regiment projecting its beams against the sky. The Brigadier of 158th Brigade having suddenly been taken ill, Major-General Ross delivered orders personally to the COs at an order group near Geffen which did not break up until 10 p.m. The road back to Bruggen was a solid traffic jam of artillery vehicles, and Lieutenant-Colonel Burden did not get back to his battalion until 11 p.m. To reach the start line on the Molen Stra, form up and attack at 1 a.m. he had a bare two hours in which to make his plan and issue orders. This much was known of the enemy's position: there was an enemy post in the *bund* about 500 yards ahead; 400 yards further on there was a defensive position linking up with another locality 300 yards to the south containing four small-calibre aa guns and some infantry; the village of Hintham was held by the enemy; finally at a ramp on the edge of the Garden Suburb air photographs showed that trenches had been dug.

Lieutenant-Colonel Burden had had no sleep for 48 hours. Owing to the boggy ground and the innumerable dykes, tank support was out of the question. The task was one for infantry, and infantry alone. Everything would have to be carried. The wider the front on which he deployed, the greater would be the risk of becoming embroiled in noisy dog fights, with consequent loss of control. He therefore decided to thrust forward on an extremely narrow front in great depth with one company on each side of the railway, each on a front of 60 yards only. Only the leading platoon of these two companies would deploy; the rest would follow in columns of threes.

Behind the left leading company would come the 'Immediate Action' Company, also in threes, followed by the Battalion Headquarters and the remaining company. If the 'aa Site' gave trouble the 'Immediate Action' Company would wheel left and 'attack it with the utmost savagery' whilst the rest of the battalion pressed on.

Even before he had finished giving his orders, some 200 guns had started on a 'milk round' of the known enemy positions. At H hour this was to cease and be replaced by timed concentrations, lifting to fit in with the battalion's advance. The Battery Commander with him could if necessary bring down the fire of the divisional artillery at any time. Forward Observation Officers accompanied each forward company. How the anti-tank guns, carriers and other vehicles were to be got forward across the dykes presented a problem which could only be solved when daylight came. Major Hussey de Burgh, the Second-in-Command, assisted by the Pioneer Platoon and an RE bulldozer, said to be on its way, was told to find the answer. The big wireless sets had to be carried forward on stretchers: rations, water, Piats, medical requirements and reserve ammunition had to be carried on the man.

Meanwhile, the Intelligence Section had gone ahead to find and mark the route to the start line on the Molen Stra. Punctually at 1 a.m. guides from this section met the battalion at Bruggen, which was still burning merrily, and led the companies forward through the darkness to their jumping-off positions a few yards behind the start line. There was time to spare. The noise of the bombardment was deafening. From the darkness ahead came bursts of machine-gun fire. Two enemy guns opened up, apparently from the enemy rear. Suddenly searchlights somewhere in the rear beamed on the clouds above, giving just sufficient light for the waiting infantry to see about 100 yards ahead. 2 a.m. had come. The 1st East Lancashires stepped off into the unknown lying ahead. It was slow going; every 100 yards or so there seemed to be a dyke full of water. Soon the whole battalion was soaked to the skin.

After about half a mile a flurry of Spandau and Bren gun fire broke out to the right of the railway: A Company in fact at a post on the bund had surprised and swamped the enemy, some of whom bolted south to be made prisoners by C Company and brought along at the rear of the column. Here there were about 20-30 bicycles which had been smashed by the British bombardment. A medium gun firing short caused some delay on the left, but A Company forged ahead. A programme of light music at great strength now blotted out all radio communication for the next half hour. Soon there was another outburst of firing on A Company's front; they had hit the enemy post at the pill-box on the embankment. This was soon eliminated with the loss of five men. On the left of the embankment there was a dugout with a light burning within. A grenade extinguished it and presumably the occupants as well — no one had time to find out.

The main body of the battalion was now passing close to the aa site and the outskirts of Hintham: both were in flames. The Germans could be seen 150 yards away running around in apparent confusion. A tank was heard approaching from the left — C Company stood ready with their Piats but eventually it moved away towards Hintham. The raggle-taggle of bewildered prisoners at the end of the column continued to grow. The Signal Sergeant, Sergeant Brindle, added more from a pill-box which had been overloaded. The pace now quickened. A Company, still in the lead, approached its objective and, brushing aside a party of the enemy, reached the houses at the east end of the Garden City. It was 4.35 a.m. and still as dark as the pit. The rest of the battalion curled up rapidly behind it into an all-round defensive position. The musical programme on the air almost simultaneously ceased: a request that the movement light should be dimmed got through and it gradually faded. There were now some 400 men of the East Lancashire Regiment in the heart of the enemy position a mile and a half behind his forward defences. The surprise was complete. Like duck shooters, they waited for the dawn flight.

Just as the first signs of light appeared in the sky a car with four German officers drove into C Company's area: two were promptly shot at 10 yards' range and two taken prisoner. Party after party of Germans drifted into the lines to receive a similar reception. Daylight revealed to A Company on the embankment to the north large numbers of Germans, blissfully unaware of their presence, shaking their blankets and proceeding with the normal business of the day. They were a sitting target of which A Company were quick to take advantage. Bewildered Germans continued to walk into the position! None got away.

Looking south, the daylight revealed an astonishing situation on the road to Hintham 500 yards away. This was screened by houses and gardens except for a gap some 60 yards long about half way between the village and the eastern edge of 's-Hertogenbosch. Along this road large numbers of men and horse-drawn vehicles were moving. On this gap D Company trained first six Bren guns and then 12. The effect was devastating. Horse-drawn guns, wagons and other vehicles persisted in trying to run the gauntlet of the murderous fire. The road was soon blocked by dead and dying horses and men and wrecked vehicles. Still the Germans persisted. Careless of cover, the Bren gunners continued to pour their fire into the shambles. Targets such as this come to an infantryman but seldom: to many only in dreams. The artillery now joined them to continue the holocaust.

With the daylight, a carrier section and two anti-tank guns which had somehow or other ploughed and towed their way over the dykes got through. A squadron of tanks was now bumping its way precariously along the steep railway embankment. Within an hour of dawn, the position of the East Lancashires was immensely strong, with a railway embankment to the north, a lake to the south and dykes to the east. Nothing could dislodge them. Their success was quickly exploited. About 7 a.m. the 1st/5th Welch arrived on their northern flank and pushed a platoon ahead to seize the northernmost bridge within the city. The Germans then blew up all the bridges at the south-east end of the town. When the tanks arrived, A Company of the East Lancashires attacked and established a bridgehead here on the far side. At 8.30 a.m. the 7th Royal Welch Fusiliers supported by two squadrons of 5th Dragoon Guards attacked the village of Hintham, and carried it: by the early afternoon they had reached the factory area south-east of the town. They then pushed on supported by tanks and Crocodiles, to secure a crossing over the nearby lock of the Zuid Willems Canal. This they held despite heavy mortaring and counter-attack. To the north 160th Brigade now took on the task of clearing the city. The road through Hintham now being open, hot food reached the East Lancashires, who were no longer for the moment in the forefront of the battle. In the houses of the garden suburb and near the bridge no amount of mortaring could disturb their sleep.

The battle was by no means over. Strongly reinforced by infantry, tanks and SP guns, the Germans were still determined to fight for 's-Hertogenbosch house by house and street by street. 25 October began with a setback. 160th Brigade's attempt to force the crossing in the north of the city struck most obstinate resistance and came to nought. It was therefore decided to put the 1st East Lancashires round the southern flank of the town to capture the bridge over the River Dommel near the Wilhelmina Park at the south-west corner and exploit northwards: meanwhile the 1st/5th Welch were to clear the centre of the town starting from the bridgehead gained the previous day in the south-east corner.

Built-up areas are easy to defend and costly to attack. Determined troops such as the Germans in 's-Hertogenbosch, can hold out even in small bodies, for a long time. House clearance is tedious and inevitably slow. Every house and every street has to be tackled methodically. The task is one in which everything depends on the quality and initiative of the junior leaders — the platoon and section commanders. Those in the 1st East Lancashires were now to prove that they were second to none. A troop of tanks of the East Riding Yeomanry now joined each company.

The initial attack, an attempt to enlarge the bridgehead at the south-east corner of the town, started about 11 a.m. and at once ran into a network of machine-gun and sniping fire. It soon became evident that progress here was likely to be unacceptably slow, frustrating and costly. Lieutenant-Colonel Burden therefore decided to outflank it by working round the canal bank on the southern side of the town. Very heavy mortar and machine-gun fire greeted this attempt: despite this, in the next three hours the leading company, fighting every inch of the way and backed by the tanks, succeeded in advancing about 500 yards. German resistance was obstinate to a degree. Lieutenant-Colonel Burden now pushed through B Company directed on the Wilhelmina Park and the bridge over the Dommel at the south-west corner of the town. Brushing aside a screen of infantry, the company approached the bridge as the light faded. Violent fire from the far bank now greeted them: a heavy anti-tank gun hit and completely destroyed the leading tank. Under cover of darkness, the battalion closed up behind them amongst the houses immediately east of the canal. The enemy's mortar and shell fire continued throughout the night. It was not until a late hour that the position in 's-Hertogenbosch became clear.

To the north three other battalions had lined up with the canal on the west edge of the city; all reported that the bridges had been blown. They had in fact closed with the position on which the enemy had decided to make his last effort to hold 's-Hertogenbosch. At dawn, Major Lake of the East Lancashires climbed up to the top of a building overlooking the bridge on this front: there were several gaping holes in it but it looked as if infantry and perhaps even an anti-tank gun could get across. The enemy covering it were dug in on the far bank and hidden in houses on the far side. The bridge on the front of the 1st/5th Welch 400 yards to the north was also found to be imperfectly demolished. The vague situation of the night before thus cleared up, the Brigadier took a hand: the 1st/5th Welch at 11.15 a.m. supported by mortar fire would rush their bridge: an hour later the East Lancashires would deal similarly with theirs, this time supported by heavy artillery fire. Owing apparently to the absence of artillery fire, the Welsh assault when it went in caught the enemy off his guard and a bridgehead of two companies was soon established. However reaction, when it came, was violent. Meanwhile the enemy forces opposite the East Lancashires were subjected to very heavy bombardment; smoke from the battalion mortars created a thin mist round the bridge. There was some delay because the four Crocodiles supporting the battalion were not ready; when they were they wasted their flame on the wrong bridge. At 1.15 p.m. the battalion rushed the bridges followed by its anti-tank guns which were manhandled across the gaps. Wild firing broke out amongst the buildings ahead; prisoners in hundreds started to pour back across the bridge, already under repair by the engineers. The 7th Royal Welch Fusiliers now passed through and, driving due north, relieved the hard-pressed 1st/5th Welch and captured the German garrison commander. Casualties around the bridges from shellfire were heavy. Fighting west of the canal with enemy tanks and infantry went on till nightfall. It was not until the evening of the following day that the last traces of German resistance were eliminated.

Thus on the evening of 27 October in heavy rain ended the battle of 's-Hertogenbosch. Quiet returned to the city; the Dutch emerged from their hiding places to resume normal life. It had been a tough four-day battle. Unquestionably the thrust of the 1st East Lancashires and 1st/5th Welch on the night of 23/24 October — the moment when Air Chief Marshal Tedder penned his memorandum expressing his concern for the morale of the army — under cover of darkness broke the back of the German defences outside the city. Nevertheless, although surprised, they had been quick to react and fight within the city itself, house by house and street by street. For the 53rd Division itself reduction of the place was a triumph of flexible command and teamwork by all arms. Nonetheless, the honours went to the infantry, the Welch Fusiliers, the 1st/5th Welch, and above all to the 1st East Lancashires — a Regular battalion with all the grim battle honours of Badajoz, Waterloo, Inkerman and the Somme on its colours — the epitome of the long and bloody history of the Infantry of the Line. But it was not the memory of past triumphs which carried it irresistibly forward: the East Lancashires fought well and overcame because they were led well by their battalion commander and the officers and the non-commissioned officers down to the last promoted lance-corporal, and because the men in the ranks were well-trained, inured to hardship and determined to end the war in the only way it could be ended — by killing Germans. In action almost continuously for five days, often cold and soaked to the skin and with little or no sleep or hot food at a cost of 25 per cent casualties, the will of these men, for the most part children of the Great Depression of the thirties and the drab streets of Lancashire, to close with the enemy never faltered. Morally, in comparison with them, the military bureaucrats in the vast Headquarters warmly housed and regularly fed looked small indeed.

Tilburg fell to the 15th Scottish Division on the evening of 27 October: the 51st Highland Division got forward on their right, the 7th Armoured Division pushed steadily to the west in vile weather. By 27 November the 15th Army had been driven across the Maas. By this time, the 1st East Lancashires were again in action 80 miles away. Here on the extreme left of the 1st US Army, US 7th Armoured Division was holding a long sector in the Peel Marshes. On the day 's-Hertogenbosch fell, with the intention of forcing the British to suspend their attack on his 15th Army, Model had attacked here with XLVII Panzer Corps and driven the Americans back for several miles.

There was considerable alarm in the rear area of 2nd Army. The 15th Scottish and 53rd Welsh Divisions were therefore quickly moved in buses to plug the gap.

6: NADIR OF THE GENERAL STAFF

But Cyrus, full of the ardour which brooks no delay, and acting on that oldest and soundest of military principles, to do that which your enemy least expects, gave his adversary no breathing spell. Winter was at hand.

Dodge, 'Alexander'

When in the second half of September the British struck north from Eindhoven towards Arnhem and the Americans towards Aachen, a huge gap inevitably opened between the two armies. This lay west of the Maas in the area known as the Peel Marshes, about 10 miles east of Eindhoven, the base of the 'Market Garden' salient. No one at the time knew much about it or what German forces it contained, but all estimates erred wildly on the side of optimism. The need to clean up the situation here and push the Germans back across the Maas being obvious and in view of Montgomery's preoccupation with the Arnhem operations, the boundary between the two armies was shifted northwards on what today seem most eccentric lines. Hodges, the Commander of the 1st US Army, inherited in fact a huge, sausage-shaped stretch of land protruding almost 40 miles into the British zone west of the Maas. Altogether it covered an area of about 500 square miles. Of all the depressing parts of Holland and North Germany, the Peel Marshes must be the least attractive on any reckoning. In a normal winter the whole area is flooded. There are very few roads and such as there are rapidly disintegrate under heavy traffic; every field is surrounded by a deep dyke.

As the historian of the 11th Hussars mournfully records: 'The country was flatter than one would have thought possible and a rise of five feet was enough to earn the designation of "high ground"; and members of the Regiment cannot be blamed for striking the Peel Country off the list of places in Europe they wish to revisit.'

It is ironic that the headquarters of shape, the successors of SHAEF, should have been banished in 1967 to the near vicinity of the Peel Marshes by the military adventurer they had brought along with their baggage to Paris in 1944.

Even more eccentric than the shape of the boundary between the Allied Armies was the choice of the force selected to evict the Germans — the 7th US Armoured Division, the 113th US Cavalry Group and the Belgian Brigade, which was entirely motorised.

The 7th US Armoured Division had arrived in Europe at the time when the Battle of Normandy had entered the pursuit phase. If possible, troops without fighting experience should be given an easy task for their first taste of action. Instead, the 7th Armoured Division's introduction had been a bitter battle on the Moselle. When it arrived in Holland in the last week of September, it was still recovering from the shock. The Intelligence estimate of the number of Germans in the Peel Marshes at the time was 2,000-3,000. In fact there were at least seven times as many — a complete corps under General von Obstfelder including the 176th Division, the Parachute Training Division and the Kampfgruppe Walter, the force which had cut the corridor to Nijmegen during the Arnhem operations. When, therefore, the 7th Armoured Division moved north through the British zone and struck south-east on 30 September towards Overloon and Venray along the only stretch of land in the area suitable for tanks with the object of clearing the west bank of the Maas, it soon ran into a strong German position stiff with anti-tank guns, mines, Panzerfausts and well-entrenched infantry. After six days' fighting and an advance of barely two miles, it became clear that the division had undertaken a task beyond its power; indeed it had not even progressed beyond the British zone. Losses, particularly in tanks, had been heavy. The Belgian Brigade and the 113th Cavalry Group attacking eastwards at the same time had got nowhere. As the operations involved a long detour through the British 2nd Army's area, one complexity would have been removed if the 7th US Armoured Division had been placed under British command from the start. At least Bradley reached this conclusion: on 8 October he handed over the whole area to the British 2nd Army and with it the Armoured Division and the Belgian Brigade, who thus now came under command of O'Connor's VIII Corps, with no apparent regret.

The 3rd British Division, supported by 6th Guards Armoured Brigade, now took over responsibility for the thrust to Venray and Venlo and on 12 October carried the village of Overloon. Resuming the attack next day, they encountered the same opposition as the Americans had done — extensive minefields, marshes, anti-tank guns, Nebelwerfer and artillery fire — and fighting all the way, on 17 October reached Venray. At this point Montgomery, in view of the need to concentrate all efforts on the Antwerp operations, temporarily suspended operations in the region. Quiet descended on the Peel Marshes.

On being relieved by the British 3rd Division, the 7th US Armoured Division and the Belgian Brigade had assumed a defensive role along the Deurne, the Needweert-Wessem and Noorder Canals. The line here was 30 miles long. Despite its length, the canals provided formidable obstacles: the only feasible approaches to them all led to the little town of Meijel in the centre.

Although Montgomery had for the time being placed operations in the Peel Marshes in cold storage, his opponent, Model, had other views. The 15th Army at Antwerp was now in desperate straits: somehow or other means had to be found to relieve the pressure on them. Montgomery's forces were widely extended, and their eastern flank along the 'Market Garden' salient was peculiarly vulnerable. A blow here from the Peel Marshes might well force Montgomery to abandon the offensive north-west of Antwerp. Model, engaged in training and rehabilitation, had available north of Aachen a force in every way suitable for a powerful armoured thrust — the XIVII Panzer Corps under General von Lüttwitz. Its main components were the 9th Panzer Division, 11,000 strong with at least 22 Panther tanks and 178 other armoured vehicles of various types, including self-propelled guns, and the 15th Panzer Grenadier Division, 13,000 strong and with further tanks. Model decided to use it against the centre of the thinly held line of the 7th US Armoured Division at Meijel and to carve out a chunk six miles deep. The weather in the last week of October was cold and overcast; the war seemed to have expired with the rapid decline into winter. It seemed as if both sides had settled down to a policy of live and let live.

Suddenly, about half an hour before dawn on 27 October, a violent artillery bombardment lasting 45 minutes descended on the posts of 7th US Armoured Division along the Deurne Canal. Hot on its tail came two armoured columns of 9th Panzer Division: one carried the town of Meijel and pushed on along the Asten road: the other thrust north towards Deurne. By nightfall both had advanced some five miles beyond the canal. At dawn next day, General Silvester, the Commander of the 7th US Armoured Division, relieved of responsibility for the northern part of his front by General O'Connor, struck back on both roads. Both these counterattacks came to naught. Early on the third day, 29 October, the Germans renewed their offensive and on the right drove the Americans back a further five miles. The situation was alarming. If the 7th US Armoured Division was wiped off the map, the rear area of 2nd Army, packed with administrative units and very few frontline troops, lay wide open to armoured attack. The alarm spread rapidly amongst the Dutch. Only 10 miles away near Helmond was the headquarters of the British 2nd Army. Bad news travels fast. For the first and only time in the campaign, the staff and clerks took to slit trenches and prepared to face a hero's death.

No one was more surprised at the speed of the advance than Model himself. Ever an opportunist, he had already pressed von Rundstedt on the second day of his attack to give him the 116th Panzer Division and six additional artillery battalions to enable him to turn what had originally been designed as a limited operation into a large-scale raid in the British back areas, of the type which Rommel had already made familiar in North Africa. Von Rundstedt would have none of it: the force had already lost some 30 tanks: it was wanted for another role; there were no signs that the thrust was drawing British forces away from the 15th Army, now *in extremis* north-east of Antwerp. What this new role was, Model in his headquarters at Fichtenhein near Krefeld, in a group of modern buildings designed as a nursing home for alcoholics, already knew. He did not think much of it — 'It hadn't got a damned leg to stand on'. Nonetheless, he had to call off the attack in the Peel Marshes. Although he did not know it, it had achieved its aim.

To plug the gap, Montgomery had already pulled out 15th Scottish Division, followed by the 53rd Welsh Division, from

North-West Holland, and they now arrived to relieve the 7th Armoured Division. Reappraising the situation, he reached the conclusion that clearing the Peel Marshes and thus closing with the Maas was obviously going to take considerable time, and the combined efforts of the VIII and XII Corps. Until this was done, he would not be in a position to carry out the task assigned to him by Eisenhower in the offensive now about to be launched towards the Ruhr.

What exactly the 'Broad Front' policy implied in practical terms, which set the pattern of Allied strategy for the rest of the campaign in the north, had been revealed to Montgomery and Bradley by Eisenhower at a conference held in Brussels on 18 October.

The 1st US Army would attack early in November from Aachen and secure a bridgehead over the Rhine south of Cologne. On its left the 9th US Army would also drive towards the Rhine, protecting the 1st Army's left flank, and then drive north between the Rhine and the Maas to meet a thrust by Montgomery's Army Group south-east from Nijmegen. Having thus closed with the Rhine, Eisenhower then proposed to encircle the Ruhr by moving 9th Army with Bradley's Army Group to the north and 1st Army to the south. Patton's 3rd Army was to protect 1st Army's right flank and the 6th Army Group in the south to advance to the Rhine at Strasbourg. Montgomery thus assumed responsibility for the preparation and launching of the 'Battle of the Rhineland' — in other words, the clearance of the area between the Rhine and the Maas. For the moment this must wait. He could, however, immediately assist the advance of 9th Army by simultaneously removing the strong German forces west of the Maas in the Peel Marshes. To this he now turned his attention.

Eisenhower and Montgomery's decisions were based on information supplied to them at the time by their Intelligence staffs. Postwar analysis and criticisms of their actions based on information which has since come to light is not only often ungenerous, but likely to be unfair as well. Nevertheless, in view of the large number of able men on their Intelligence staffs, it is surprising that they were so ill-served at this stage of the war. Their Chief Intelligence Officers were men who would have been outstanding in almost any walk of life, and in some cases were. When wars break out, the magic word 'Intelligence' attracts dons and schoolmasters like insects to a lighted lamp in the darkness — even the intellectual athletes in Arts of the older universities. The crux of the problem which faces every commander before a battle is: what is the character of my opponent and what, with the resources available to him, is he likely to do? In the last months of 1944 the opposing commander was Hitler himself. His record for the past 12 years was available in the greatest detail: in *Mein Kampf* he had revealed the secrets of his soul; the effect of his military decisions in Russia, North Africa, Italy and Normandy was known. And yet when these able men addressed themselves to the key question, they got the answer wrong. In fact it was simple enough, indeed almost to the point of absurdity. This may well be why in the complexity of their own thought, and forgetting they were no longer dealing with spotty adolescents, but forced for a brief interlude in their lives to the necessity for reaching a firm conclusion, they failed to perceive the obvious. Of the many courses open to Hitler in the autumn of 1944, they failed to consider the one he actually took.

Throughout the Normandy operations it had been evident that all decisions for major operations were made by Hitler himself, not only in principle but down to the smallest detail. It is inconceivable that any German general would have staged the mad thrust from Mortain to Avranches at the time of Bradley's breakout which finally sealed the fate of the 7th Army. The 20 July plot had further convinced Hitler of the fact that he could not trust his Generals not to stage another *coup d'état* against him and that he must retain control in his own hands. Nothing, not even defeat after defeat, could shake his faith in his own military genius.

An omnivorous and self-taught student of military history, he found in it a mine of apparent precedents which he used incessantly to confront the arguments of those who dared to suggest alternatives to conclusions on which he had already made up his mind. As a result of his studies he had convinced himself that success in war depended on the application of a few simple rules. Offensive action is the secret of successful war: negotiation must proceed from strength, that is after a victory, never after a defeat. The keys to military success are surprise and concentration of overwhelming force at the decisive time and place: this often is the point where two allied armies join. The will to conquer, if ruthlessly and inflexibly maintained, will triumph in the end. Brooding over the past he had convinced himself that he alone possessed the secret of how to apply this bleak and crude doctrine.

In fact he had little conception of the nature of mid-twentieth-century warfare. His visits to the back areas behind the fronts were rare. He visualised operations in terms of his own experience as a corporal in the 16th Bavarian Regiment in 1918. This he had made clear in *Mein Kampf*:

> It was my luck to be in the first two and the last offensives [of 1918]. They made on me the most tremendous impressions of my whole life; tremendous because for the last time the struggle lost its defensive character and became an offensive

as it was in 1914. In the German Army's trenches and mine galleries men breathed anew again when, after three years of hell, the day for squaring the account at last arrived.... For the last time the Goodness of God smiled on his ungrateful children.

In March 1918, Ludendorff had launched 40 divisions against 21 of Haig's about St Quentin aimed at Amiens, a vital point in the Allied railway communications and virtually along the boundary between the French and British. In 10 days' fighting he had driven the British back approximately 40 miles. The exhaustion of his troops and the breakdown of his supply system had prevented him from separating the two Armies and driving the French towards Paris and the British to the coast. In this offensive the attacking troops had been concealed behind the flank of the front attacked until the last possible moment, when they were moved up to their assault positions under cover of darkness. The actual attack had been preceded by an overwhelming artillery bombardment. In this battle, Hitler concluded, lay the prescription for victory. Another along the same lines, with Antwerp substituted for Amiens as the objective, would be equally successful. The fact that Ludendorff's Army had to cover only 40 miles, whereas it was 150 miles to Antwerp with the Maas to be crossed *en route*, was a detail which could be ignored. Nothing in Eisenhower's record indicated that he was less gullible than Haig. In any case, Hitler had a poor opinion of professional soldiers. In May 1940 he had overridden their advice and shifted the point of breakthrough from north to south of Liège. Key features in this operation had been airborne operations to secure the Maas bridges and the move of XV Armoured Corps through the Ardennes, an area considered impracticable for operations by orthodox military opinion, whether British, French or German.

There followed von Manstein's lightning campaign, the collapse of France and the Dunkirk evacuation.

What the Germans could do in 1918 and 1940 they could do again. The massing of great numbers of guns to open the fighting had long since ceased to be a feature of German tactics; to revive it would confront the Americans with an overwhelming bombardment for which they were psychologically unprepared. The short hours of daylight would enable the concentration of the troops and guns for the offensive to be concealed. The likelihood of bad flying weather at this time of the year would offset the weakness of the Luftwaffe. Above all, resumption of the offensive would remove the threat to the ultimate source of German material strength — the Ruhr. Delivered in this way through the Ardennes in early December by the Strategic Reserve, there would be time to snatch victory in the West and redeploy to meet the Russians when the ground had frozen hard enough to permit mobile operations in January. The Ludendorff concept of 1918, with some of the 1940 modifications, was thus the solution, delivered this time from the Ardennes. Accordingly Jodl, on 9 October, was ordered to work out the details and produce a plan couched in the language of the General Staff. He had served too long in closer contact with Hitler than any other officer of the General Staff for any thought of protest to enter his head. At his trial at Nuremberg, he stated that the plan was Hitler's own: it was merely his function to provide his master with the necessary data and translate his orders into action. The general impression in the Wehrmacht that he was merely Hitler's tool is probably correct: that he was also a highly competent staff officer there can be no doubt. Equally certain is that close association with Hitler had destroyed whatever moral sense he may ever have had.

The German layout on the Western front had now reached the form it was to retain for the rest of the year. In the north, Student's Army Group H held Holland, roughly facing Montgomery's 21st Army Group. In the centre, Army Group B under Model, comprising the 5th Panzer Army and 7th Army, confronted Bradley's 12th Army Group, which now included from north to south the 9th, 1st and 3rd Armies on the German frontier where it touches Belgium and Luxembourg. Army Group H, now under Balck, facing 6th US Army Group defended Alsace and Lorraine. Behind Model's Army Group B a further Panzer Army, the 6th, was forming.

In response to an order from Jodl, Westphal and Krebs, Chiefs of Staff to von Rundstedt and Model respectively, reported at Hitler's headquarters in the Wolf's Lair in East Prussia on the morning of 22 October. Immediately on arrival they were ordered to sign an undertaking binding them to the utmost secrecy concerning a mysterious operation named *Wacht am Rhein* (Watch on the Rhine) and informed that if any details of the plan leaked out, they would be shot. They meekly swallowed the insult. The title of the plan was aptly chosen, giving as it did the impression that it concerned the next American offensive now obviously imminent on the Aachen front. A long list of troops due to arrive on the Western front in late November and early December was handed to them at the same time.

At noon, they attended Hitler's daily conference. Routine business was quickly dealt with and the majority of the staff dismissed. The two Chiefs of Staff then found themselves in a much smaller meeting presided over by Hitler himself. As Chief of Staff to Rommel in North Africa, Westphal was no stranger to fantastic proposals. What the Führer now revealed, however, took even his breath away. Hitler intended to go over to the offensive in the West on the front of Army Group B in the Eifel area where the Americans were weak and drive on Antwerp, splitting the enemy front into two and surrounding the British and American forces north of the line Bastogne-Brussels-Antwerp. The operation would be carried out in two phases: in the first, bridgeheads over the Maas would be seized; in the second Antwerp would be the objective. Model would have at his disposal the 5th Panzer Army under Hasso von Manteuffel and the 6th Panzer Army under Sepp Dietrich, which would spearhead the attack: the 7th Army would cover their exposed flank. Preparations would be complete by 25 November, a date expected to coincide with the end of 10 days' continuous bad weather, which was likely to ground the Allied Air Forces. For planning purposes, Westphal and Krebs were to count on receiving from the Strategic Reserve additional reinforcements in the shape of 13 infantry divisions, two parachute divisions and six Panzer-type divisions. Meanwhile von Rundstedt was to withdraw from the Western front three infantry and six armoured divisions. By these means 18 infantry and 12 armoured divisions would be made available to Model for the Grand Assault.

Hitler then ran through the list of additional reinforcements that had already been ordered: five anti-aircraft regiments, 12 Volks Artillery Corps, 10 Nebelwerfer Brigades, and other units. He emphasised that these reinforcements would definitely be forthcoming and promised that the Luftwaffe would support the operation with 1,500 fighters, including 100 jets which were superior to anything the British and Americans could produce.

Keitel now gave his word of honour that four and a quarter million gallons of petrol and 50 trainloads of artillery ammunition would be set aside for the offensive.

Meanwhile, said Hitler, von Rundstedt must hold his ground and keep out of the defensive battle all troops earmarked for *Wacht am Rhein*. Westphal and Krebs, their automatic obedience assumed as if they were mere clerks, were then dismissed, with orders to submit draft plans for the first phase, the advance to the Maas, and to be sharp about it.

The plan was audacious, but no more audacious than some of a similar character which had brought victory to Sherman in the American Civil War, to von Manstein in Russia and to Rommel in Africa. Furthermore, commanders well qualified to conduct a desperate adventure were at hand. Von Rundstedt, now a mere figurehead, could be relied upon to put his rubber stamp on instructions from the Wolf's Lair. His Chief of Staff, Westphal, in his own sphere, was at least as competent as any other survivor of the General Staff. In any case, they were expected to work miracles. The real commander would be Model who, unlike von Rundstedt, had not lost the creative urge; he was in the prime of life and had proved his reputation in many a tight corner. Foul-mouthed and apparently always in a rage, he could be relied on to drive the troops to the limit. An ardent Nazi, clever and ambitious, he had staked his all on the personal fortunes of Hitler: more important, he was not a member of the inner circle of the General Staff and was therefore politically reliable.

Sepp Dietrich, Commander of the 6th Panzer Army, had an equally spectacular fighting record. In World War One, this Bavarian butcher's boy had risen to the rank of sergeant. He had been one of the first to join forces with Hitler in 1923. During the 'Night of the Long Knives' on 30 June 1934 he had commanded the SS Guard battalion which assassinated Hitler's rivals, the SA, in Munich. Thereafter promotion had been rapid. In Russia his reputation as a tough leader in a rough house was almost legendary, and as a corps commander in the great battles on the Falaise road, he had at least avoided losing it. His personal courage, tenacity and drive were outstanding. Despite his impatience with the complications of staff work, he was a good trainer. Given the means, there seemed to be, at any rate to Hitler, every reason to believe that this super sergeant-major would be able to handle an army as well as he had handled a corps.

Hasso von Manteuffel, in sharp contrast to Sepp Dietrich, came from the upper ranks of pre-1914 German society. Born in Potsdam in a family with a long Prussian military tradition, he had entered the army as a cadet in the socially exclusive Zeithen Hussars and become a member of the Reichswehr show-jumping team. This fondness for the horse did not, however, prevent him soon making his mark as an exponent of armoured warfare. Although he was not a member of the General Staff, this had not handicapped his rapid rise on sheer merit as a leader in North Africa and Russia, from a regimental to an army commander. His personal courage endeared him to his troops: his staff were devoted to him. Modest and of small stature, he embodied the frigid virtues of the Prussian aristocracy at its best. Distaste for politics and politicians combined with shrewdness, and luck, had enabled him to avoid incurring Hitler's suspicion. This man was formidable.

No written record survives of what must have been the most dramatic briefing of the war. Confirmatory orders reached von Rundstedt's headquarters by special courier on the night of 2 November. They included a note in Hitler's own hand: 4The intention, organisation and objective of this offensive are unalterable.' In the next few weeks Model must not only beat back the massive American onslaught on the Siegfried Line which was now known to be imminent, but concurrently plan and mount a grandiose armoured counter-stroke as well.

7: NOVEMBER

The name of the slough was Despond. Here therefore they
wallowed for a time, being grievously bedaubed with dirt; and
Christian, because of the burden that was on his back, began
to sink in mire.

Bunyan

Blissfully unaware of what the Germans had in store for them,
Eisenhower and his two United States Army Group
Commanders, Bradley and Devers, now pressed on with the
preparations for their own offensive — an attack on the axis
Aachen-Cologne designed to close with the Rhine, as a first
step towards the envelopment of the Ruhr. Further south,
Patton's virtually independent attack on the Saar had already
started.

In retrospect, as Antwerp was not yet open, and in view of
the rapid onset of winter, it might have been wiser to defer
launching the offensive until the late winter, when good tank
going in frosty conditions could be expected on both their own
and the Russian fronts. Three reasons prompted them to
discard this course of action: German losses at the time were
said to be running at the rate of 4,000 per day; a few more
months' delay would give the enemy a chance to train their
new divisions; above all the Germans might recapture
command of the air with the new jets now known to be
coming off the assembly lines.

The November battle immediately east of Aachen occupies
in the history of the American Army a place and significance
similar to that of the Somme in the history of the British. It

absorbed in the end some 17 divisions, it was fought in vile weather and in country which favoured the enemy, it resulted in heavy casualties, and it placed a severe strain on the morale of the troops. When it finally fizzled out, the Americans had nothing to show for all their efforts beyond a few miles of tree stumps pock-marked with shell holes, shattered buildings and swamps. In this ghastly battle the men of the British Army played only a minor part: it did however give some of them an opportunity of judging the fighting quality of the individual American soldier. Early in November, Horrocks' XXX Corps had taken over from the American 84th Division (the Rail-Splitters) some 17 miles of the front extending from the Maas to the town of Geilenkirchen on the extreme left of the 12th US Army Group. Considerable good-natured *badinage* had characterised the relief: the 84th Division, fresh from the United States, would soon learn what war was really like; the British, given the slightest excuse, sat down and drank tea. Allies usually underrate each other.

This new area north-east of Maastricht formed a rough triangle between the Maas and the Roer with its apex at Roermond. For Guards Armoured Division and 43rd Wessex Division this was their first sight of Germany. They were struck by the almost uncanny quiet and the strangeness of their surroundings. The villages seemed sinister and alien: even the *Gasthauser* had a funereal air. The churches with their bulbous spires seemed outlandish and dark without and forbidding within. To the astonishment of the troops, the inhabitants were still in residence and even doing their autumn ploughing in front of the forward positions. Within a few hours it was brought home to them that a change of management had taken place. The British did not share the trust of their American predecessors that the local population would not betray them to their compatriots only 1,000 yards away, as indeed would have been their duty. Military police appeared and ordered them to go. Bewildered parties of old men, women and children pushing a few possessions, usually including a bright red bedspread, moved painfully back through the rain to the frontier where they were taken by military government detachments to a camp in Holland at Vught, housed and fed. Their arrival was understandably unwelcome to the Dutch, but they were luckier than most other refugees earlier in the war when overrun by the German Armies. The comfort in which they had been living right up to the fifth year of the war astonished the British, accustomed as they were to strict rationing of clothing and fuel and Spartan fare. They left behind them flocks of geese, crowded pigsties and hen-houses, larders full of food. Their attics were stuffed with clothes and footwear; their rooms so full of new furniture as to be overcrowded. They were plump and healthy-looking. There were cellars full of French wine and brandy; huge stocks of coal and wood were at hand — plenty such as the British had not seen for years. All agreed that if war has to be waged it should be in countries other than your own or that of your allies.

Bradley's preparations for his great offensive were now practically complete. South of Aachen, his 1st Army veterans of the Normandy battle, now numbered 300,000 in 12 divisions, three of which were armoured. This was to make the main effort in the drive to the Rhine. The newly arrived 9th Army, starting from immediately north of Aachen, had the task of advancing simultaneously towards the Roer and thus protecting the exposed northern flank of the 1st Army.

Some seven miles ahead, traversing the front, lay the River Roer. This formed the initial objective of both armies. To reach it 1st Army had to fight its way through the Hürtgen forest, about three miles deep. On its flanks were complex industrial areas. The country in front of the 9th Army was much more open; it consisted of farmlands and isolated villages and offered greater opportunities for the use of tanks and, incidentally, for controlling the large forces now to be engaged. It seems therefore strange that Bradley should have selected the intricate Hürtgen forest area for his main effort. When this point was raised with Bradley after the war, he said 'You don't make your main effort with your exterior force'. With this cryptic remark posterity must be satisfied.

Like Haig at the Somme and Passchendaele in World War One, Bradley's intention to attack at Aachen had been blatantly obvious for a considerable time: Model had taken every possible step to deal with it when it came. Barring the way ahead he had the 5th Panzer Army and the 7th Army. The former was particularly strong in artillery, centrally controlled, well-concealed, and increasing as the battle developed to an estimated 1,000 guns. There was ample ammunition. The losses of the early autumn had been made up, admittedly in many cases by reinforcements with comparatively little training, but nonetheless formidable in a defensive role. Finally, as a 'fire brigade', he had the XLVII Panzer Corps withdrawn from the Peel Marshes. Model's aim was crystal-clear: in no circumstances would the Americans be allowed to cross the River Roer.

Like Haig before him in not dissimilar circumstances, Bradley placed his hopes on overwhelming fire rather than subtlety and surprise to shatter his opponents' morale: unlike Haig, he had in addition to his artillery a plan for 'the largest air/ground cooperative effort yet undertaken'. Twelve hundred US heavy bombers had the task of 'taking out' the towns of

Duren, Julich and Heinsberg on the Roer. Seven hundred and fifty fighter-bombers were to be on call by the forward troops. Elaborate precautions were taken to ensure that this avalanche of high explosive was not deposited on the wrong side of the line, as had happened on the Falaise road. Given clear skies, the plan seemed to have all the ingredients for a rapid breakout.

The northern boundary of the 9th Army with the British ran along a mean, sluggish tributary of the Roer appropriately called the Wurm. Here a salient of the Siegfried Line projected like a wedge to the small town of Geilenkirchen. To develop their advance to the Roer the use of the roads passing through it was vital to the 9th Army. The task of eliminating the salient was given to the XXX British Corps with the 84th US Division under command in addition to the 43rd Wessex Division. Originally the operation was planned for the second day of the main offensive: in fact it came a day later.

Vast fleets of bombers heading east passing over XXX Corps about midday on 16 November revealed that the 'last big offensive necessary to bring Germany to her knees' was under way. The Strategic Air Forces at any rate were playing their part. News of the progress of 1st Army did not filter through to XXX Corps till the late afternoon. It was unexhilarating — the bombs, for safety reasons, were dropped so far behind the German forward troops that they almost completely missed them. No more than three per cent of the enemy seem to have been hit. The attacking troops, despite the support of some 1,000 guns, found themselves greeted by murderous small-arms, artillery and mortar fire. It was no consolation to them that the three towns on the Roer six miles ahead had been virtually destroyed. Marked up on the talcs of staff officers and adjutants of XXX Corps, the gains seemed unimpressive. By the following day it had become evident that a battle as obstinately contested as the fighting in the early days in the bridgehead, and not the expected breakthrough, had developed on the whole American front about Aachen.

With ample time to prepare for his own part in the battle, Horrocks ensured that not a moment was wasted. Patrols probed the enemy's defences and accurately pinpointed the main centres of likely resistance: reconnaissance parties in the brick works at Gilrath and the church spire of the village of Teveren scanned the country ahead. The Intelligence Officers of each of the attacking battalions constructed large-scale models and with their aid every man had the part he was expected to play thoroughly explained to him. To the preparation of the actual fire plan, Major-General G. I. Thomas of the 43rd Wessex Division brought a lively and original mind, probably unequalled in this respect by any other commander of similar rank in the Allied Armies. His division was organised and trained not to think and act in terms merely of their own arm but as teams combining the effort of the infantry, artillery and tanks. Each of his three brigades had a field regiment of 25-pounders and a regiment of the 8th Armoured Brigade permanently 'affiliated' to it. Their COs lived with the brigadiers. Each battalion had a battery and squadron of tanks which it regarded as its own. The infantry spoke of 'our gunners' and 'our tanks'. There had thus grown up a feeling of mutual confidence and, it must be added, mutual admiration. This delegation of command in no way deprived the senior artillery and tank commanders of the power to concentrate their resources according to the requirements of the battle.

Technically, the Royal Artillery at this stage of the war had reached a standard of efficiency unequalled by any other army in World War Two. There were more gunners than infantry in Montgomery's Army. Their radio communications and discipline were superior to those of both the Germans and Americans. An infantry brigadier, using the code word 'Victor' could bring down the fire of 300 guns within a minute on any given point. In view of the shortage of manpower, the need had been foreseen for vast supplies of ammunition, to enable the infantry to close with the enemy with the minimum possible loss. The volume and weight of accurate fire which the British could produce astonished the Germans: the amount of punishment the Germans could take equally impressed the British.

The ground east of the River Wurm was considerably higher that that on the west, where the 43rd Wessex Division's attack was due to go in. It was therefore planned that the 84th US Division should attack first to take the high ground about a mile and a half ahead near the village of Prummen. Its right flank thus secure, the 43rd Wessex Division would then thrust forward to a depth of about two and a half miles and complete the encirclement of the town of Geilenkirchen, which 84th Division would then mop up. To complete the wiping-out of the enemy salient, a further advance of about one and a half miles was contemplated on both sides of the Wurm, to the villages of Hoven, Mullendorf, Wurm and Beek.

Men who have been deprived of sleep for several days, subjected to exposure to the weather in wet slit-trenches and denied regular food can be expected when finally attacked to display less enthusiasm than rested troops, advancing on full bellies. Continuous artillery bombardment can boost morale, but it is expensive, and in any case sufficient artillery ammunition was not available at the time. This did not deter Major-General Thomas: he had other weapons in his armoury

— 3- and 4.2-inch mortars, 70 all told, his Vickers machineguns, the 17-pounder guns, 216 in number, of the 8th Armoured Brigade; the 54 40-mm. guns of his light anti-aircraft regiment; the 48 6-pounder and 17-pounder guns of his anti-tank regiment. This massive array which General Thomas called his 'pepperpot', opened up at nightfall on 16 November and for the next 40 hours or so poured a continuous stream of shells and bullets into the positions held by the German 176th Division and 183rd Volksgrenadier Division around Geilenkirchen. Some of the shells and bombs were incendiary and fires soon lit up the night sky.

An hour before dawn on 18 November in the hazy light cast by the searchlight beams of 357th Searchlight Battery, Royal Artillery, two troops of Flail tanks moved forward into the minefield south of Geilenkirchen and despite the greasy mud flogged two lanes through it. An hour later under cover of a sharp five-minute bombardment, two battalions of the 84th US Division moved through. What they lacked in experience they more than made up by their outstanding courage; fighting their way forward supported by the Sherwood Rangers Yeomanry of the British 8th Armoured Brigade, by midday they reached the concrete defences of Prummen. Large movements of reserves behind the German lines were promptly halted by spectacular attacks of 'typhoons' from the 'cab-rank' in the sky.

With all thus going well on his right flank, Horrocks, soon after midday, released the 7th Somerset Light Infantry and 1st Worcestershires towards the villages of Neiderheide and Tripsrath. An avalanche of fire descended on the village of Bauchem, a suburb of Geilenkirchen, on their right flank. Crashes and spurts of smoke ahead showed where the gunners were hammering the German positions. Streams of tracer fire from machine and Bofors guns poured ahead. The tanks of

4th/7th Dragoon Guards did all they could to keep up with the advance, but were soon bogged down in the mud. Fighting transport endeavouring to follow became hopelessly stuck down to the axles. Nonetheless the infantry forged ahead, despatching their prisoners to the rear. Neiderheide fell to the Somersets on schedule. The Worcesters pressed on towards Tripsrath. Suddenly two SP guns in a small wood ahead emerged and shot their carrier platoon to ribbons — in a flash 31 men had fallen. The commanding officer, Lieutenant-Colonel Osborne-Smith, was hit; there was a check. The final objective was still 1,000 yards ahead. Major Ricketts now took charge and made a fresh fire plan. As night fell the Worcesters fought their way into their final objective.

Meanwhile the 5th DCLI had crashed their way through the congestion at the gaps in the enemy minefield and moving through the Somerset Light Infantry pressed on for two and a half miles. They then swung south and as the light faded, cut the main road running north-east out of Geilenkirchen at the hamlet of Bruggerhof. On the right beyond the Wurm the 84th Division were now in Prummen but not completely masters of it. Behind them Bauchem had fallen after a formidable bombardment to the 5th Dorsets.

Geilenkirchen was surrounded. Amongst the large number of prisoners moving to the rear were members of the 9th PZ Division: the enemy had committed at least part of his reserve. When night fell, both the British and the American divisions had taken all their objectives. Skilled planning and flexible fire support can accomplish much: put into execution by troops with stout hearts, it had enabled the 84th US Division in their first battle to step off on the right foot and the 43rd Wessex Division to gain all their objectives — and on time.

The battle had only just begun; in fact it was to continue for another five days. That night it rained, converting the fields into quagmires. The whole front now felt the weight of the guns in the Siegfried Line. Next day the 84th Division entered Geilenkirchen, driving the Germans into the fire of the Bren guns of the 5th DCLI. Meanwhile the Dorsets on the left of the 43rd Division fought their way through the thick woods to the northern edge west of Tripsrath: the 7th Somerset Light Infantry in the woods east of the village advanced another mile. The 84th Division, however, found themselves faced by overwhelming fire from the concrete emplacements blocking the way forward to their final objectives, the villages of Mullendorf, Wurm and Beek. First-class German troops, the 15th Panzer Grenadier Division, now barred the way. It was galling to see their tanks with their broad tracks manoeuvring over muddy fields impassable to our own. Somehow or other carrying parties of the 43rd Wessex Division got hot food, rum and ammunition to the Dorsets, the Somersets, the Worcestershires and the DCLI. Their spirits never flagged. The DCLI's official historian writes:

> Years after the event those who survived could recall the intensity of the enemy fire and the sloppy ground over which they had to move to reach their objective. What is difficult to describe is the physical agony of the infantryman when fighting forward against two enemies at once: men and their lethal weapons and vile weather. The former could be assessed and partly avoided, the latter not at all. The days and nights were wet. The November rain seemed piercingly cold. After exertion when the body warmed, the cold air and the wet seemed to penetrate the very marrow of every bone in the body, so that the whole shook as with ague, and then after shaking would come a numbness of hand and leg and mind, and a feeling of surrender to forces of nature far greater in

strength than any enemy might impose. Only the inherent claim of self preservation and the determination to do one's duty kept men alive and active.

A damp, grey mist hung over the pill-boxes on the eastern bank of the Wurm and the rain-soaked field and woods to the west of it, where the 43rd Division were now a mile ahead of the Americans. The latter resumed their attack in a downpour on the 21st and aided by British Crocodiles closed with the Germans on the concrete defences of Suggerath and thrust onwards towards the next village, Mullendorf, 500 yards ahead up a gentle falling slope, only to be held up. Until a way could be found through the ruins of Suggerath for the tanks further progress was impossible.

For the 22nd, Horrocks ordered a supreme effort on both sides of the Wurm to carry the final objectives of Mullendorf, Wurm, Beek, Hoven and Kraudorf. After four days' close fighting both British and Americans were reaching the limits of endurance. Only those with actual experience of such circumstances know the moral struggle over their own emotions which the battalion and brigade commanders had to endure and overcome. It was not easy to order the rain-soaked soldiers of the DCLI once more into action in the dripping woods. Fierce fire greeted them from the trees ahead: as they worked their way forward men fell thick and fast. Germans in their rear who had been missed in the advance continued firing behind them. Stretcher bearers struggled amongst the trees to extricate the men who had fallen. Undeterred as the grey light deepened into darkness the survivors fought their way into the houses of the village of Hoven, reorganised and prepared to meet counter-attack. A nightmare night now began: prisoners had to be despatched to the rear; the wounded had to be got out. The slightest move brought a burst of Spandau fire.

Nonetheless they were ready to fight on. They had done what they had been ordered to do; provided the Americans on their flank got forward when daylight returned all would end well.

It was not until long after dark that the critical nature of the situation became clear; until the debris in Suggerath could be pushed aside by a bulldozer, the tanks supporting the Americans could not get forward. It failed to arrive. At length British Crocodiles got through and with their support the 84th Division carried three pill-boxes. At nightfall, however, they were still 500 yards from Mullendorf. The DCLI in Hoven were thus at the tip of a pencil-like salient, a mile and a half ahead of the Americans. If the 84th Division did not renew its attack at dawn, the chances of survival of the DCLI were slim.

About midnight, a tall figure dripping with rain arrived in a jeep at the headquarters of the attacking brigade in Geilenkirchen. It was Horrocks, the Corps Commander himself, true as ever to his instinct of being at the critical point at the critical time. He and the Brigadier had no illusions. If the Americans resumed the attack in the morning all would be well: if they did not the DCLI in Hoven were doomed. Horrocks gave his decision: if the Brigadier wished to withdraw the DCLI now while there was still time he could do so. If he chose to stay and gamble on the Americans resuming their attack at dawn, whatever happened, he would have Horrocks' backing. The Brigadier elected to stand fast: the DCLI had never since the early days in Normandy fought otherwise than to the bitter end. They would not do so now. Horrocks departed through the night to urge the Americans once more into the attack.

Just before dawn fighting flared up in the headquarters of the company holding Hoven. It was beaten off, but a grenade smashed the wireless set and thus cut off contact with the guns. A German tank outside ran over the telephone line which had been laid during the night. The company was on its own. As the light improved, large numbers of Germans could be seen advancing along the hedgerows. They were greeted with withering fire. For two and a half hours the fight went on. Then came another attack, this time supported by two SP guns. Captain Spencer, leaning over a window-sill in an upper room, engaged a tank in the street with a Piat only to be wounded by fire from the tank. Meanwhile, a further force of Germans had closed with the company in the rear of Hoven, which was thus surrounded. The battle continued at heavy cost for both sides. Hoven was soon choked with British and German wounded; many houses were in flames. British ammunition ran out; the dwindling body of defenders fought on with both weapons and ammunition taken from the enemy. Eventually only Major Lonsdale and 15 men were left. He decided, rather than surrender, to fight his way out, taking with him such wounded men as could walk. Aided by the smoke from the burning buildings, they cut their way through to the position held by what was left of the battalion some 700 yards in rear of the village. Here the line held. They left behind them as prisoners only wounded men who could not be removed. The enemy who belonged to 10th Panzer Division, apparently reinforced by two companies of 21st Panzer Division despatched from the far side of the Wurm, treated the British wounded with the same consideration as their own, spoke ruefully of their own heavy losses and expressed their own admiration for the DCLI.

It had been a gallant fight to a finish. The attack by the 84th Division beyond the Wurm came to nothing; they too had fought to the limit of exhaustion. So far as the British were concerned, apart from holding Hoven, the contract had been fulfilled. The Geilenkirchen salient had been cleared: there was no further point in continuing the offensive on this part of the front. The 43rd Wessex Division had maintained its reputation: the 84th US Division, lacking previous battle experience at the start, had gained British and German respect. What surprised the British was the apparent indifference of the American Commanders to the physical needs of their men in winter warfare. In these conditions, hot food once a day is as vital as ammunition: in the first few days the infantry of the 84th Division were expected to exist on packets of odd items such as eggs and bacon compressed into tablets, gum and candy with nothing hot to drink. Men fight with greater cheerfulness even on the cheapest form of pig's belly of transatlantic origin masquerading as bacon, if hot, or the bully beef and tea and biscuits which maintained the British. They also need a pair of dry socks every day. It is not surprising that the 84th Division had 500 casualties, mostly from trench-foot, which is a preventable disease.

Both sides compare the fighting on the US 9th and 1st Army fronts to the Somme and Verdun. In Hürtgen Forest conditions rivalled the horrors of Passchendaele. One German officer recalled later that 'great losses were caused by numerous frost bites. In some cases, soldiers were found dead in their foxholes from sheer exhaustion.' The village of Hürtgen changed hands 14 times and the village of Vossenack eight times. In at least one American battalion, morale cracked under the strain. An attacking company came suddenly under a heavy concentration of artillery fire, heightened as always in the forest by deadly bursts in the trees and followed by a sharp local counter-attack. The strain of the previous days' fighting apparently had unnerved both men and officers of the company. The men fell back. Colonel Jeter promptly relieved both the company and battalion commanders involved in this incident and a day later had to appoint a third company commander when artillery fire cut down the second. These were first in a wave of summary 'reliefs' (sackings) touched off by the inconclusiveness of the regiment's advance. In four days a total of three company commanders lost their commands. In one company all officers were relieved or broke under the strain. A second battalion commander also was replaced. One platoon commander who refused to order his men into the line was placed under arrest. Unless the regiment could find some way to break the impasse, heads higher up also might roll. Two days before, for example, the Army Commander had 'made it quite clear to General Stroh that he expected better results'.

Justified or not, the reliefs were due in large measure to the misery and incredible difficulty of forest fighting.

> It was attrition unrelieved. Overcoats soaked with moisture and caked with freezing mud became too heavy for men to wear. Seeping rain turned radios into useless impedimenta. So choked with debris was the floor of the forest that men broke under the sheer physical strain of moving supplies forward and evacuating the wounded. The fighting was at such close quarters that hand grenades were often the decisive weapon. The minefields seemed endless. A platoon would spend hours probing, searching, determining the pattern, only to discover after breaching one minefield that another, just as extensive, lay 25 yards ahead. Unwary men who sought cover from shellfire in ditches or abandoned foxholes might trip over lethal booby traps and turn the promised sanctuary into an open grave. When a diabolical enemy planted a booby trap underneath one seriously wounded soldier, the man lay motionless for 72 hours, driven almost insane in his efforts to maintain consciousness in order to warn whoever might come to the rescue.

Added to all the other miseries was a constant reminder of the toll this bloody little plateau had exacted. Because concern for the living had from the first taken precedence over respect for the dead, the swollen bodies of the fallen of three other regiments still lay about in grotesque positions.

These isolated incidents, despite the vivid description of the conditions in which the Americans had to fight, do less than justice to the majority of the soldiers of the 1st and 9th Armies. During the battle many officers and men of Guards Armoured Division were exchanged with the Americans. Their impression, writes their official historian, was that 'their methods might be somewhat curious and unorthodox, but there could be no doubt about the excellent results when put into practice. Divisions such as the 29th and 30th Infantry who fought in this battle could have challenged comparison with the finest of our own.'

This ill-starred re-creation of the slaughter, mud and misery of the Western front of World War One dragged on well into December. Why Bradley chose to make his main effort in the shambles of the Hürtgen forest, instead of over the easier going on the 9th Army front, remains an enigma. Better still he could have attacked through the Ardennes to the immediate south where the Germans were known to be in no great strength.

That this area was practicable for military operations would soon be demonstrated to him in dramatic form. In the event he chose to attack where the Germans were numerically strongest and where they had every advantage in the form of concrete defences and thick forests — a military problem new to his troops and for which they had not been trained. His intention to attack where he did had come as no surprise to the Germans. The gigantic air support plan was a mere copy of similar programmes in Normandy: if it softened up the Germans the effect was not apparent to the troops on the ground. Condemned to a battle of attrition, the infantry sustained such losses that divisions quickly exhausted themselves in action: every possible expedient both in Europe and the USA had to be adopted to keep them up to strength. It is astonishing in retrospect to record that the American Army, late arrivals in the war, should have been confronted by a manpower crisis so soon.

The most serious feature of the battle, however, was the failure to capture the seven dams at the head waters of the River Roer near Schmidt. So long as the Germans held these dams they could at will release flood waters which would make Allied advance beyond the river impossible for at least a week. Both ground attacks to capture these dams had failed: the RAF had attempted to burst them with their heaviest bombs — to no effect.

By the end of November, the 9th Army had reached the Roer river from Julich to Linnich, but it was another two weeks before the 1st Army closed up to the river opposite Duren. Thus, after a grim month's fighting, Bradley's Armies were only eight miles deeper into Germany: they had set out in high spirits to reach the Rhine.

Model's intention had been to stop the Americans on the Roer subject to the limitation that he must not commit the 6th Panzer Army and the other troops detailed for the coming counter-offensive. Of these he only had to call upon the 10th Panzer Division. By mid-December, using for the most part second-class troops, whom in any case he regarded as expendable, he had succeeded in bringing the Americans to a halt on the west bank of the Roer. He had achieved his aim: by contrast Bradley had sustained a severe reverse. How severe he was soon to learn.

8: DREAR-NIGHTED DECEMBER

Things and actions are what they are, and the consequences of them will be what they will be: why then should we desire to be deceived?

Bishop Joseph Butler

What the consequences would have been had Montgomery's concept of the Narrow Front been adopted in early September will never be known: those of the Broad Front policy actually adopted were now, in the dismal weather of early December, evident to all, including the Germans. The Allied Armies were bogged down and reduced to the semi-static warfare it had always been their object to avoid. Until spring dried the ground and reinforcements arrived from America, they were little better situated than their predecessors had been in 1917.

Six weeks before the first convoy of 19 large ships sailed up the Scheldt and safely berthed in Antwerp docks on 28 November, the bombardment of the port by V1s (pilotless aircraft) and V2s (long-range rockets) from sites in Western Holland had started. It was to continue throughout the winter and early spring. After London, the civil population of Antwerp suffered more than any in the war. Altogether 2,900 civilians were killed and another 5,433 seriously injured.

Of some 6,000 of these missiles which landed within an eight-mile radius of the docks only 302 fell within the boundaries of the port. Casualties to Allied soldiers were 734 killed and 1,078 seriously wounded, including 490 on 16 December when a V2 hit the Rex Cinema. Altogether the anti-aircraft defence of the city consisted of some 18,000 troops and 500 anti-aircraft guns.

Despite this sinister bombardment the courage of the citizens of Antwerp never flagged. When the first convoy sailed in, 7,000 dock workers immediately presented themselves for work. Thanks to their efforts, the discharge of cargoes and the turn-round of ships was never seriously interrupted. On occasions the port handled 25,000 tons a day. The welcome given by the Belgians to their liberators far exceeded that of the French. The troops remarked that whereas as they passed through France, the people showed them the craters the Germans had left in the roads, when they entered Belgium the big holes had already been filled in. Situated as they were in the cockpit of Europe, occupation by a foreign army was no new experience to the Belgians. A strong resistance movement had sprung into action almost from the very moment when King Leopold and the Army had been forced to capitulate in 1940. They now turned to the rehabilitation of their country with a will. Before the last German had been driven out, the mines were working, the tramways were running and the harvest of sugar beet and potatoes was in full swing. The big stores of Brussels plied a lively trade, the cafes and cinemas were crowded, the breweries were in full spate. Belgium, cynically described by some as a political compromise for making money, had the will to survive — a resilience which four years of German occupation had in no way impaired.

From the point of view of defence, 21st Army Group was now established to the satisfaction of Montgomery, roughly behind the great loop of the Maas from Roermond to Walcheren. On the extreme left 1st Canadian Army, with 1 British Corps, held the line of the Lower Maas as far east as

Maren, north-east of 's-Hertogenbosch — an economical front which demanded the minimum of troops. On their right II Canadian Corps had taken over the 'Nijmegen Salient', the legacy of the Arnhem operations and the most important on the British front, including as it did the vital bridge at Grave across the Maas and the other across the Waal at Nijmegen. It thus offered a sally port from which an attack could be launched against the northern flank of the German armies west of the Rhine and, in the 'island' between Nijmegen and Arnhem, a base from which an attack northwards could be mounted over the Neder Rijn.

This low-lying fertile strip, which in September had seemed to XXX Corps, in their attempt to relieve the 1st Airborne Division, the very epitome of advanced horticulture, with neat orchards of every description, and modern housing, had now in the teeming rain become a veritable Slough of Despond. Every polder bore the scars of graves and wrecked vehicles and the signs of the divisions who had fought there — the Wyvern of the 43rd Wessex, the Pithead of the 53rd (Welsh) the HD of 51st Highland, the 'Eye' of Guards Armoured, the TT of 50th (Northumbrian) and the Screaming Eagle of US 101st Airborne Division. The slit-trenches were flooded; the brick roads had disintegrated into bottomless quagmires; the attractive houses with their neat gardens had become piles of rubble; scarcely one brick stood on another. An occasional burst of German shell fire added to the general misery. To add to the discomfort of the garrison, the 51st Highland Division and 49th West Riding Division, the Germans on 2 December blew the dykes north of Elst and west of Arnhem. The waters slowly rose, forcing the infantry to evacuate their slits and form strongpoints amongst the ruins of the houses. The floods spread slowly. The few remaining Dutch farmers glumly loaded their belongings into farm carts and drove their cattle back to the great bridge across the Waal. The 51st Highland Division had to be evacuated in storm boats. At the end of three days only Elst and the south-eastern corner of the island were above water. The Germans either out of sheer spite or ignorance of the Yorkshire proverb, 'nowt for nowt and damn little for sixpence', chose this moment to attack the 1st/7th Duke of Wellington's Regiment, disposed in isolated positions for the defence of the bridge. They got a typically Yorkshire reception, which cost them 50 killed and 100 prisoners. The losses of the Duke's were 10 killed and 19 wounded.

With most of the island now under water, the prospects of an offensive northwards vanished, leaving the headquarters of 1st Canadian Army free to concentrate on planning and preparation for the next offensive, 'Veritable' — a thrust eastwards to Cleve and then southwards between the Maas and the Rhine to meet the 9th US Army striking north-east towards Krefeld.

Whilst XXX Corps had been occupied in the Geilenkirchen offensive with the Americans, the other two corps of 2nd Army, VIII and XII, had methodically proceeded with clearing the Germans from the west bank of the Maas north of Roermond. Here there were only three roads, all of which converged at Venlo. The mud, the large number of mines laid by the enemy and the need for considerable efforts by the engineers to make the limited roads capable of taking military traffic, inevitably resulted in a large number of minor actions with unspectacular but nonetheless eventually satisfactory results. By the end of November both corps had closed with the line of the Maas except at Blerick opposite Venlo, where the Germans still retained a strongly fortified bridgehead. This finally fell to the 15th Scottish Division, with strong support from the 79th Armoured Division. The German defensive system of wire obstacles, mines, an anti-tank ditch and trenches was 600 yards deep. The Flails and the infantry led the assault and cut six lanes through the wire protecting the anti-tank ditch. When they reached it the AVREs advanced with the bridges they carried, laid them and then moved on with the infantry in Kangaroos. When the short December day ended, the infantry had finally wiped out all traces of enemy resistance opposite Venlo. The cost in casualties was only 50. The Army had every reason to be thankful to Major-General Hobart, the Commander of 79th Armoured Division, whose inventive genius, drive (often in the face of official opposition) and foresight had ensured that when the need arose the necessary assault engineer equipment was available. It is not surprising therefore that with this evidence of efficiency in the High Command, the morale of the infantry, despite the depressing weather, mud and the general discomfort, was at this time as high as at any time in 1944. The recollection of one infantry company commander is typical of the spirit of the period.

The river was badly in flood and the water came right up to the position from which an excellent view could be obtained over all enemy activity on the far side. So good was the OP that after a short time the Boche hardly dared to show himself at all.... We were in the unique position of receiving under command a troop of light anti-aircraft guns. They were about to be disbanded to provide infantry reinforcements and the battalion had requested the loan of their services before they gave up their guns. They were used to 'pepperpot' the village of Beesel on the opposite bank, particularly the windmill and the church steeple there, which had already been hit several times but appeared to be almost indestructible. My intention was to destroy every possible German op. The LAA troop was sited well away to the left flank. Each time they did their stuff, the red tracer fairly ripped through Beesel, the windmill and the adjacent area. Then they nipped off quickly — and wisely. Soon enough the retaliatory 'hate' came back from the ubiquitous SP guns and Nebelwerfers on the very spot where the LAA guns had been. It was on the whole a very happy period for the Company.

Thus by 3 December, Montgomery had fulfilled all the tasks given him by Eisenhower on 18 October, with the exception of clearing the Heinsberg triangle between the Maas and the Roer south of Roermond. This he was preparing to do when a period of heavy sleet and snow, making cross-country movement practically impossible, caused this particular operation to be postponed.

On the American front, the situation was far more alarming than anyone on the Allied side capable of expressing an authoritative opinion realised. South of the 9th and 1st Armies concentrated on either side of Aachen, a 75-mile gap, occupied only by four divisions separated them from Patton's 3rd Army on the Saar. They were thus in a peculiarly vulnerable position — how vulnerable no one realised more fully than Model. Throughout November, whilst devoting all his energies to the preparation of Hitler's grandiose plan of a thrust by the 5th and 6th Panzer Armies through the Ardennes across the Maas, he had advocated instead that the two Panzer Armies, on reaching the Maas, should swing north toward Liège, using the river to guard their west flank; simultaneously the 15th Army, attacking due south from the Heinsberg triangle, would also strike for Liège. This pincer movement offered the prospect of surrounding some 15 Allied divisions in the Aachen pocket. His final effort to get this 'small solution' accepted came on 2 December when he, Dietrich and von Manteuffel were summoned to meet Hitler in the Reich Chancellery in Berlin.

Here, well-prepared and with all the factual data at his finger tips, he argued his case with masterly ability. Even Hitler failed to interrupt him! Nonetheless, at the end the Führer remained unmoved — *Antwerp must be the objective*! The original plan must be carried out to the letter. No decision was taken with regard to an attack by the 15th Army to coincide with the main thrust of the Panzer Armies. It was indeed fortunate for Eisenhower and Bradley that the last word lay with Hitler himself and not with Model.

As events were to prove, Bradley's dispositions were fundamentally unsound, whether described as a 'calculated risk' or in any other way. That Eisenhower accepted responsibility for them ever afterwards does more credit to his willingness to back up his subordinates than to his strategic thinking.

Whilst the 9th and 1st Armies were attacking in the last weeks of November, the 3rd Army had isolated Metz and continued with its own offensive. On the extreme right of the Allied front in the Vosges, the French Army, reborn, had reappeared on the scene. On 19 November de Lattre de Tassigny broke out in the Belfort gap and reached the Upper Rhine at the outskirts of Mulhouse. This lightning thrust weakened the entire German line in the Vosges. Three days later the US 7th Army in turn broke through the Saverne gap and with the 2nd French Armoured Division in the van, swept on to liberate Strasbourg, splitting the front in two and isolating what remained of the 19th German Army in the Colmar pocket. If this could be eliminated, the Allies would now be able to close with the Upper Rhine from Strasbourg to Basle. Unfortunately, however, Eisenhower, assured by Devers that the 19th German Army had ceased to exist as a tactical force, now agreed to the 7th Army swinging north to assist Patton on the Saar. As a result the Colmar pocket presented a task beyond the resources of the 1st French Army and the Germans succeeded in maintaining a bridgehead west of the Rhine. Worse still, although reinforced, Patton made little or no headway against the strongest part of the Siegfried Line on the Saar.

The Allies were fully aware of the fact that the Germans had built up a substantial armoured reserve in the 6th Panzer Army. They all seem to have assumed, however, that von Rundstedt was in charge on the Western front and that, in view of the restraint with which he had handled his forces since September, he was unlikely to gamble with it. This view, that, to quote the sentence passed from mouth to mouth at the time amongst the more junior commanders 'the Boche may stage a counter-attack: he is incapable of staging a counter-offensive', was generally held throughout both Allied Armies.

That the command arrangements were unsatisfactory and that since September Eisenhower's policy of attacking all along the line instead of striking a single concentrated blow aimed at the Ruhr had resulted in dispersion of effort and was likely to end in stalemate, had been apparent to Montgomery for some time, and he spared no effort to keep Alanbrooke, the CIGS, informed of the fact. When Eisenhower on 28 November came to stay a night with him at his Tactical Headquarters near Zonhoven, he made it clear that in his opinion the Allies had suffered a strategic reverse. They had set out to secure both the Ruhr and the Saar and failed. A new plan was therefore necessary. Furthermore Eisenhower, in electing to act not only as Supreme Commander but also as Commander of the Land Forces, had taken on a task beyond the powers of any commander to fulfil satisfactorily. The Allies must abandon the doctrine of attacking all along the front and concentrate on a single powerful thrust. Finally, Montgomery thought that the battle area was divided naturally by the Ardennes into two distinct fronts. Therefore there should be one Commander north of the Ardennes and one south. Eisenhower for his part refused to countenance the proposal of a single Commander of the Land Forces. He did however agree that the other points raised by Montgomery should be examined at a conference between himself, Tedder, Bradley and Montgomery at Maastricht.

The lovely old city of Maastricht, fortunately undamaged by the fighting, had been one of the cornerstones in the life of the great Duke of Marlborough. Here he had first seen active service as a young officer. The city, with its almost impregnable fortifications and vast depots, had played a vital part in almost all his great campaigns in the Low Countries in the War of the Spanish Succession. When stripped of all his high offices and banished from England in 1712, he found the whole Dutch garrison drawn up to greet him on his way through to exile. If he, or his ghost, could have attended the conference which now assembled here on 7 December, he would have noted that whilst in 300 years there had been vast developments in the techniques of war, in the vital matter of relations between allies, all present would have profited by a study of his own campaigns. Montgomery urged that the plan for future operations must be aimed at isolating the Ruhr and forcing the Germans to conduct mobile operations. The only area where this could be ensured was in the north. All available effort should therefore be concentrated to this end. Eisenhower agreed that the Ruhr must be isolated but maintained that there should also be a strong subsidiary thrust on the line Frankfurt-Kassel. In other words there would be two offensives, one round the north of Ruhr under Montgomery and the other under Bradley from the south. He also had no intention of closing down Patton's operations on the Saar. When Montgomery pressed his own case for taking charge north of the Ardennes, Eisenhower flatly refused to alter the existing arrangements. That Montgomery's reference to a strategic reverse caused offence there is no doubt. Equally certain is the fact that Montgomery felt that Eisenhower, Bradley and Tedder had joined forces against him. That night he wrote to Alanbrooke:

> I played a lone hand against the three of them; they all arrived today and went away together. It is therefore fairly clear that any points I made will have been put right by Bradley and Tedder on the three-hour drive back to Luxembourg. I can do no more myself.... If we want the war to end within any reasonable period you will have to get Eisenhower's hand taken off the land battle. I regret to say that in my opinion he just doesn't know what he is doing. And you will have to see that Bradley's influence is curbed.

Posterity owes Montgomery a debt in that he recorded his own version of the conference that very night in his diary. Unquestionably on purely military grounds he had a very strong case. The Allies had indeed lost the strategic initiative and their command arrangements were fundamentally unsound: one commander was needed to coordinate all operations north of the Ardennes and another to the south — Model would demonstrate the naked truth within the next fortnight. In endeavouring to play the role of Supreme Commander and Commander of the Land Forces at the same time, Eisenhower had missed the chance of at least securing a bridgehead over the Rhine before Christmas.

On political and personal grounds, however, Montgomery was in a fatally weak position. The order of battle in the West at the time showed a total of 68 divisions, of which 15 were

British and Canadian, eight were French or French African, one Polish and the remaining 44 American. In the end, whatever the other Allies might urge, the American will would prevail — a fact made abundantly clear in the American press at the time. It is an axiom of democracies that the voice of the people is the voice of God and God is on the side of the big battalions.

Few at the time, and least of all Montgomery, seem to have realised the extent to which he had antagonised the American generals. If there was to be a separate Commander of the Land Forces, this could only be Montgomery. This solution the American generals and particularly Bradley, whose influence with Eisenhower was very strong, would not accept. Regrettably, considerations of personal prejudice, national prestige and professional rivalry overrode the common Allied military need. Nonetheless, Montgomery, whatever may be said of his lack of diplomatic finesse and political insight, had faced the unpalatable military facts and expounded his own convictions with all the uncompromising clarity and force of an Old Testament prophet at loggerheads with the Kings of Israel. So far as he personally was concerned, they had at least been warned of the wrath to come.

None of the somewhat bogus *bonhomie* which prevailed at the time in Anglo-American military relations characterised the confrontation of Hitler and his generals, down to and including divisional commanders, on 11 and 12 December at the 'Eagle's Nest' near Zeigenberg west of Bad Nauheim. They left Koblenz after dark in a bus which twisted and turned through side roads to prevent the occupants knowing where they were going. On arrival, understandably in view of what had happened on 20 July, they were made to deposit their arms and brief cases before entering the Conference Room. Hasso von

Manteuffel, who attended on the 11th, says they arrived to find von Rundstedt, Model, Sepp Dietrich and a number of SS Generals already there. There were not enough chairs for all, and the SS Generals, surprising to relate, politely remained standing. This created the impression that an SS Officer was posted behind each Army officer's chair for reasons other than good manners. One of the Army generals at any rate was afraid even to reach for a handkerchief. The assembly presented a striking contrast. On the one side the hard-faced, highly capable commanders in the field: on the other, Hitler, the Supreme Commander, pale and puffy, crouching in his chair, his hands trembling and his left arm twitching violently. Obviously a sick man, he dragged one leg behind him when he walked. Beside him, Jodl seemed prematurely old, mentally and physically exhausted.

Only a few pages of the stenographer's record of Hitler's interminable harangue have survived. He spoke without notes for well over an hour and a half, at first in a low and hesitant voice, but later warming to his subject. For well over an hour these tense, hard-bitten professionals had to endure a rambling dissertation on the Treaty of Westphalia, the Treaty of Munster and the encirclement of Germany, parliamentary democracy and Churchill's instigation of the 'Holy War' against the Reich. The enemy might have made temporary territorial gains, but the price he would have to pay would be so terrible that he would become demoralised and collapse. The situation which faced the Germans was similar to that of Frederick the Great who in the seventh year of war despite the pleadings of his ministers elected to fight on to ultimate victory. In 1940 he, Hitler, had been the only one to insist on offensive action: the result had been the overthrow of France. Now, apart from the Luftwaffe, there was little difference in the strength of the opposing forces. The Americans had lost 240,000 in three weeks; the German tanks were superior. Once they had broken the Americans all they would find in the rear areas would be bank clerks dressed as officers. The enemy had no reserves; given surprise and bad weather success was certain.

He then once more outlined the coming operation. In essence it was virtually unchanged from the plan first put forward in October. The aim was to destroy the Allied forces north of a line running from Luxembourg to Brussels and Antwerp. Some 30 divisions were available.

Model's Army Group B was to act as spearhead of the attack. It would cross the Maas between Liège and Namur, seize Antwerp, and then destroy all the British and American forces in this area, thereby cutting off the rest of the Allied forces from their main lines of supply. Within Army Group B the main effort would be made on the right by Dietrich's 6th SS Panzer Army who were to advance on the axis Liège-Antwerp fanning out the while to form a front extending from Maastricht to the Albert Canal. On the left von Manteuffel's 5th Panzer Army was to thrust forward on a roughly parallel axis, Namur-Brussels. Both these armies were powerful forces, each possessing four armoured and five infantry divisions. 7th Army, with one armoured and four infantry divisions, had the responsibility of protecting the left flank. In the Aachen area the 15th Army was to launch a series of holding attacks to tie down the Allied reserves and later to stage a subsidiary attack to destroy them.

Parachutists under von der Heydte were to be dropped to block the roads north of the Ardennes. The versatile Skorzeny, who had snatched Mussolini out of Allied hands, was to use his special troops to seize bridges across the Maas.

The initial attack was to be made between Monschau and Echternach by infantry with strong artillery support. Thereafter, Hitler emphasised, every formation should continue to advance, regardless of what might be happening on its flanks and would push forward with all possible speed. He hoped to strike hardest at the national seam between the British and American forces and thus create inter-Allied friction.

'The only positive contribution to the forthcoming operation which I took away from the conference', says von Manteuffel, 'was Hitler's own appreciation of the enemy. From his point of view — and he alone had access to all the Intelligence sources — the prospects for a successful operation looked favourable.' He adds: 'Then we returned to our troops. They and we went into action in a mood of complete determination, ready to fight to the best of our ability, and, if need be, to die.'

Eisenhower, Bradley and their Army Commanders had at their disposal greater sources of Intelligence and staffs apparently better qualified to collect, sort and interpret it than any previous commanders in history. How then did it come about that on the morning of 16 December, they were completely outwitted by a cover plan devised by an amateur who in his military service had never risen above the rank of corporal — the build-up of the Panzer armies immediately behind the Aachen front, where Bradley was attacking, to create the impression that in due course they would be fed into the battle there?

To them the inevitability of the triumph of overwhelming American military might had become an article of faith. Bradley's Intelligence summary of 12 December asserted: 'It is now certain that attrition is steadily sapping the strength of the German forces on the Western Front.' Their optimism was heightened by reports that the enemy no longer possessed the petrol, aircraft, tanks and ammunition to stage a counter-offensive.

German operations since von Rundstedt had reassumed command in the West had been conducted with the skill to be expected of a commander of his reputation. It was natural therefore for Eisenhower and Bradley to assume that he was fully in command and that he would act on sound and orthodox military lines, husband his resources and place his strategic reserve, the 6th Panzer Army, in a position where it could intervene at the point of greatest danger astride the route to the Ruhr. He, they were convinced, would be the last person to stake his reserves on a hazardous adventure. They accepted as an axiom that the rugged nature and winding narrow roads of the Ardennes ruled out the possibility of armoured attack here.

Seven incidents suggesting the possibility of attack here had been reported; only one, a report of abnormal traffic, had reached Bradley's headquarters. No one there seems to have seen any significance in it. Despite the bad weather, a considerable amount of information from air sources was also available. This was interpreted as reinforcements of the 6th Panzer Army for counter-attack on the Roer front.

Bradley and Eisenhower thus got an appreciation of likely enemy action which they themselves were already conditioned to believe. In accepting uncritically the opinions of the men they employed to do their thinking for them, they got the answer they deserved.

9: ARDENNES

Great God who through the Ages
Has braced the blood stained hand,
As Saturn, Jove or Wodan,
Hast led our warrior band,
Again we seek thy council,
But not in cringing guise,
We whine not for thy mercy —
To slay: God make us wise.
General George S. Patton in 'Women's Home Companion'

The first snow fell on 9 December: thereafter the days were chill and the skies overcast. At 5.30 a.m. on 16 December 13 infantry and seven armoured divisions advanced through the forest of Eifel, followed by a further 10 supported by 2,000 guns. They had about 1,000 tanks. Counting the 15th Army, the total force numbered 29 infantry and 12 armoured divisions. Facing them between Monschau and Echtemach on a 100-mile front, Bradley could only muster some four and two-thirds divisions, two new to battle and two which had been badly mauled in the fighting in the Hürtgen forest. Model had achieved a surprise equalled only by Napoleon before Waterloo. All, from the American soldier in the front line to Eisenhower himself, were caught off balance. So good had been the German security precautions that even Montgomery had no inkling of the coming offensive. His Intelligence summary, circulated that very morning, stated: '3. The enemy is at present fighting a defensive campaign on all fronts; his situation is such that he cannot stage major offensive operations. Furthermore, at all costs he has to prevent the war from entering on a mobile phase; he has not the transport or the petrol that would be necessary for mobile operations, nor could his tanks compete with ours in a mobile battle.' Tedder, visiting Bradley's headquarters during the preceding week, had studied the map showing the layout of the Army Group and noted 'the relative weakness in the centre', but had been satisfied with Bradley's explanation that adequate forces could be drawn up from the south should the Germans attempt anything.

Throughout the 16th the situation on the Ardennes front remained obscure. Late that day, Eisenhower and Bradley had received only fragmentary reports. Bradley thought it was a spoiling attack designed to forestall Patton's offensive in the south. Eisenhower took a more realistic view, and ordered the 7th US Armoured Division from the 9th Army in the north and the 11th US Armoured Division from the south into the Ardennes. That night German paratroops, landing near Spa, added further to the confusion behind the American lines. It was not until the evening of the 17th that Eisenhower ordered forward the 82nd and 101st Airborne Divisions from the Rheims area, to which they had been belatedly withdrawn on conclusion of their brilliant contribution to the Arnhem operations in September.

Montgomery, in his team of liaison officers, had a ready means of ascertaining the true nature of the situation which the American commanders lacked. These young officers lived with him at his actual headquarters. They were all men of character, initiative and courage; all had considerable experience of command of troops in action. They were therefore peculiarly well qualified to grasp a situation and to sense the atmosphere of the various parts of the American front to which they were now despatched. He had selected them all with considerable care: all were notable for their good manners. None ever forgot the courtesies of civilian intercourse which are as important on the field of battle as in normal life. In the British Army their arrival was welcomed at every headquarters they visited: it was reassuring to many a battalion and brigade commander to know that his own appreciation of the situation would be passed on, undiluted by the comments of staff officers, to Montgomery himself. On their return from a mission, he too knew that he could rely on their giving a frank and realistic report. In addition to all the information reaching him from other sources, he got a picture of the fighting as seen through the eyes of youth, with practical experience of battle. He was thus able, far earlier than Bradley and the commanders in his Army Group, to make an accurate appreciation of the situation in the Ardennes.

By 18 December, the threat to the security of his own Army Group was apparent. Steps must be taken to secure his own right flank and right rear. At the time he was in the process of moving XXX Corps from the Maastricht area to the Nijmegen area, where it was to join the 1st Canadian Army for the 'Veritable' operation planned for 12 January. Advance parties, including Horrocks, the Corps Commander, had already left for the north. Montgomery therefore cancelled the move and ordered XXX Corps to assemble west of the Maas between Louvain and St Trond, where they were well placed to deal with any attempt by the Panzer Armies to cross the river between Namur and Liège. Reconnaissance troops were despatched to the line of the river and covering parties established on all bridges. The 29th Armoured Brigade, which was then reequipping in Western Belgium, was ordered to take back the tanks it was discarding and to concentrate at Namur.

By the 19th he had available three infantry divisions, the 43rd, 51st and 53rd, all battle-experienced and all rested, four armoured brigades, and the Guards Armoured Division — some 90,000 men, 1,200 tanks and over 500 guns, a force more than adequate and eager to deal with any German attempt to cross the Maas and led by a light-hearted commander, on whose dash and courage he could rely. Under Horrocks' direction the division and brigade commanders, immediately on arrival, reconnoitred the ground to the west of the Maas and started to plan for a battle in which everything seemed to be in their favour. The Maas about Huy is a formidable obstacle: the west bank dominates the east. The ground is the best tank going in Belgium. Spirits were high: the enemy had shown his hand at last. If he reached the Maas and attempted to cross it, the prospects of inflicting on him a decisive defeat seemed good indeed.

By the 19th Montgomery had a clear picture of the situation in the Ardennes. In the north, the extreme right of Dietrich's 6th Panzer Army had been brought to a standstill by two divisions of the US V Corps: further south, however, the US VIII Corps had virtually collapsed. At first the American commanders had assumed that they were faced by nothing more than a spoiling attack staged with a view to holding up Patton's offensive on the Saar. Later they took the view that provided they could hold the flanks of VIII Corps' front, the situation could be restored by an attack by Patton from the south, directed on Bastogne and Houffalize. This Eisenhower had ordered that very morning at Verdun: it could not be expected to produce any effect for several days. He had further indicated that as soon as possible he would also stage another attack from the north to meet Patton at Houffalize and thus cut the head off the German penetration. Bastogne and St Vith were still holding out, but the general picture on the night of the 19th showed that the 6th Panzer Army was within 15 miles of Liège and that the 5th Panzer Army had reached Houffalize. There was every indication that the German thrust towards the Maas was moving fast, by-passing the island of resistance and getting closer to some of the American supply dumps.

There was real danger of Bradley's Army Group being cut in half long before Patton could intervene. At the same time it had become obvious that Bradley, with his headquarters at Luxembourg, was in no position to control the battle. His communications with 1st US Army were virtually cut and he had not visited Hodges since the start of the battle.

If Eisenhower's plan for eventually attacking from the north as well as from the south was to succeed, there would have to be a change in the command arrangements. All troops taking part in the northern attack must be under the command of one man. That man could only be Montgomery, who was on the spot and more fully in the picture than any of the American commanders. Eisenhower's decision to order Montgomery to assume control of all British and American forces north of a line from Givet to Prum, including the 1st and 9th Armies, raises his stature both as a commander and a man. Bradley and Patton and their staffs were bitterly opposed to it on personal grounds — dislike of Montgomery dated back, in some cases, to the war in North Africa. Then and subsequently, according to Major-General Kenneth Strong, Eisenhower's Chief of Intelligence and a British Army officer, they made no attempt to conceal it. This hostility was shared by some of the leading American staff officers at Eisenhower's headquarters. Major-General Strong relates that on the night of the 19th he and Major-General Whiteley, another British officer who was temporarily acting as head of the Operations Section, were so disturbed by the situation that they went to the quarters of Lieutenant-General Bedell-Smith, got him out of bed and told him that in their opinion Montgomery must be placed in charge of the north.

> Bedell-Smith telephoned Bradley straightway and told him what we had said. Bradley replied that he doubted whether the situation was serious enough to warrant such a fundamental command change, especially considering the effect it might have on opinion in America. He admitted, however, that if Montgomery had been an American commander it would have been the logical thing to do. It was a difficult moment for us all. We fully realised the mistrust of Montgomery among many senior Americans... Nevertheless, I did not feel that this should alter my judgment of the situation.
>
> Bedell-Smith then intimated that because of the view we had taken of the situation, neither Whiteley nor I could any longer be acceptable as Staff Officers to General Eisenhower. Next day instructions would be issued relieving us of our appointments and returning to the United Kingdom. This looked like being a sad ending. Next morning, however, Bedell-Smith, at the normal daily briefing, recommended to Eisenhower that the change they proposed should be put into effect. Eisenhower listened without speaking to what he had to say, and then raised the telephone and spoke to Bradley. The latter was left in no doubt that these were his orders.

Later in the day Bedell-Smith handsomely apologised for the events of the night before.

The attitude adopted by the American commanders added little to their stature. It must be admitted, however, that had the breach occurred on the British front and an American commander been appointed to coordinate the operations, the feeling of the British subordinate commanders would probably have been equally strong if less articulate.

Fully aware of the inevitable outcry there would be in the United States and of the apparent slur his decision cast on the professional reputations of the senior officers in his own army, Eisenhower chose to ignore all considerations of national prestige, and to face the situation as an Allied Commander-in-Chief, and give a vital decision on military grounds alone. This magnanimous step was to prove the turning point in the Ardennes battle.

The Ardennes was an American battle and the laurels were American. The British Army played only a very minor part in it. Many British officers, however, had the good fortune to see something of the fighting and their evidence does much to dispel the fog of myth which exaggerated reporting, at the time and subsequently, has built up around this battle.

Montgomery actually received Eisenhower's order to take over command in the north at 10.30 a.m. on the morning of the 20th. The news flashed around XXX Corps with amazing speed. On arrival in their new concentration area, they had found the civil population in a state of acute alarm, bordering on panic. This had no effect on the troops. In their opinion all foreigners were excitable and therefore prone to display emotion on the slightest provocation in an un-English manner. They had acquired by various means poultry, destined to provide their Christmas dinner. Their main anxiety, therefore, was that operations would interfere with the celebration of the most important festival of the year. The majority, however, felt that 101st and 82nd Airborne Divisions, whose ability to fight they had witnessed in the Arnhem operations, were perfectly capable of dealing with the situation. Nonetheless, the news that Montgomery had taken over relieved them of any need to speculate on the outcome of the battle. If he considered a battle necessary, then the poultry could wait a little longer.

Anyhow, in their eyes, whatever he chose to do would end in victory — so why worry?

Montgomery appeared in person about 11.30 a.m. in the market square in the little town of Bilsen, which was packed with troops. Here Dempsey, the Commander of the 2nd Army, met him. The two withdrew to a brigadier's caravan, conveniently parked nearby. Half an hour later Montgomery emerged alert and smiling. He was, in fact, *en route* to the headquarters of 1st US Army, where he had arranged to meet Simpson, commanding the 9th Army, and Hodges at 1 p.m. Standing in the square, he accepted a cup of tea. He then ordered all the troops nearby to gather around a brigade Intelligence officer's truck at the tail of which was a large map. He proceeded to describe what had happened in the Ardennes, and displayed even more than usual self-confidence and ability to sort out the essentials of a complex situation, to explain what he proposed to do and to show what the inevitable outcome must be now that he had the reins in his hands. His manner was paternal and unhurried: he radiated confidence. In this respect, with an audience of troops, he could stand comparison with Hannibal or Napoleon. About noon he departed slowly in his jeep through the crowded square, in which soldiers automatically sprang to attention, meticulously acknowledging the salutes of the officers.

Montgomery's main personal contribution to the Battle of the Bulge can be expressed in a few words: from the outset he saw the situation as a whole as opposed to viewing it as a series of isolated incidents. Secondly, he made sure that the vital rear areas were safeguarded. Finally, he realised that before an offensive counterattack could be launched, adequate reserves would have to be assembled and that this would take time.

Both at the time and later, criticism of his actual handling of the battle was mainly directed against his decision on 23 December to abandon the St Vith salient and to withdraw the 82nd US Airborne Division from Vielsalm. His intention in doing this was to convert a series of isolated individual battles into a coherent whole. He proposed to use the US VII Corps for counter-attack: it was essential that they should be pulled back into reserve, given the opportunity to reorganise and sufficient time to plan for the counter-attack in the north. He did not therefore go over to the offensive until 3 January: the American commanders, who were more emotionally involved in the contest than he was, considered that in thus delaying he was unduly cautious. In postponing the battle until he was certain of victory, he had the backing of Eisenhower. Viewed dispassionately and in retrospect, there can be no doubt that his was a wise decision: nothing would have been gained by precipitate action.

His use of the US VII Corps rather than the British XXX Corps which was readily available, also attracted heated American press criticism, based on the well-known newsworthy principle that miseries should be equally shared. In fact, to have put XXX Corps into the Bulge in the first 10 days of the battle would have raised acute difficulties of supply — the administrative axis of the British corps would have cut right across those of both the 1st and 9th US Armies. Further difficulties would have arisen in the vital matters of artillery and air support: procedures in the two Armies were widely different. The Americans and the British also used different types of ammunition.

A further reason for Montgomery's reluctance to commit XXX Corps was that they were due to play a major role in 'Veritable' in the very near future and, if he was not to risk postponing it, he had to move them north to the Nijmegen area as soon as possible. He was also short of men: if he lost a lot in the Ardennes, he would have to go short in 'Veritable'. There were no fresh British divisions arriving in the theatre as there were American. Finally, it was undesirable in the climate of popular opinion in America at the time that irresponsible British commentators should be put in a position to claim that their troops had saved the Americans from disaster. Tact in dealing with allies was not always Montgomery's strong suit, but on this occasion it must be admitted that he showed enlightened concern for American susceptibilities.

The major credit for the victory, however, goes to the American soldiers whose staunch resistance, especially at St Vith and Bastogne, defeated the utmost efforts of the cream of the German Army, commanded by generals of great ability such as Hasso von Manteuffel and Bayerlein. Their staunchness too in attack in the later stages of the battle in conditions of biting cold and wind at least equalled that of any other army, Allied or German, at any time during World War Two. How grim conditions were is well illustrated by the experience of the East Lancashires, put into the battle on the right flank of the US VII Corps thrust to Houffalize immediately west of the Ourthe in the first week in January.

> The Regiment now found itself deployed in very tricky fighting country. With their steep undulations and thickly wooded slopes, the Ardennes are certainly no paradise for attacking infantry and tanks. On the Verdenne-Marenne front the woods were extensive and irregular. The undergrowth hindered all movement and the trees consisted mainly of young firs with abundant low branches, which reduced visibility to a matter of feet. Very few tracks led upwards into these woods, which rose 400 feet in a distance of about 2,000

145

yards: such tracks were steep, narrow, ice- and snow-covered. Inside the woods they frequently deteriorated to small paths, making movement of men and vehicles most difficult.

Within the forest, movement was generally restricted to an advance in file or single file along the main tracks. Any deployment involved physically forcing a way through snow-laden undergrowth, which was slow, tiring work and resulted in an immediate loss of control from platoon level upwards. There were no visible landmarks so the locating of position was largely a matter of guesswork and to emerge at any point from the shelter of the wood into an open space was to risk a heavy toll of casualties from concealed positions beyond....

Before the battalion took over (on 3 January) very little seemed to have been ascertained of the exact enemy dispositions on this front. Patrols were therefore sent out before first light to comb through the small woods ahead. But the hazards of such patrols were unusually great as the thick snow background made concealment doubly difficult, and in some cases, impossible during the day. Snow camouflage suits were afterwards issued for patrols and met with great approval, but they — like the excellent tins of self-heating soups — came too late to be of use in the Ardennes battle. Movement at night was almost as hazardous. A stationary and camouflaged enemy position could rarely be spotted at any time until it had opened fire. Such difficulties of movement, as well as the biting cold, were to make life singularly unpleasant during the operations which followed.

Soon after first light on 4 January, the battalion advanced in a violent blizzard to capture the ridge some 1,600 yards ahead. There were six inches of snow on top of the slippery ground, which made it almost impossible for the supporting tanks to keep up with them. All went well for the first 1,000 yards. The rifle companies then found that under cover of the blizzard, they had superimposed themselves on the forward troops of the 116th Panzer Division. Nevertheless, before nightfall they fought their way through to the final objective in a series of minor battles at close quarters against pockets of the enemy not only to their front, but in their rear.

'The remainder of the battalion then settled in on the objective for the night — if such an expression is permissible to describe digging in a frozen ground with snow falling fast; uncertainty of the strength and intentions of the enemy and an urgent growing demand for food for the inner man.' The men remained in their slit trenches, frozen to the marrow in a temperature well below freezing point and without any sort of cover, waiting for the snow to stop. Owing to the state of the ground it had proved impossible to get blankets or additional clothing up from Verdenne and, needless to say, it was far too cold for anyone to sleep.

Apart from an iced haversack ration about midday, nobody had eaten since about 6 a.m. and the hot meal cooked back in Verdenne during the afternoon was still on its perilous way up through the forest. Wheeled vehicles had proved useless for the job. Carriers seemed the most promising form of transport but every few yards one of them lost a track and as soon as that happened on the narrow icy paths through the thick forest, all traffic had to wait while a repair was carried out. Finally the effort and delay proved too great and the QM, with a team of willing helpers, valiantly handled the heavy food containers for the greater part of the way and reached the battalion about 3 a.m. — even cold stew can provide a delectable diet on the appropriate occasion. Soon afterwards, John Moore (the Quartermaster) struggled up again with a warming cargo of rum, which he personally had carried all the way from Verdenne like some great St Bernard dog.

When daylight came the battalion resumed the advance in the face of heavy close-range shell fire.

> Intermittent falls of snow and the bitter cold continued and on the high ground a thick damp mist set in. Already cases of frost bite and physical exhaustion began to appear and a close watch had to be kept on the incidence of 'trench foot'. The routine daily change of socks had no value since the men's boots were already wet through, and there existed no means of drying either socks or boots in the forest. Similarly woollen gloves had quickly become saturated and frozen. All such problems of administration — particularly ammunition, feeding and evacuation of wounded — assumed the proportions of a nightmare as the weather deteriorated. The solution could only be found in some new special form of transport.
>
> Fortunately on 5 January the battalion received a small number of 'Weasels', a vehicle not unlike a carrier but with broader tracks... these vehicles were frequently able to get through where other tracked vehicles failed and they produced a tangible proof of contact with the outer world — which cheered everyone — when they brought up the Company Cookers in time for the evening meal! Thereafter they brought up daily rations so that cooking could be organised forward with the Companies.

On the 6th orders arrived to continue the attack on the morrow and take the village of Grimblimont over a mile ahead and nestling out of view behind the crest a hill 1,500 yards to their front; both of which dominated the enemy's escape route to Laroche. Between their start, the Rau de Grimblimont, the ground rose sharply and destitute of cover to the crest. Patrols during the night and prisoners taken confirmed that the 60th Panzer Grenadier Regiment of 116th Panzer Division was holding the position in strength and was supported by tanks. It snowed steadily for the remainder of the night.

'At 11.50 hours on the 7th, the battalion began to form up. The blizzard howled and raged with ever increasing intensity and not even the massive Christmas tree regalia which the fighting soldier dons for battle, could in any way relieve the numbing effect of the Arctic wind.'

A shell fell on the Advanced Battalion Headquarters, killing the Adjutant and two lance-corporals and wounding 11 of the Commanding Officer's party. Only Lieutenant-Colonel Hill, his Intelligence Officer, and one orderly escaped. A large shell fragment virtually degutted his wireless set, forcing him henceforward to rely on personal contact alone to control his companies. H Hour came at noon. At this very moment the support squadron of tanks reported that they could not get across the Rau de Grimblimont. Nonetheless A and D Companies, punctually on the hour, plunged forward into the snow, followed by the remainder of the battalion across the completely open ground. An immense weight of artillery and mortar fire, as intense as any experienced in Normandy, descended on them, including air-burst shells which exploded with a particularly vindictive bang and produced large clouds of black smoke. The Company wireless sets were soon knocked out; casualties began to mount, but all pressed on. At last they reached the crest: now there was a check on the front of the left forward Company, D Company — three enemy Mark IV tanks, in hull-down positions, barred the way: enemy machine-guns on their flank opened up. The Company went to ground. Without the aid of their own tanks and gunners, further advance seemed suicidal. It was now that Major D. H. Macindoe, commanding the battery in support, although wounded, came to their aid. Somehow or other he manoeuvred his half-track forward to a position immediately below the crest and engaged the enemy tanks and machine-guns holding up the infantry. At the same time Lieutenant R. S. Tuffnell led what remained of his platoon down the reverse slope of the hill. As soon as they got within Piat range of the nearest tank, Private C. W. Wride calmly sited his weapon in full view of the enemy and scored a direct hit with his first shot which jammed the turret of the nearest Mark IV tank. The remaining tanks withdrew. Major Lake, the Company Commander, now gathered the remnants of his company, formed them into one platoon and fought his way forward into the houses on the edge of the village of Grimblimont. Meanwhile on his right, A Company disregarding the hold-up on their left had struggled up the hill in the face of fierce machine-gun fire. When they reached their objective, the high ground north-west of the village, only Major Cetre, the Company Commander, and 25 men had survived. The other two companies of the battalion now passed through into the village; the enemy fought well. Every house had to be systematically cleared. How many Germans were killed is not known, as the falling snow obliterated them in a few seconds. The battalion's six anti-tank guns now came up. Although they had lost 11 officers and 232 men, nothing could now dislodge the 1st East Lancashires from the sheltered village of Grimblimont. After five days' exposure, with practically no sleep, to vicious enemy fire and abominable weather, they were nonetheless ready to fight on.

This infantry battle has been dealt with in detail because it is typical of the struggle in the Ardennes: the majority of the Americans encountered equally appalling conditions. Most of the Germans fought with equivalent courage and fortitude and with considerable skill. Their losses have never been accurately assessed but probably reached a total of 80,000 killed, wounded and missing — roughly the same total as the Americans. In sheer valour there was little to chose between friend or foe. The Wehrmacht at any rate exhausted the supply of decorations. Signed photographs of von Rundstedt were therefore offered them in lieu. Their reactions can be inferred in a report from a division to Corps Headquarters.

> The division reports that no result has been achieved by the distribution of signed photographs of Field-Marshal von Rundstedt as individual rewards for services in battle. No request for them has been received. The Division does not consider that this type of reward has any effect in encouraging the infantry to fight. The Divisional Commander considers that the choice of this reward is unfortunate. The soldier cannot carry the Field-Marshal's photograph around with him in the line. The majority of the men cannot send it home since many families have evacuated owing to the bombing. In those cases where it does reach home it is more likely to be forgotten.
>
> The Divisional Commander thought that better results would be achieved by the grant of special leave for bravery and by the distribution of some visible decoration.

The actual comments of the German soldiers are, perhaps, wisely, not recorded. Those of British troops, in similar circumstances, would have been unprintable.

Although the forward infantry got little direct help from the Air Force, the praises lavished on them immediately after the battle and subsequently, were on the whole well-earned. When the cold, dry east winds cleared the skies on Christmas Eve the 2nd and 9th US Tactical Air Forces were able to concentrate on the soft-skinned vehicles moving up the narrow wintry roads and thus deprive the Panzer Divisions of petrol. Attacks on tanks were less successful. Subsequent investigation showed that only one tenth of the number claimed by fighter bomber pilots was justified. The attacks by the strategic bombers on marshalling yards east of the Rhine and the rail communications west of the river undoubtedly had a crippling effect. So great was the degree of air superiority attained that on 26 December Model was forced to forbid major troop moves in daylight. The Luftwaffe completely failed to defend their supply lines west of the Rhine, and their only large-scale attacks on the Brussels and Eindhoven airfields on New Year's Day, although mildly disconcerting, cost them dearly. In fact it merely delayed the normal compassionate leave traffic to England by a few hours. Thereafter Allied dominance of the skies over the battlefield went unchallenged.

According to Galland, the Commander of the Luftwaffe Fighter Command: 'The Luftwaffe received its death blow at the Ardennes offensive. In unfamiliar conditions and with insufficient training and combat experience, our numerical strength had no effect. It was decimated while in transfer, on the ground, in large air battles especially during Christmas, and was finally destroyed.' Over 1,000 aircraft were lost.

The claim, however, that the Allied Air Forces succeeded in completely isolating the Panzer Armies in the Ardennes cannot be sustained.

The influence of the forces employed to operate behind the Allied lines on the course of the battle was greatly exaggerated by war correspondents. The records of British regiments and divisions in the neighbourhood devote ample space to the difficulties of staging their Christmas dinners on the appropriate date but generally fail even to mention the alleged panic behind the lines. In fact there were two forces: Lieutenant-Colonel Baron von der Heydte's parachutists, and Skorzeny's Group.

Von der Heydte's exploits as 'fire brigade' to Student's Panzer Army in October have already been mentioned. He was not warned about this operation until 8 December: the troops placed under his command were a scratch collection of some 1,200 strong, hastily assembled at Sennelager Camp on 12 December; only 300 had ever jumped before. The parachutes were of an unfamiliar type. Sepp Dietrich was obviously drunk when he briefed von der Heydte to drop on the Hohes Venn astride the Eupen-Malmedy road to assist the advance of 6th Panzer Army. The actual drop on the night of 16/17 December was hopelessly scattered: von der Heydte only succeeded in collecting one tenth of his men. They wandered helplessly for three days and exerted virtually no influence on the battle. Von der Heydte, sick and disillusioned, was captured on 23 December.

Skorzeny's Group in captured vehicles and American uniforms, the Führer's own personal contribution to the Art of War, numbered about 2,000. Their task was to seize the bridges over the Maas above Liège at Engis, Amay and Huy. Eight groups seem to have penetrated the American lines on 16 December. The remainder were eventually used as a normal military formation near Malmedy. Neither party achieved anything of purely military significance beyond cutting telephone wires and interfering with signposts. They did, however, succeed in producing an element of confusion in the rear areas and perhaps even anxiety, amongst the rear services, which in any army seldom, if ever, achieve personal contact with the enemy and even less frequently wish to do so. Their ignorance of the more recondite features of American life was usually their undoing. Knowledge of the love-life of American film stars had not been included in the curriculum of their preliminary course of instruction: none could say what was the capital of Illinois. One indeed had the effrontery to act as a military policeman controlling traffic in Liège. The main result was a number of embarrassing encounters between the British and the Americans, both of whom became highly suspicious of each other. This was particularly true of the Americans. In the north, according to the official historian of the 94th Dorset & Hants Field Regiment, they

> suddenly became incredibly security-conscious, especially the coloured ones, and we were eternally giving the password to suspicious GIs. Captain Hancock, who visited Captain Clarke with the Somersets on Christmas Eve, was warned to go carefully, as the coloured sentries on the Liège bridge had already shot one American and two Belgians (though to their credit they had arrested three German saboteurs in a captured jeep).

A number of innocent American officers not concerned with the battle, who had decided that Christmas was a good time to visit their girlfriends north of Maastricht, found themselves temporarily in custody: similarly, several British officers' ignorance of leading personalities in American football resulted in a similar short period of arrest. Even one of Montgomery's liaison officers found himself for a short while the subject of British suspicion. The precautions taken for the security of Eisenhower himself were exaggerated and aroused his justifiable wrath.

In fact the difference of opinion between the British and the Americans never rose above the level of a domestic squabble. By contrast de Gaulle, when the need to evacuate Strasbourg on purely military grounds was being considered, provoked an international issue. On 26 December, Devers commanding 6th US Army Group, confronted by the need to take over the

154

front of Patton's 3rd Army now thrusting towards Bastogne and Houffalize, and to meet a German counter-attack known to be imminent, requested the 1st French Army to side-step north. This was beyond their power. Devers therefore proposed a withdrawal from the plain of Alsace to the Vosges, which meant exposing some Frenchmen to German reprisals. Juin, the Chief of the French Defence Staff, informed de Gaulle on 2 January, and he immediately sent a telegram of protest to Roosevelt and Churchill. Roosevelt considered that the issue was purely military and left the decision to Eisenhower. Churchill, however, with clearer insight into the political issues at stake and the character of the French Head of State, immediately flew over to Eisenhower's headquarters at Versailles, where the two had, in Churchill's words, 'an informal conference' with de Gaulle, the upshot of which was that the proposal to withdraw from Strasbourg was abandoned. There can be no doubt, however, that Churchill's personal influence tipped the scale and that his comment in the telegram to Roosevelt to the effect that Eisenhower had been 'most generous' to de Gaulle was not only justifiable and sincere but also politically wise. De Gaulle's attitude was, according to Juin, entirely in character. He said in his account, 'On getting back into our car, I could not help remarking to de Gaulle that Churchill had some right to expect at least a word of thanks. Bah! he said and relapsed once more into gloomy contemplation. He was obviously vexed with everything connected with this unhappy incident.'

In retrospect it is surprising that a plan so misbegotten and grandiose should have achieved such success as it did in the first days. Hitler, fighting for his own survival and that of the Nazi regime, aimed at winning a favourable bargaining position for securing an acceptable peace and took the offensive

155

because, according to his ill-digested study of history, this was invariably the recipe for victory. The Wehrmacht of 1944 was not the Wehrmacht of 1941-1942 which had carried the German armies to the shores of the Black Sea and threatened Cairo. Far too many good soldiers had gone to their death in Russia, North Africa, Italy and Normandy. The 7th Army in particular was too weak and undertrained to carry out its task of protecting the southern flank and attacking towards Luxembourg. The available resources in material, particularly petrol and lubricants, were hopelessly inadequate. The 1,000 tanks destroyed were irreplaceable. Above all, the Luftwaffe were incapable of securing, even for a few hours, the local command of the air. As von Manteuffel said: 'When the weather cleared the enemy enjoyed the same unlimited air superiority that he had had in Normandy.' Model from start to finish was hamstrung by the tight and inflexible control exercised by Hitler and the clique of toadies around him who were completely out of touch with conditions at the front. For political reasons, Hitler, when von Manteuffel seemed for the moment to have the ball at his feet, refused to transfer to him Panzer divisions from Sepp Dietrich's 6th Panzer Army. Throughout, he blatantly ignored the advice of his battle-experienced generals, who were as good as any in the Allied Armies, particularly Model. His 'small solution', which aimed at swinging north the Panzer Armies when they reached the east bank of the Maas to meet a simultaneous attack south-westwards from Geilenkirchen might, given luck and a free hand, have isolated some 14 Allied divisions. About Geilenkirchen, where the defences were flimsy in the extreme, only 7th Armoured and 52nd (L) Division stood in the way, with their backs to the Maas.

Above all, Hitler completely underrated the courage and tenacity of the American soldier, fighting in isolation in countless small battles, and particularly at St Vith and Bastogne. His obstinate resistance put the Panzer thrusts completely out of gear; to him goes the major credit for the victory.

At the outset, Eisenhower was caught at a disadvantage. His Intelligence staffs, in failing to warn him of the offensive, served him badly. They had considerable information both of ground and air sources, indicating an attack on the Ardennes front, but failed to make the correct deductions from it. In particular, those charged with interpreting the information gained by the Air Forces, let him down: they were, according to Tedder, completely at fault in concluding that the Germans lacked transport and fuel for a major offensive. With a virtually open front before the battle, it should have been easy for the four divisions initially in line to have sent out medium- and long-range foot patrols into the Eifel and thus secured warning of the coming assault. This elementary and routine precaution was not taken. Thereafter, in his prompt action in committing 82nd and 101st Airborne Divisions in the gap and in appointing Montgomery to coordinate the operations in the north and backing his subsequent decisions, Eisenhower dominated the battle and displayed political sense of a very high order.

At most, the Ardennes battle delayed the Allied advance into Germany by six weeks. When, on 6 January, Hitler pulled out 6th Panzer Army to meet the imminent Russian offensive, the Germans in the West were already beaten. As von Rundstedt said: 'the backbone of the Western front was broken.' So far as the British Army was concerned, the main result was to postpone the 'Veritable' operation, originally designed to go in between 12 January and early February. Had it gone in on the original date in conditions of hard frost, giving good tank going, it is highly probable that it would have achieved quicker results that it did later on, when the thaw had set in.

There is no justification for the Russian claim that in putting forward the date of their offensive to 12 January they helped the Western Allies. In fact, the Western Allies, by writing off some 100,000 Germans, exhausting their rapidly dwindling supplies of petrol and destroying vast quantities of material, helped the Russians.

10: WINTER WAR

It all depends on that article whether we do the business or not. Give me enough of it and I am sure.

The Duke of Wellington in the Park at Brussels before Waterloo,
pointing to a British soldier

Experience in World War One had shown that prolonged periods of static defence, unless aggressively conducted, can sap morale. On the French front particularly between the great battles a policy of 'live and let live' had in many places been allowed to develop between the two sides. As a result, troops in the forward area had been given time to brood in idleness with disastrous results. Montgomery and his commanders were fully aware of this danger. Consequently, from one end to the other of the front of 21st Army Group no opportunity was missed to make life unbearable for the Germans sitting in their strong defences behind belts of mines and antipersonnel bombs. Throughout January the weather was unspeakably bad, hard frost alternating with falls of snow, fog and occasional thaws.

Whilst the Ardennes battle dragged on to its inevitable end, Montgomery took the opportunity to overrun the one remaining area still held by the Germans west of the River Roer. This was the Heinsberg salient, a roughly equilateral triangle with sides about 20 miles long and with its apex at Roermond and its base along the Saeffelen Beek running into the Maas at Maeseyck. From Sittard, two main roads led to Heinsberg and Roermond, both part of the Siegfried Line. The two German divisions holding it, 176th and 183rd, were not in the same class as those put into the Ardennes offensive. They were however, well supported by the heavy artillery in the Siegfried defences, skilfully sited and fully aware of the fact that any display of reluctance to fight on their part was likely to result in the imposition of the death penalty.

This operation, known as 'Blackcock', called for meticulous staff work on the part of XII Corps, a high standard of leadership by infantry regimental officers, and courage and endurance by the troops themselves. All were forthcoming. There was little or no scope for air support: the tanks were hamstrung on many occasions by the bad going and the vast number of mines, of which the enemy had an apparently inexhaustible supply.

The main burden of the attack fell to the 52nd (L) Division, entrusted with the main effort towards the heart of the enemy's defences — Heinsberg; the 7th Armoured Division on their left and the 43rd Wessex Division were allotted subsidiary roles. Mindful of the need to conserve manpower for the advance into Germany and with a view to familiarising the infantry with the techniques of working with the Flails, Petards, Crocodiles and Kangaroos of 79th Armoured Division, Mongomery provided support on a formidable scale. In case of need the fire of eight field regiments, six medium regiments and some heavy and super-heavy guns could be called upon. A further novelty was a Canadian invention, the 1st Canadian Rocket Battery, which could fire a salvo of some 350 rockets, each equivalent to one 5'5-inch shell, known to the troops as the' Canadian Mattress' or 'Flying Bedstead'. This made a weird whistling sound before impact and produced an explosion like the crack of doom. Finally there was a troop of searchlights, whose beams reflected from the sky produced

'Monty's Moonlight', giving enough light to enable troops assaulting in the dark to see their way.

For the troops snow suits provided admirable camouflage; tanks and other vehicles were painted white. Every phase of the operation was planned in great detail and previously rehearsed. Troops were put into action, rested and fed: every man understood the part he had to play. The response between 16 and 24 January was what it has always been in similar circumstances and what it should always be with well-trained British troops — success.

The action of Fusilier Dennis Donnini, of the 4th/5th Royal Scots Fusiliers, who won the Victoria Cross at the crossing of the Saeffelen Beek, illustrates in concentrated form the spirit of his regiment and the 52nd (L) Division as a whole: the German position, which was covered by the half-frozen Saeffelen Beek, was protected on the far bank by a deep belt of mines and wire. A sudden thaw made it impossible for the supporting tanks to cross the stream. Private Donnini's platoon, as they left their trenches to assault a small village, came under concentrated machine-gun and rifle fire from the houses and he was hit in the head. Recovering consciousness after a few minutes, he charged 30 yards down an open road and threw a grenade in the nearest window. The enemy fled, pursued by Donnini and the survivors of his platoon. He and two companions then, under fire at 70 yards range, crossed an open space and reached the cover of a wooded barn, 30 yards from the enemy trenches. Still bleeding copiously from his wound, he then went into the open under intense close-range fire and carried one of his wounded companions into the barn. He took a Bren gun, firing as he went. He was wounded a second time, but recovered and went on firing until a third bullet hit a grenade he was carrying and killed him.

Donnini, a youth of 19, had only been a soldier for seven months. He was the son of an Italian confectioner in a Durham mining village, who had never even taken out naturalisation papers but who gave three sons to his adopted country and the lives of two of them.

Apart from the Victoria Cross, the reputation of no decoration was more scrupulously safeguarded than that of the Distinguished Conduct Medal. To gain it, a soldier had to display not only conspicuous courage but also outstanding initiative. None was better earned than that of Lance-Corporal Alexander Leitch of the 4th KOSB in the bitter fighting at Heinsberg on 24 January. In the fields to the west of the town his company was caught in the open in a hail of fire from accurate and well-concealed mortars. His Company Commander was wounded; the Second-in-Command was killed; the Company Sergeant-Major was badly hit. Communications with the outside world had collapsed; even the gunners were out of touch. Then to the guns through the frantic din on the air came a clear Scottish voice, coolly calling for covering fire. It was the voice of the Company Signaller, Lance-Corporal Leitch, effectively directing the guns on to the energy mortars. When help arrived and the stretcher bearers were moving off with the wounded, he asked whether they would be coming back. When asked why he put the question he replied quietly: 'I think I have been wounded in both legs.' One in fact had been almost severed: the other was badly damaged. These wounds had been received before he took charge and called for the support of the guns.

'Blackcock' ended on 26 January with the fall of Heinsberg and the majority of the 176th and 183rd Divisions who survived in the prisoner of war cages. 52nd (L) Division's casualties were light — 101 killed and 752 wounded. During the battle, despite the Arctic weather, only 258 men were evacuated owing to sickness — one and a half per cent of the fighting force. Sick rates in the other two divisions of XII Corps, likewise exposed to the elements, were similarly light.

Throughout January on the rest of 21st Army Group front few opportunities were missed to subject the enemy to persistent sniping and to raid his lines with the object of obtaining prisoners for Intelligence purposes. On the Canadian front small patrols regularly crossed the Maas at night by boat. The sniper nuisance was removed by sniping the enemy with greater intensity. Mortar bombs and shells fired into the British lines brought at least threefold retaliation within minutes. Moral ascendancy was complete. By the end of January the Army, whose spirits had sagged somewhat in October at the prospect of a long winter war, had attained a standard of offensive eagerness as high as at any time in World War Two, and higher than in 1917 and the last months of World War One. The foundations on which this high standard of morale was based therefore merit consideration.

The infantry of 1944/5, on whom the main burden of the fighting had fallen since the D-Day landing and was still to fall, in no way resembled the PBI of World War One. By 1944 the fact had been recognised that the infantry required men of higher standard than the technical arms, that the stress and discomfort they meet in battle is greater than that encountered by all other branches of the Army, and that their duties such as fighting at night or in built-up areas and forests call for a higher standard of individual courage and initiative than is needed by those arms that always fight in groups. By the last year of the war, the selection procedure instituted by the Adjutant-General, Sir Ronald Adam, had borne fruit — at least to the extent that the infantry was no longer burdened with men who were emotionally unstable or of low intelligence. The methods used were by no means perfect, but they were at least an improvement on previous techniques based on the principle of 'choosing Guardsmen by the yard'. It was also recognised that just as a truck wears out after a number of miles, there comes a point in a long campaign when an infantry soldier, temporarily at any rate, reaches the end of his tether. The Americans thought this stage was reached after 200-240 combat days: the British estimated that a rifleman would last 400 days. Where possible, therefore, veterans were sent home or found employment behind the lines. As a result the quality of the infantry was high: furthermore, they were conscious of the fact. If they had realised that they, who bore the main burden of the battle, constituted only 14 per cent of the BLA, they would have held their heads even higher than they did.

No nation in any war ever had a clearer aim than the British in World War Two. All were convinced, thanks to Churchill's leadership, that they were fighting in a great cause for which they must be prepared if necessary to die. They were not fighting for abstractions such as the Balance of Power in Europe, national prestige or any ideology. Their task was to purge the world of the moral disease of Nazism as personified by 'that wicked man' Hitler and the SS. The German Army in front of them must therefore be destroyed with all speed and by all available means. Essentially civilian at heart, their one desire once their task was accomplished was to return to their families and live their lives in peace. This conviction animated the whole of Montgomery's Army. If ever a general was entitled to speak, as many did, of 'my Army' it was Montgomery.

No commander of a British Army in history, except perhaps Marlborough, ever established a greater ascendancy over the minds of his troops than Montgomery. They saw him: he talked to them in words they could understand, face to face and without a note. He told them what he intended to do, convinced them that his plans were good, assured them that the tools at their disposal were more numerous and effective than they had ever been and that, provided they played their part, success was certain. Above all, he convinced them that under his leadership and that of his subordinate commanders their lives, unlike those of some of their fathers in World War One, would not be thrown away unnecessarily.

The corps, divisional, brigade, battalion and regimental commanders were all of his own selection: he made it his business to know them all. In his relations with them he was correct and formal. Contrary to popular belief, he never sacked them without good reason. The element of chance plays a big part in war: no commander can expect to be successful every time; many were given a second chance. If however, they had lost the confidence of their troops, then they had to go. The knowledge that he had a pool of potential commanders readily available and eager to replace those who fell by the wayside was an added stimulant.

One of the outstanding features of Montgomery's Army at this stage of the war was the youthfulness of the majority of battalion commanders, on whom the greatest strain in battle fell. Nearly all were in their late twenties or early thirties. For the most part they were regular officers sprinkled with a proportion of brilliant Territorials, many of whom were, after the war, to achieve distinction in civil life. The junior war-emergency officers, for the most part, were a cross section of British society — approximately one quarter the products of public schools and three-quarters of grant-aided or state schools. There were also a considerable number of promoted

NCOs who had won their commissions in the cannon's mouth. School and social position counted for nothing: the sole criterion was eagerness to get to grips with the enemy.

Nothing astonished British troops coming into contact with the Americans more than the large notices about two miles behind the front to the effect that anyone found not wearing his steel helmet, whatever his rank, would automatically be fined 50 dollars. In the matter of niceties of dress, Montgomery showed even less interest than his predecessor Wellington. In insistence on the vital importance of discipline as the only means of achieving the conquest of fear, he was, however, as implacable as the Iron Duke.

Instant and unquestioning compliance with orders was expected: even in the front line, if humanly possible, men had to shave; hair was cut short — every company had its own so-called barber with a pair of shears and the results of his labours frequently lacked finesse. The interests of hygiene and the doctors dealing with head wounds were however met. The infantryman's inescapable companions of World War One, the louse and the nit, were unknown. To inculcate discipline, training went on continuously, even when in the line. The majority of divisions had their own battle schools where reinforcements on arrival where possible, were taught the finer points of tactics peculiar to the theatre. In reserve, a good unit could always be recognised by the noise of small-arms fire, grenades and mortar bombs coming from its area. In one battalion, a large draft of reinforcements on arrival were 'given a taste of things to come by being invited to dig themselves in, whereupon they were assisted in fulfilling the purpose of the exercise by the mortar platoon, which landed some sixty bombs with skill and precision some sixty-five yards away from them'. So intense was the training given in one division that it was facetiously said of them that death must have come to many as a happy release.

Before 1939 regimental tradition had always been regarded as a mainstay to good morale: so far as regular officers and NCOs were concerned, it undoubtedly had considerable influence. The branches of the War Office concerned with postings involved themselves in fantastic complications in the endeavour to maintain it. By this stage of the war, loyalty to the division to some extent had replaced it, especially in the English as distinct from the Scottish regiments, although in the case of the latter, divisional pride was also strong. This development had the advantage of embracing all arms and services within one individual loyalty. The infantry could talk of 'our gunners', 'our engineers', 'our RASC': they in their turn spoke of 'our infantry'. They fought well not because their ancestors had distinguished themselves in the assault on Badajoz, but because they were well led and had developed a corporate sense in the unit in which they happened to serve.

By this stage of the war, so widely was the officer element of the prewar Regular Army dispersed that so far as fighting ability was concerned there was often little, if any, difference between units with the titles of the Regular Army and those which had started their life in 1939 as a result of Hore Belisha's expansion of the Territorial Army.

Although adamant in insisting on the instant and whole-hearted compliance with his orders affecting operations, no commander showed less interest in the prevention and punishment of petty crime than Montgomery. Within most British soldiers lurks the eternal Boy Scout: there is an element of truth in Tolstoy's theory that war is an excuse for humanity to wander about more freely. On the battlefield abandoned pigs, hens and geese roamed in search of food. The plight of cattle, often wounded by shell and mortar fire, was pitiful: in their attitude to unnecessary suffering on the part of animals, the British display sentimentality greater than that of the inhabitants of the Continent. Public opinion in the ranks therefore demanded that suffering animals should be put out of their misery: common sense, stimulated by monotonous rations and the almost insatiable appetite created by hard exercise and exposure, equally dictated that good food should not be wasted. To a man accustomed to a breakfast of baked beans and greasy bacon and a dinner of stew and strong tea, the prospect of a roast chicken or a pork chop represented the last word in luxurious living. In the forward area in the lulls between actual fighting, men shifted for themselves. Thus engaged, they had no time to brood on their likely future prospects in eternity. Many a dish of chips was cooked in the ruins of houses damaged by shell fire. German prisoners on surrendering usually prominently displayed their cash balance when they put their hands above their heads: it would have been out of character not to accept a gift so freely offered. The possession of a watch, too, adds to a soldier's efficiency.

Although a firm believer that 'hardship and privation are the school of a good soldier: idleness and luxury are his enemies', Montgomery applied his policy with common sense. Out of the line he insisted that troops should be quartered as comfortably as possible. A particularly gracious and rewarding act on his part was the provision of caravans for brigadiers for their use when battle conditions permitted. He expected them to plan at least one battle ahead: clear thinking is difficult amid the din and traffic of a forward headquarters. No commander is at his best in conditions of personal discomfort. At a crisis, when those under his command are tired and suffering from exposure, he must be, or appear to be, at the top of his form.

Montgomery at least ensured this. He himself lived in austere but not uncomfortable dignity and gave himself time to think. At no time during the campaign did he show the slightest sign of fatigue.

Of all the peoples on the Continent, the British found themselves most at home with the Dutch. The Netherlands Military Administration, based on the government which had fled to England in 1940, and which was now endeavouring to restore the civil life of the country, was not popular with the people and soon ran into difficulties. Many of the local officials had been removed to Germany or had cooperated with the invader: some of the provincial capitals were still in enemy hands. The ministers returned from England had difficulty in reasserting their authority and were soon at loggerheads with the resistance movement. Above all there was a chronic shortage of the necessities of life and an acute refugee problem.

These difficulties amongst the Dutch themselves in no way affected the warm-hearted welcome given to the British and Canadian troops when out of the line. Two hundred and fifty years before, the links between the two peoples had been very close. Under the Captain-General of the Netherlands, the Great Duke of Marlborough, the Dutch Horse had struck the decisive blow at Ramillies; at Oudenarde, the Dutch Army under Overkirk had completed the envelopment of the French Army in a circle of flame when night closed in on the battlefield; the combined English and Dutch fleets had swept the French Navy from the seas. Few of either nation were conscious of this close association: nevertheless, despite the difficulties of language, the affinity of outlook between the inhabitants of the neat little houses of the Netherlands and the mass of British soldiers was soon apparent. Despite shortages of food and the humiliation of occupation, they never complained. Their generosity to the troops was unparalleled: their menfolk were pale and drawn, their women tired and worn and their children pale and anaemic; nonetheless what they had, they gave. On arrival in a village or housing estate, allotment of individual billets was unnecessary. Companies were marched to the end of a street or block: thereafter the men billeted themselves. Above all, the Dutch had the virtue of kindness as understood by the British. When men were killed and buried by the roadside, the women and children placed flowers on their graves. When they came out of the line to rest, the women, as formidable as many of their own mothers, hurried to dry their greatcoats, mend their clothes and do their washing. Within their houses, the troops were somewhat awed by the spotless red tiles, the general tidiness and the fact that they were expected to remove their muddy boots before entering. In sharp contrast to the comparative laxity in manners and morals of wartime England, the Dutch retained strict Victorian standards with regard to relations between the sexes. The soldiers were quick to conform: anyone who wished to take a girl for a walk was expected to take her brother as well, or her fiancé if she had one. Most of the girls sported scarves made from the violently incandescent yellow celanese triangles carried by the troops to indicate their position to aircraft. It was all very correct — the proprieties were satisfied — at least so far as the eye could see. Most of the soldiers' sweet ration went to the children and surreptitiously, some of their rations as well.

A man can face the monotony and hardships of battle all the better if he can look forward to a break in the near future. In the Peninsular War, Wellington had decided that 48 hours in Lisbon was adequate: Montgomery saw no need for a more lengthy period in Brussels. The arrangements made there however, in view of the Field-Marshal's widely publicised hostility to any form of self-indulgence or frivolity in wartime, astonished everyone in the army. No less than 17 good hotels were requisitioned for the troops and operated under the supervision of NAAFI, with remarkable efficiency. For 48 hours all ranks enjoyed the comforts of civilisation: the turnover, which was liberal, was only suspended for a few days during the Ardennes offensive and went on to the end of the war. The shops in Brussels were crammed with goods which had long since disappeared in England. The Germans had travelled free on the trains and the Belgians saw no reason why their liberators should not do the same. It was good to be a British soldier in Brussels that winter: a man felt and was treated like a conqueror. The entertainments provided by ENSA in the theatre were lavish and free. For 48 hours a man on leave could do whatever he pleased — subject naturally to the maintenance of normal peacetime standards of military behaviour. The extremely smart and efficient Military Police saw to that. The Field-Marshal himself habitually went to bed at 10.30 p.m. After this hour anyone found in the streets, whatever his rank, was liable to arrest, and deservedly so — Brussels had nothing of which Montgomery would approve to offer after such a time.

A characteristic expected in any great commander is ability to grasp the implications of the specialised knowledge of the expert and to apply them with humanity and common sense. By this stage of the war considerable experience had been gained in the treatment of psychiatric cases, which in Normandy had risen to 10 per cent of the total battle casualties. The fact was recognised that, with men continually exposed to danger, especially continued shell and mortar fire, casualties of this sort are inevitable, but that much can be done by early diagnosis, rest, sedation and reassurance. To this end, Montgomery had set up exhaustion centres in divisions and corps, where it was found that after a few days' treatment up to 70 per cent of men could be returned to their units. He himself and his subordinate commanders kept a sharp eye open for the slightest sign of imminent breakdown amongst those serving under them. A remarkable fact amongst the troops themselves was their own insistence on the removal of any of their comrades who had, in their own words, lost their nerve. Since World War One great advances had been made in the field of psychiatry: nonetheless, the contrast was striking between the attitude of the apparently callous and inhuman commanders of World War One and that of Montgomery. When the need arose he could be as ruthless as his predecessors: nevertheless he knew how to temper the wind to the shorn lamb.

In World War One, the staff with their conspicuous red tabs, worn even by staff captains, and highly polished field boots, were regarded with loathing and contempt by the fighting troops. Under Montgomery all this was changed. They lived hard and worked incredibly long hours. Only the very highest standards of staff work sufficed: the needs of the fighting troops were the only consideration. So intense was the drive from the top that to return from staff duty to a fighting unit was as refreshing as escape from the tensions of city life to the breezes of the open sea.

In Normandy the performances of the divisions which had served in the 8th Army in North Africa and Italy had compared unfavourably with that of those which had spent the greater part of the war in the United Kingdom. The sharp contrast between the open spaces of the desert and the closely wooded country and continuous mortaring of the *bocage* had in some cases been too great for men who after two years of continuous action had understandably lost their first enthusiasm. By this stage of the campaign, thanks largely to changes in command, they were back in their old form. In the process a number of commanders had been replaced: some felt, with what appeared to them good reason, that they had been unjustifiably removed. The fact remains that they were not missed. By the late autumn, the morale and efficiency of all the divisions in 21st Army Group was uniformly high: naturally they differed in character: some excelled in deliberately planned operation, others shone in exploitation and the impromptu battle. The fact that some thought themselves better than others was a powerful stimulant to gain further renown.

Thus, with a well-found and well-trained Army, based on sound administrative foundations, shorn of the weaker brethren and eager to end the war in the only way it could be ended — by destroying the enemy in front of them — Montgomery faced the way ahead with equanimity.

11: PRELUDE TO 'VERITABLE'

The general must know how to get his men their rations and
every kind of stores needed for war.

Socrates

To mount and sustain the Ardennes offensive, Hitler had
starved the Eastern front: he, like Bradley, had taken a
'calculated risk' (a cliché much in use at the time both in
North-Western Europe and Italy by commanders to laugh off
lack of foresight) and it also had not come off. The best of the
new divisions raised since September had gone to the 5th and
6th Panzer Armies. Twice as many tanks and assault guns had
been sent to Model as had reached the Eastern front. It was
not until 22 January that Hitler agreed to withdraw the 6th
Panzer Army from the Ardennes to the Hungarian front.
Finally, in January the Western Allies were engaging almost as
many German divisions as the Russians on the long front from
the Danube to the Baltic. When, therefore, on 12 January, the
long-awaited Russian winter offensive erupted, the German
collapse was complete. In the centre Koniev and Zhukov's
Army Groups, with a fivefold superiority of men, tanks and
guns, broke out and with complete air superiority advanced
over 250 miles in three weeks into Hitler's other main
industrial area, Upper Silesia. In the north, Rokossovsky
reached the Gulf of Danzig and cut off 25 German divisions.
By the end of the month, Zhukov was only 40 miles from
Berlin and the roads leading westwards from Frankfurt-an-der-
Oder were choked with refugees. When, therefore, Roosevelt,
Churchill and their entourage met Stalin at Yalta in the first

week of February they had, in sharp contrast to the Russians, little to show in the field of military achievement. Understandably, the fact that they were about to reach the positions they had held the previous November and had lost some 80,000 men and more tanks than the Germans in the process failed to impress Stalin. His claim that his offensive had helped them, however, had no foundation: they, on the contrary, had helped him — although certainly not by design.

Chester Wilmot, writing at a time when Russia was' considered to be threatening the very existence of the West, has described the Yalta conference as 'Stalin's greatest victory'. This can now be seen to be an overstatement. At the time, in British and American eyes, and especially those of Roosevelt, the USSR was still an ally. Their main aims were to reach agreement with regard to the occupation zones, to decide on the fate of Austria and so far as the Americans were concerned to reach a settlement which would allow them to remove their army of occupation from Germany as soon as possible after the end of hostilities. They also wanted Russian aid to finish the war against Japan. Both Western Allies hoped that the USSR would become an effective partner in the United Nations organisation. The conference broke up with the Western Allies believing they had succeeded in reaching a moderately satisfactory working agreement. At Britain's request, France was allotted an occupation zone: it was clearly understood that the boundaries between the zones could be crossed if necessary during the final military operations. Churchill makes this point abundantly clear: 'It was well understood by everyone that the agreed occupational zones must not hamper the operational movements of the armies. Berlin, Prague and Vienna could be taken by whoever got there first.' The Western Allies agreed to keep the Russians informed of their future military plans and hoped for similar information from their enigmatic ally. Beyond reaffirming the doctrines of 'unconditional surrender', nothing else was decided. Eisenhower was given no guidance whatever with regard to the territorial objectives he must gain in order to place his political masters in a good bargaining position at the end of hostilities. If Yalta was the most important inter-Allied conference of the war, then it was important not for what was decided but for what was not.

On the eve of the Yalta conference, the British Chiefs of Staff had met the United States Chiefs of Staff at Malta, to reconcile their divergent attitudes with regard to Eisenhower's plans for the final destruction of the German Armies in the West. In the hope of defending the Ruhr, Hitler still had some 85 divisions west of the Rhine. Eisenhower therefore envisaged 'one more great campaign aggressively conducted on a broad front' with the preliminary aim of destroying these forces and closing with the entire west bank of the Rhine. Thereafter the Allies were to cross the Rhine in force, their main effort being to the north of the Ruhr. Having done this, he intended to make three separate thrusts across the Rhine, the main effort being made by Montgomery's Army Group with the 9th US Army under command across the Lower Rhine into the North German plain. This force was to consist of 35 divisions, the maximum which his logistic staff considered could be sustained in this area. A complementary effort was to be made by Bradley's 12th Army Group with 'such forces, if adequate, as may be available after providing 35 divisions for the north and essential security elsewhere'. Advancing from the Mainz-Frankfurt area to Kassel, the Ruhr would thus be enveloped from the north and south. A third, but subsidiary, effort was to be launched by Devers' 6th Army

Group, also with 25 divisions. This Army Group, having cleared the Germans out of the Moselle-Saar area, was to cross the Rhine near Mainz and then help the 12th Army Group with the southern envelopment of the Ruhr. By capturing these objectives in the south, Eisenhower hoped to draw enemy forces away from the vital thrust in the north.

At Malta, Alanbrooke strongly objected to the first part of Eisenhower's plan on the grounds that clearing the whole west bank of the Rhine would absorb so many divisions that the attack in the north would be jeopardised. Discussion was prolonged and obstinate. The almost undisguised lack of faith in Eisenhower's judgment by the British aroused intense American resentment, particularly from Marshall, the revered US Chief of Staff. Eventually, thanks to the diplomatic skill of Bedell-Smith, Eisenhower's Chief of Staff, a compromise was reached whereby it was agreed to go ahead in the north without waiting to close with the Rhine throughout its length, and to leave the 9th US Army under Montgomery's command. The British also chose this moment to revive the controversy concerning the need for an overall ground commander. So sensitive were the Americans on this subject that it was never formally considered at the conference but only secretly discussed by the Combined Chiefs of Staff without recorded minutes, if the appointment was to be made, it could only be filled by Montgomery who was unfortunately quite unacceptable not only to Marshall but to Bradley and Patton as well. Both national prestige and personal jealousies were involved. The war had, in fact, reached a stage at which the Americans considered it more important to conciliate the Russians than to remain on good terms with the British. In fact, the latter were in no position to reveal at the conference the main reason for their anxiety. There seemed to be a real risk that the Russians might well reach the Elbe and the North Sea before the Western Allies. If that were to happen, the Russians would gain the ports and naval bases in North Germany and thereby threaten vital British interests. Nonetheless, it was tactless to revive the command issue at this late stage of the war. The whole controversy illustrates the manner in which operations by allied forces are almost inevitably influenced by personal rivalries, national ambitions and prejudices, as well as political factors.

Backed by both governments and by the Western Chiefs of Staff, Eisenhower was now free to fight the last campaign as he wished. A firm, comprehensive and integrated plan now existed for the whole front, together with provision for a central reserve to ensure flexibility. Provided the troops themselves played their part, victory was inevitable.

There was nothing novel in the task allotted to Montgomery. It had in fact been under spasmodic consideration by his planning staffs ever since October. The plan adopted displayed all the characteristics of the Montgomery technique at its best — an aim so simple that every private soldier could understand it, meticulous preparation down to the last detail, the maximum possible material backing, the concentration of overwhelming support by the artillery and the air arm and a subtle element of surprise calculated to catch the enemy 'off balance'. In brief, he proposed to seize the western bank of the Rhine from Nijmegen to Dusseldorf by converging attacks, one by 1st Canadian Army from the north ('Veritable') and the other by 9th US Army ('Grenade') striking north-east from the Roer river. The German forces would thus be caught in a vice. If they chose to fight west of the Rhine, they would be destroyed. If they decided to pull back, the 21st Army Group would be admirably placed to force the crossing of the river. In any case, as all their communications centred on the bridge at Wesel, they were likely to be so badly mauled that they would be unable to hold the line of the Rhine in adequate strength. The cover plan suggested an attack due north to liberate the Dutch, now near starvation: somewhat surprisingly it succeeded. The target date for 1st Canadian Army to attack was 8 February: 9th US Army, which was not yet concentrated, was to attack 48 hours later, by which time it was hoped that 1st Canadian Army would have attracted most of the enemy's reserves. Further to the south, Bradley's Army Group was made responsible for the protection of 9th US Army's southern flank.

Freed at last from the embarrassment of the Ardennes, Bradley could now concentrate on the task which had baffled him since October — to capture the Roer dams. So long as the Germans retained control here, they were at liberty at any time to smash the discharge valves and swamp 9th Army's battlefield.

Since October, the front line east of Nijmegen had been stationary, facing the dark mass of the Reichswald — a forest of young pines, about seven feet apart, eight miles long and four miles wide and traversed by one metalled road. Running west from Cleve within the forest was a belt of higher ground. North of this again was a wide belt of flooded polders stretching to the Rhine, with villages a foot or so above the water dotted here and there. South of the forest extended a further belt of sodden fields, through which flowed the River Niers to the Maas. Before, therefore, 1st Canadian Army could strike southwards along the belt of dry ground about 10 miles wide between the two rivers, it would be necessary to clear the bottleneck leading to Cleve. From here three roads ran southwards to Goch, Udem and Calcar, whence the ground over which it was possible to manoeuvre expanded to a width of 20 miles. Flanks virtually secured by the great rivers with their flooded banks gave the attacker no alternative to frontal assault. A more unpromising area for mobile operations in wet winter weather could scarcely have been found.

To this uninviting terrain, the Germans had applied with considerable skill all the experience in the laying-out of defences gained in both World Wars, exploiting the advantages of the ground favourable to themselves and concentrating their strength where it seemed to favour an attack. The defences themselves were based on three main zones. The first was the outpost position to the main Siegfried defences — a double series of trenches covered in front of the Reichswald by an anti-tank ditch. All the villages and farmhouses had been converted into strongpoints: every house had its cellar with a machine-gun emplacement at ground level. Connecting trenches linked the whole of this complex system to a depth of 2,000 yards from the forward minefields to the edge of the forest. The two main roads were particularly strongly defended by road blocks, dug-in anti-tank guns and obstacles.

Three miles to the rear of the outpost system was the northern end of the Siegfried Line, the main belt of which traversed the Reichswald from north to south, then skirted the southern edge as far as the town of Goch. The corridor in the north to the town of Cleve, known as the Materborn gap, was defended by a series of trench systems reaching back to the high ground immediately west of the town. Covering Cleve from attack from the south, a further trench system completed the all-round defence of the Reichswald area. So far as the construction of concrete defences was concerned, the work had never been completed. There were, however, a number of large bunkers designed to hold about 60 men each near the

Materborn. Goch itself was a formidable fortress, surrounded by anti-tank ditches with houses reinforced by concrete.

The third defended zone, some 11 miles further south and known as the Hochwald layback, was a series of entrenched systems with anti-tank ditches about a mile deep and protected by a continuous belt of wire. All the towns and villages were designed to provide individual islands of resistance.

Holding this intricate network was the 84th Division under Major-General Fiebig, reinforced by three battalions of the 2nd Parachute Regiment. The latter were first-class troops drafted from Göring's Luftwaffe. The same cannot be said for the 84th Division, about 10,000 strong, reformed after destruction in the Falaise gap from the debris of worn-out infantry divisions and the scrapings of the German manpower barrel. The only armour at Major-General Fiebig's disposal consisted of 36 self-propelled assault guns. Altogether he had about 100 guns. It was estimated, however, as it turned out with remarkable accuracy, that General Schlemm commanding the 1st Parachute Army could reinforce the defence within six hours of the assault with the 7th Parachute Division and the 15th Panzer Grenadier Division, and rapidly build up a total of 11 Panzer and Panzer Grenadier divisions. In the eyes of the Commander of the 1st Parachute Army, the 84th Division were expendable. Provided they could put up some sort of resistance for a few hours, no one, except the men themselves, cared what happened to them. The first essential, therefore, was to seize the Materborn gap before the Germans could bring up these reserves. For this reason Horrocks, the Commander of XXX Corps, charged with the initial assault, decided to use overwhelming force at the outset, assaulting with five divisions in line, supported by a vast concentration of artillery.

Normally, military historians and commentators, either through impatience with or sheer ignorance of the mechanics of handling large forces, give scant attention to the very foundations on which tactics and strategy are based — the factors of supply, movement and maintenance. In this case the problem which faced the administrative services and staffs was formidable. Fortunately Montgomery and Crerar had available many officers of great ability in this field, who after the war reached high positions in the industrial, commercial and political world. The strength of the 1st Canadian Army was to rise to 450,000 men. Ammunition equivalent to the bomb drop of 25,000 medium bombers had to be brought up and dumped. If this had been stacked side by side and five feet high, it would have stretched for 30 miles. A stock of one and a half million gallons of petrol had to be built up. All this, plus a vast quantity of other stores, had to be brought over roads frequently flooded and constantly collapsing under the strain of heavy traffic and alternating weather conditions of hard frost and rapid thaw. Altogether, their maintenance absorbed the efforts of nearly 50 engineer companies and 29 pioneer companies. Road conditions were at their worst when the troops themselves were brought forward into the congested area around Nijmegen for the coming battle. All this traffic had to pass by night over the only bridges over the Maas at Grave and Mook. The staff work involved was intricate to a degree: over 1,600 military police were involved on traffic control alone. The strain on the RASC drivers was so great that many crashed through sheer fatigue.

The problem of providing camouflage to conceal this vast concentration was peculiarly exasperating. In the days preceding the offensive, the weather changed abruptly and often from snow conditions to rapid thaw. Infinite pains therefore had to be taken to whitewash the tanks one day and smear them with mud on the next. In the event the experts excelled themselves. Ammunition was sited in unrecognisable groupings simulating hedgerows, kitchen gardens and irregular patches of scrub. All British aircraft were warned off the area. As a result, when the day came, as Horrocks remarked: 'Odd though it may seem, we did achieve surprise.'

Much of the credit for this must go to the RAF, who completely dominated the skies before 'D-Day', bombing railways, bridges and ferries leading to the battle area. On the night before the battle, the towns of Cleve and Goch were to be completely destroyed by Bomber Command. These two fortresses were the linchpins of the enemy defensive system and therefore legitimate targets. Model and Schlemm were aware of this: responsibility for the deaths of their civil populations rested squarely on their shoulders. Horrocks had to secure the bottleneck at Cleve before the German reserves arrived. Faced with the alternatives of losing the battle and many of his own soldiers' lives and inflicting suffering on women and children, he rightly chose the latter, repugnant though it was. Unfortunately Cleve, like Caen in Normandy, in view of the importance attached to the large concrete defences on the Materborn, was overbombed by Bomber Command as will be seen.

For planning purposes Crerar envisaged the battle in three phases: the clearing of the Reichswald and the capture of Cleve; the breaching of the enemy's second defensive system hinged on Goch; and finally a break through the Hochwald layback and an advance to the line Geldem-Xanten to meet US 9th Army thrusting forward from the Roer. The first phase he entrusted to Horrocks' XXX Corps, attacking on a seven-mile front with five infantry divisions, the 51st (Highland), the 53rd

(Welsh), the 15th (Scottish), and the 2nd and 3rd Canadian from right to left supported by an immense weight of artillery fire from well over 1,000 guns, Guards Armoured Division, 43rd Wessex Division, three armoured brigades and 11 regiments of Hobart's specialised armour — just under half a million men. There was no room for manoeuvre: Horrocks must blast his way through.

In the planning period what could be foreseen was foreseen. In every battalion, regiment and company, officers assembled their men and on rough models explained the task ahead. Everywhere the troops saw the signs and portents of the battle: in every field, on every road vehicles were waiting under their camouflage nets or moving. The air above was busy with the drone of aircraft. The tension could be felt. An immense and general feeling of confidence prevailed. There was hard and bitter fighting ahead — the Boche would die game. The fact that the battle had obviously been brilliantly planned did not absolve every officer and man from using his initiative within his own sphere and they knew it. The will to close with the enemy reached its highest level in the whole campaign. Every man knew that he was fighting in a great cause — the destruction of the very embodiment of evil, the Nazi blight on the continent of Europe. Every man felt that what he was and what he did mattered. He was convinced that the Parachute Army could be beaten: the evidence of the efficiency of his own army was before his eyes. At every level the hard school of war had brought forward leaders he could trust. He knew that whatever hardships might come, his life would not be lightly thrown away. Everything possible which could be done to provide the weapons and equipment for the task ahead had been done. Montgomery's personal message read out to the troops on the eve of the battle echoes the spirit of this supreme moment of the war:

> The operations of the Allies on all fronts have now brought the war to its final stage. There was a time, some years ago, when it did not seem possible that we could win this war; the present situation is that we cannot lose it; the terrific successes of our Russian allies on the Eastern front have brought victory in sight.
>
> In 21 Army Group we stand ready for the last round. There are many of us who have fought through the previous rounds: we have won every previous round on points; we now come to the last and final round; and will want, and will go for, the knockout blow.
>
> The rules of the last round will be that we continue fighting till the final count; we must expect him to fight hard to stave off defeat possibly in the vain hope that we may crack before he does. But we shall not crack; we shall see this thing through to the very end. The last round may be long and difficult, and the fighting hard; but we now fight on German soil; we have got our opponent where we want him; and he is going to receive the knockout blow; a somewhat unusual one from more than one direction. You will remember the poem written by a soldier of the 8th Army in Africa before going into battle, in one verse of which he described what he was fighting for:
>
> *Peace for the kids, our brothers freed,*
> *A kinder world, a cleaner breed.*
>
> Let us see to it that we achieve this object, so well expressed by a fighting man of the British Empire. And so we embark on the final round, in close cooperation with our American allies on our right, and with complete confidence in the successful outcome of the onslaught being determined by our Russian allies on the other side of the ring. Somewhat curious rules you may say, but the whole match has been most curious; the Germans began this all-out contest and they must

185

not complain when in the last round they are struck from several directions at the same time.

Into the ring then let us go. And do not let us relax until the knockout blow has been delivered. Good luck to you and God bless you.

These simple words written with burning sincerity by a fundamentally unsophisticated man reached right down to the hearts of the rank and file of the British soldiers who made up almost 80 per cent of the 1st Canadian Army. He had never failed them: they would not fail him now.

12: 'VERITABLE'

And the waters prevailed exceedingly upon the earth.

Genesis

The battle between the Rhine and the Maas in February 1945, called the Battle of the Rhineland by Montgomery but generally known by its code name of 'Veritable', has, in comparison with the Battles of Normandy, Arnhem and the Bulge, attracted little attention. Originally intended as a double-headed punch by the 1st Canadian Army in the north striking southward to meet a similar thrust northwards very soon afterwards by the 9th US Army from the south, for the first 14 days the battle developed into a lone struggle between the 1st Canadian Army and 10 German divisions, three of which were armoured. As a result, when at last the drying out of the floods on the Roer enabled the 9th US Army to advance, they found themselves opposed by a mere four weak infantry divisions. The underlying theme of the battle is therefore strikingly similar to that of the Battle of Normandy in July and August 1944, the attraction of the enemy's reserves to one flank by one army to enable another army to break out on the other. It lasted for 28 days and nights in almost unspeakable conditions of flood, mud and misery. The troops were soaked with almost incessant rain; there was no escaping it and no shelter. They met on virtually equal terms in the 1st Parachute Army the last remaining German indoctrinated youth fighting with undiminished courage on German soil, supported eventually by the fire of some 700 mortars and over 1,000 guns. The volume of fire developed by both sides was the heaviest experienced by

British troops in the whole campaign. Not only had the Siegfried Line, rehabilitated by five months' work, to be pierced: thereafter the battle had to be continued along the length of it.

From the start it failed to proceed 'according to plan'; it abounded in unanticipated situations and bizarre incidents and it called for the very highest degree of improvisation and ingenuity on the part not only of the troops but of the staffs as well. The tanks were confronted by virtually insurmountable obstacles, dense forests, bogs, craters, road-blocks, mines and every form of demolition. As the historian of the 11th Armoured Division remarks, 'Although they struggled on to the limit of their capacity, they were virtually impotent'. Close air support, owing to weather conditions, was impossible on 19 out of the 31 days' fighting. Conditions therefore closely resembled those of the last battles of World War One, in which every 100 yards was important to the men who gained them. According to the Coldstream Guards, the fighting was the toughest they had ever known. Veterans of the 51st Highland Division who had fought through the desert campaign were agreed that the Hun, on his own soil, was the stiffest proposition they had met. 'It was real honest-to-God infantry stuff', said a senior officer, 'with no punches barred.'

From the outset, the will to close with the enemy had risen to a higher pitch than at any time during the campaign. The mood of disillusion of the autumn had passed. The ghastly side of war had ceased to shock. The issue was clear: there was only one way to end the war and that was by killing the enemy man for man.

By nightfall on 7 February, the concentration was complete. The woods and eastern suburbs of Nijmegen were packed with troops, guns, vehicles, workshops and tanks. Heavy guns, medium guns, field guns, tanks, anti-aircraft guns, mortars and machine-guns, all stood side by side ready to fire the greatest bombardment of the war. The tension could be felt — the kind of feeling which runs through the crowd before the Derby. As the night wore on, and the drone of the heavies of Bomber Command on their way to Cleve and the Stirlings and Lancasters of 84th Group to Weeze, Udem and Calcar could be heard overhead. The eastern sky was fit up by the fires they started: the sound of exploding bombs came from the direction of Cleve. Men said to each other with satisfaction: 'Bomber Harris is out tonight.' A feeling of immense confidence surged through the waiting soldiers of 51st Highland, 53rd Welsh, 15th Scottish and 2nd Canadian Divisions. There could now be only one end to the war.

It was still dark at one minute to five, though grey enough for the black silhouettes of the guns and tanks to be just discernible. Sixty seconds later it was light enough to read a book. The historian of the 4th/7th Royal Dragoon Guards describes the scene thus:

> It was a fantastic scene, never to be forgotten by those who were there: one moment silence and the next moment a terrific ear-splitting din, with every pitch of noise imaginable, little bangs, big bangs, sharp cracks, the rattle of machine-guns and the ripple of Bofors, intermingled with the periodic swoosh of a rocket battery. The night was lit by flashes of every colour and the tracer of the Bofors guns weaving fairy patterns in the sky as it streamed off towards the target.

Dawn broke with low clouds and rain. At 7.30 a.m., after a smokescreen had been laid across the whole front, came a brief lull of 10 minutes. This lured the enemy into manning his guns and bringing down his defensive fire against the expected attack. This was the opportunity for the sound rangers to locate one of his batteries and 19 mortar positions. Then once more the bombardment thundered out. Through the din came the noise of armour grinding forward and of aircraft droning overhead. About 9.30 a.m. the covering barrage began to descend on the opening line. Slowly it built a screen of smoke mingled with high explosive along the north-western edge of the Reichswald. At last, one minute before H Hour at 10.30 a.m., a line of yellow smoke shells indicated that the time of the assault had come. 'It was impossible to see more than half a mile ahead in the swirling eddies of smoke that drifted over the battlefield. Then khaki figures, Scots, Welsh and Canadians, filed out of the buildings below, accompanied by their squadrons of Churchills, and advancing steadily behind the barrage disappeared into the smoke towards the dark woods of the Reichswald.'

So shattering was the bombardment that except on the front of the 51st H Division, advancing on the right where a fresh battalion of the 180th Infantry Division brought into the line had to be summarily dealt with, there was little enemy resistance. Dazed prisoners of the 84th Division told their interrogators that the bombardment had created 'an impression of overwhelming force opposed to them which, in their isolated state, with no communications, it was useless to resist'.

A German soldier's letter captured later said: 'When Tommy began his attack he started such a terrific artillery barrage that we took leave of our senses. I shall not forget my experience in the Reichswald for a long time.' In fact, on this day it was not the enemy who slowed down the advance, but the mud. On the 53rd Division front the Flails, whose task it was to clear the mines ahead of the infantry, bogged down on the start line. Of all the tracked vehicles, only the Churchill tanks, with their broad tracks, succeeded in mastering the mud. Nonetheless, the infantry forged ahead in the soaking rain and by the afternoon had seized the commanding ridge at the north-west corner of the Reichswald. 'An almost overpowering smell of spent explosive hung like a cloud inside the forest; trees lay smashed and shattered, their broken branches strewn about, leaving stumps like grotesque scarecrows.' Aided by the pale light of searchlights shining on the low cloud and moving on compass bearings through the tangled undergrowth, they reached the road from Kranenburg to Hekkens astride the Siegfried Line.

On the 15th Scottish front only one Flail reached the start line. Nonetheless the attacking infantry, disregarding the mines, kept well up to the barrage and by 6.30 p.m. had taken Kranenburg, conspicuous with its onion-shaped church tower on the main road from Nijmegen to Cleve, and the Galgensteeg ridge immediately south of the town. The tracks behind them now completely collapsed and the force charged with the breaching of the Siegfried Line defences did not get through till the early hours of the morning.

Further to the north, the 2nd Canadian Division carried Den Heuvel without difficulty apart from casualties from SCHU mines, but the capture of Wyler cost the Calgary Highlanders 60 men.

It was on the extreme northern flank, however, that the operations took their most unorthodox turn. Here it was the task of the 3rd Canadian Division to clear the flooded area between the main road from Nijmegen to Cleve and the Rhine and thus protect the Corps' left flank. Since 3 February the waters of the Rhine had been slowly rising to an unprecedented height. Two days later the Germans had breached the main dyke at Erkelom four miles east of Nijmegen and through this gap poured the waters of the Rhine. By the day of the attack practically the whole of the area of operation was under water, with the exception of the village of Zyfflich and the Quer dam a mile to the east of their start line. Here the Regina Rifles, attacking by the light of 'Monty's Moonlight', and accompanied by a Crab of the 1st Lothian and Border Horse which flailed its way down the village street, firing its guns as it went, rounded up about 100 prisoners. A party of the enemy at the Quer dam showed more fight and were not finally liquidated till dawn the next day. Thereafter the troops embarked in Buffaloes and set sail to do battle with the German garrisons marooned in the villages still above the water. It is not surprising that in the darkness there were errors in navigation.

Thus in the first day and night, hampered more by the forces of nature and the mines than by the 84th Division, XXX Corps had broken through the main Siegfried defences. The problem was now to seize the Materborn gap before the enemy reserves arrived. Ominously, the maintenance routes behind the divisions had collapsed. Between 1 p.m. and midnight the water level north of the main road from Nijmegen to Cleve had risen 18 inches: it continued to rise.

It rained all night and it rained all the next day. Except on the main road in the north, all the tracks were now impassable except to men on foot. Here the breaching force by dawn had bridged the huge anti-tank ditch at Frasselt and over it the Lowland Brigade of the 15th Scottish Division pressed on into the heart of the main Siegfried Line and by mid-morning had cleared the concrete defences of the villages of Schottheide and Nutterden. Owing to the mud and mines rather than the resistance of the enemy, the division was now 10 hours behind schedule. Owing to the congestion in the rear arising from the collapse of the communications, there was no hope of getting the other two brigades of the division through in time to carry the Materborn heights before dark. Major-General Barber therefore ordered the Lowlanders to press on. As the light faded, they carried the commanding heights of the Bresserberg and Esperance about a mile west of Cleve. On their right within the forest the 53rd Welsh Division, without tank or artillery support, fought their way through the trees. As night fell, carrying parties manhandling ammunition and food struggled forward. In the southwest corner, where the 51st Highland Division continued their obstinate battle, one vehicle only got through to them — it was a Weasel carrying 500 tins of self-heating soup. That was all the hot food the infantry of XXX Corps got that day. For the rest it was cold stew delivered in the early hours of the morning.

On this day, a long way to the south, the 1st US Army at long last carried the Roer dams to find that the Germans had opened the sluice gate of the Schwammenauel, causing the river to burst its banks across the whole front of the US 9th Army. There could now be no help from that quarter until the floods subsided. Von Rundstedt was thus free to concentrate his reserves against the 1st Canadian Army. The 7th Parachute Division was already arriving on the front of the 51st Highland Division. It was vital therefore to seize Cleve and thus get possession of the Materborn gap with all speed. Just before last light Horrocks ordered the 43rd Wessex Division — which, crammed together shoulder to shoulder in the eastern outskirts of Nijmegen, had been waiting at one hour's notice to move for the past 48 hours — to advance, take Cleve and push on to Goch, Weeze, Kevelaer and beyond. At this time, the one and only usable road to Cleve was jammed nose to tail not only with the transport of 15th (Scottish) Division but also of quite a representative proportion of the vehicles of 1st Canadian Army. Tanks, Flails, Crocodiles, carriers and wheeled vehicles, lay inert in the mud all over the battlefield. Of this decision Horrocks wrote later:

> This was one of the worst mistakes I made in the war. The 15th Scottish had not got nearly so far as had been reported and one of their brigades had not yet been employed at all. There was already too much traffic on this one road, and it was impossible to deploy across country owing to the boggy ground. The arrival of the extra division caused one of the worst traffic jams of the whole war, only equalled, I believe by the scenes in the Liri Valley in Italy after the last battle of Cassino. The language heard that night has seldom, if ever, been equalled.

Was it however a mistake? Battles in fact, despite the narratives of many historians, do not proceed in a neat and tidy manner. A battle is chaos in which the factor of chance and the human element play a vital part. Churchill, who although unsound on technical detail, knew all about the spirit in which battles should be conducted, would quote time and time again from Nelson's Trafalgar memorandum: 'No Captain can go very wrong if he places his ship alongside that of an enemy.' If Horrocks had not committed the 43rd Division the course of events might have later taken a very different turn — XLVII Panzer Corps now coming forward, might, as will be seen, have converted the ruins of Cleve into another Cassino.

The night was bitterly cold with showers of icy rain and driving sleet as the 43rd Wessex Division, riding on tanks of the 8th Armoured Brigade, took the road from Nijmegen to Kranenburg and Cleve. The Luftwaffe chose this moment to stage a raid on Nijmegen. The sky was sprayed with fountains of glowing tracer shells, till there seemed to be curtains of floating red dots over the whole sky. In fits and starts the dense column jerked forward. Now and then a few German aircraft bombed the road by the light of flares. To the north an occasional gunflash lit up the great expanse of water north of the road. At Kranenburg the road itself was awash: the floods were obviously rising fast. Here Lieutenant-Colonel Corbyn, commanding the leading battalion the 4th Wiltshires, found the headquarters of a brigade of the 15th Scottish Division. Apparently the main road ahead was blocked two miles west of Cleve, but a secondary road branching off about three miles further on through a gap in the woods was said to be clear. The column trundled on through the darkness and, as he had been told, found this road. It was blocked by a fallen tree. A Spandau sprang to life: the troops were off the tanks in a flash and at close grips with the enemy, who were eventually overwhelmed. The column pushed on into the darkness and were soon amongst the houses on the southern outskirts of Cleve. Firing into every house as they passed, by dawn the 4th Wiltshires reached the south-eastern exits of the town. 'There were bomb craters and fallen trees everywhere, bomb craters packed so tight that the debris from one was piled against the rim of the next in a pathetic heap of rubble, roofs and radiators. There was not an undamaged house anywhere, piles of smashed furniture, clothing, children's books and toys, old photographs and bottled fruit, were spilled in hopeless confusion from sagging crazy skeletons of houses.' In this chaos the 129th Infantry Brigade, isolated from the rest of the Division, in small groups throughout the day and the following night, fought a series of sanguinary battles with the 16th Parachute Regiment which had just arrived from Arnhem, backed by Tiger and Panther tanks. They had, in fact, passed right through the outer defences of Cleve and superimposed themselves on the headquarters of Major-General Fiebig, who was struggling at the time to restore the situation with reinforcements now coming up.

The position of Major-General Thomas of the 43rd Wessex Division with his Tactical Headquarters in the column a few miles back, was hardly more enviable. Behind him stood a vast motionless traffic jam: the road was flooded and the water was rising rapidly. Through this confusion Major-General Barber of the 15th Scottish was endeavouring to pass his 227th Brigade to complete the task of capturing the Materborn heights and the town of Cleve. The meeting between the two commanders lacked cordiality. Major-General Barber, who was about seven feet tall, could personally contemplate the rising water with greater equanimity than Major-General Thomas, who was more in the jockey class. In the early dawn, after an exchange of argument notable more for forceful expression than urbanity, it was eventually agreed that the 43rd Wessex Division should clear the road to enable the 15th Scottish reserve brigade to struggle and work its way round the south of the town. A day of nightmare traffic congestion ensued. It is not surprising therefore that the 15th Scottish Division's plan for capturing Cleve on this day had to be abandoned. By nightfall the axis of both divisions at Kranenburg was three feet deep in water.

It is impossible to withhold a measure of professional sympathy for all three major-generals, both British and German, involved in this predicament: Major-General Barber, baulked of his prey by the descent of a vast and virtually immobile mass of troops and tanks of another division between him and his enemy; Major-General Thomas, in his leaky reconnaissance car, stuck in the mud by the roadside contemplating the steady downpour and the ever-rising waters; Major-General Fiebig, surrounded in the chaos of Cleve by bewildered and belligerent Westcountrymen engaged in a free-for-all shooting match around his headquarters like a riot in a Western town. By dawn on the 11th, however, the two British divisions at Cleve, now disentangled, were able to resume the attack. On their right 53rd Welsh Division fighting all the way in almost unspeakable conditions in the Reichswald, pushed on and by nightfall had crossed the road from Cleve to Hekkens. By the afternoon the 15th Scottish Division were masters of the ruins of Cleve. Attacking at 2 p.m. the DCLI carried the village of Materborn to the immediate south.

Two miles south of Cleve is a ridge of high ground about the village of Hau which commands the main road running due south from Cleve to Goch. Hot on the heels of the DCLI came the 7th Somerset Light Infantry and, as light faded, pressed on ahead for 1,000 yards.

> Four hundred yards ahead lay the junction of four roads — one from Materborn, one going north to Cleve, the Goch road and one going due east — later to be known as 'Tiger Corner'. At the cross-roads stood a burning SP gun. Other SP guns and many Spandaus opened up on Major Durie's Company. One of our tanks was hit, but the rest of the squadron (4th/7th Royal Dragoon Guards) now saturated the enemy infantry with fire. A brilliant attack fought inch by inch amongst the houses by No. 13 Platoon under Lieutenant E. Lawson finally left the cross-roads in our hands. The light was failing and heavy sleet had begun to fall.

Lieutenant-Colonel Ivor Reeves now arrived. There was still another 1,000 yards to go. Ahead the road to Hau, bare of cover, ran straight into the darkness. Spandaus seemed to answer every move. The troops were almost dropping with fatigue. However, Lieutenant-Colonel Reeves decided to press on without his tanks. In fact this was a sound decision, as the tanks could have done little in the dark. B Squadron of 4/7th Royal Dragoon Guards therefore pulled back a few hundred yards whilst the battalion, still led by Major Durie, fought its way slowly down the burning road, dealing with each house in turn by the light of burning tanks. By midnight his men had almost reached the limit of fatigue. He therefore took a bold decision — to advance straight down the road to his objective… By 2 a.m. he had reached the bend of the road at Hau. On his right stood the eastern fringes of the Reichswald; in front on his left, stood Forst Cleve. The road and railway ran side by side through this gap. He had reached his objective. 'Fighting continued for the rest of the night; by 5.30 a.m. after thirteen hours of continuous fighting in the dark, the battalion was firm in its objective.' With the dawn came the 1st Worcestershires and without artillery support in the face of fierce resistance pressed on to complete the capture of the ridge. They were just in time.

XLVII Panzer Corps, under General von Lüttwitz, had been moving forward during the night with orders to launch a counter-attack to recover Cleve and the heights to the west. Because he was short of tanks — he had only 50 — von Luttwitz decided to attack westward into the Reichswald where the Allied superiority in tanks and artillery would be less effective, with 15th Panzer Grenadier Division on the left and 116th Panzer Division on the right. On reaching the road from Cleve to Hekkens, the corps was to concentrate on a drive due north to carry the Materborn heights. The operation was mounted in a hurry and although timed for 6 a.m. did not get under way till 9.30. When it did get going it withered away before the fire of the 53rd Welsh Division in the forest, the

Somerset Light Infantry at Hau, and the Worcestershire Regiment.

Next morning, von Luttwitz, his men fought to a standstill, conceded defeat and reverted to the defensive on the four-mile front of the Eselsberg, a low range of hills about four miles long between Moyland and Forst Cleve. This he held with the remnants of 84th Infantry Division, reinforced by a fresh regiment from beyond the Rhine and the battered divisions of XLVII Panzer Corps. Thus began the bitter struggle, fought continuously for five days and five nights, to smash this line.

The problem of the Commander XXX Corps was not only that of destroying the enemy in front of him but that of keeping his men, exposed to the elements, alive and fed. A journey from the A Echelon, where the food was cooked, to the front line took anything up to 18 hours. This is the experience of Captain and Quartermaster J. F. Moore of the 1st East Lancashires:

> The 53rd Division's Axis was hopeless and I decided to go via Kranenburg again. I got through but the water was over our mudguards. I could not contact the battalion that day but found the cooks under Captain Whiteside near Frasselt. Going back to A Echelon, no roads could be seen or even signs of any: it was just like a lake and the Dukws were being used for wounded and ammunition. We could have got through, because I had a pretty good idea where the submerged road was, but our luck was out and Bean, the driver, ran into one of the Jerry slit trenches on the side of the road. No one would stop to help — you could not blame them — so I had to get out and decided to make my way on foot. The water was up to my thighs and the Dukws kept giving me their wash but I survived and made the high ground near Nijmegen. Here I got the Transport Sergeant to take me back with a three-tonner and we managed to get through to

Bean, who by that time had given up all hope of ever seeing me again.

The suffering of the wounded, manhandled through the dripping forest and then exposed to a hazardous journey through the floods, cold and wet, were great. Once Cleve was taken some respite from the weather could be found for reserves in the cellars: for the troops of 53rd Welsh Division in the forest there was none. Somehow they survived to bring XLVII Panzer Corps to a standstill and eventually beat them back.

Meanwhile from the southern flank came encouraging news: the 51st Highland Division, back once more in its old desert form, was forging ahead to open the road from Mook to Goch via the Hekkens cross roads, to give the corps another supply route. Gennep on the Maas fell to the Black Watch, sent across the swollen Niers river in assault boats on the night of 10/n February. In the streets there was rough and terrible fighting, into which the Highlanders entered with zest. Next day, the 154th Brigade approached Hekkens. This village, surrounded by trees, constituted one of the strongest fortified areas in the main Siegfried defences. Night fighting amidst the Reichswald with all the paths blocked by the trees which had fallen would have been hopeless. The brigade, therefore, attacked at 3.30 in the afternoon, which gave it just 90 minutes of daylight, supported by every gun in XXX Corps. If ever a battle resembled World War One it was this. The infantry kept so close behind the barrage that they were amongst the enemy before they knew what had hit them. An hour after dark had descended it was all over. Two nights later the brigade crossed the swollen Niers river south of Hekkens in Buffaloes and established a bridgehead after bloody fighting west of Kessel.

To the north in the flooded area the 3rd Canadian Division in Buffaloes continued their strange aquatic war and by the night of the 11th had reached their objective — the Sploy Canal which joins Cleve to the Rhine. They had well earned their title of the 'Water Rats'. In the next two days they cleared the entire area right up to within 2,000 yards of the Emmerich ferries. When Montgomery visited them on the 15th, he toured the whole area in a convoy of amphibious vehicles. 'Veritable' was unquestionably the most uncomfortable battle the army ever fought in World War Two, but it was never dull — 'Age cannot wither nor custom stale its infinite variety'. From the start of the battle, the operations of the 3rd Canadian Division had been screened from observation from the far bank of the Rhine by four smoke companies of the Royal Pioneer Corps — 1,350 devoted men ineligible for any other arm of the service, with a sprinkling of intellectuals considered to be of no military value elsewhere and grouped under a headquarters known as 'Smoke Control'. Altogether they expended 8,500 zinc chloride generators and about 450,000 gallons of fog oil — to the satisfaction of all concerned except the Germans.

Meanwhile the struggle south-east of Cleve to break through the German position astride the Udem and Calcar roads reached ever-increasing intensity. On the 13th, the 46th Brigade, brought in on the north flank of the 43rd Wessex, found itself brought to a halt by intense mortar and artillery fire in the woods around Moyland. Here the 6th Parachute Division had reinforced the defence. There was bitter close fighting amongst the fir trees. This continued day and night for the next four days. The brigade voted it 'the worst experience they had endured since the campaign began'. The experience of the 43rd Wessex Division was equally grim — here von der Heydte's paratroops stubbornly held their ground. By the morning of the 16th it seemed that a deadlock had been reached; there was no sign of a break in the enemy's morale. During the morning however, the 130th Brigade succeeded in advancing about 600 yards between the hamlets of Blacknik and Berkovel, in the face of intense fire from SP guns. Here in the early afternoon the 214th Brigade emerged into the open fields and assaulted with the 7th Somerset Light Infantry on the right and the 1st Worcestershires on the left. They got off to a ragged start — fighting on their jumping-off line compelled them to abandon their prearranged fire plan: the tanks were late; but once started, nothing could stop them. Fighting all the way, by 5 p.m. they had advanced two miles and reached the village of Pfalzdorf within a mile of Goch. Prisoners of the 15th Panzer Grenadier Division were streaming to the rear — unescorted: there was more important work ahead. The 5th DCLI in Kangaroos and B Squadron 4th/7th Royal Dragoon Guards now emerged from Bedburg and in the fast-fading light, vanished amidst the bursting shells and smoke of the battlefield. The mass of armour surged due south in five columns; directed on the villages of Imigshof, Bergmanshof and Schronshof, at last by 8 p.m. cut the road from Goch to Calcar.

The enemy's front was cut in half. Meanwhile, at Pfalzdorf, the battle was not yet over. Half an hour after midnight, the 4th Somerset Light Infantry continued the advance and by dawn had reached the escarpment overlooking Goch on a front of 1,000 yards. The 1st Worcestershires and 7th Somerset Light Infantry resumed the attack at dawn and, fighting every inch of the way in a series of bitterly contested company and platoon battles, by the late afternoon had seized the whole escarpment and could look down on the chimneys of Goch on a front of 4,000 yards. The total of prisoners taken by this brigade had passed the thousand mark — all good troops.

The majority came from the 15th Panzer Grenadier Division, a *corps d'élite* with a magnificent fighting record in North Africa under Rommel. In Sicily, after fighting a bitterly contested rearguard operation, they had withdrawn intact and in their own time, to the mainland. At the Salerno landing, they had almost tipped the scales against the invaders. In January 1944 they had flung back the 36th (Texas) Division on the Rapido and in the following three months maintained their line at St Angelo against all efforts by the 5th Army to evict them. Transferred to North-West Europe, they had driven back the 7th US Armoured Division in late October in the Peel Marshes and in the Ardennes battle come within an ace of taking Bastogne. Their dead and abandoned equipment now littered the sodden field.

The 43rd Wessex Division had defeated as fine a division as any in the German Army and created a deep salient in the front of the XLVII Panzer Corps nearly five miles deep. At Moyland Wood however, where the 3rd Canadian Division had now taken over, the struggle continued for a further four days of costly fighting. Here four fresh parachute regiments put up an obstinate resistance amongst the trees, as costly to the Canadians as any engagement in the campaign. Counter-attack succeeded counter-attack; flamethrowers had to be brought in; shells bursting in the tree tops added to the general horror. It was not until the morning of the 22nd that the road to Calcar was at last opened.

From the cellars of the ancient castle emerged the aged Baroness Steengracht von Moyland, who had taken refuge in the vast cellars with 50 or 60 of her retainers. Sitting proudly in her armchair she complained that no notice had been taken of the white sheets hung out of the windows, and when it was pointed out that our troops had grown exceedingly wary of white flags of surrender, she sighed and said, as we so often heard, that the SS Troops were not like the old Wehrmacht.

Meanwhile the 15th Scottish Division and the 53rd Welsh Division from the north, and the 51st Highland Division had closed in on Goch. The town itself is divided into two parts by the River Niers and was guarded on three sides by an inner and outer anti-tank ditch. The place was a mass of bomb rubble, but the concrete defences were still intact. By the afternoon of the 18th all was ready for the final assault. In the north, the 44th Brigade using the six crossings over the outer ditch, seized by the 214th Brigade, advanced for the final kill in Kangaroos and by nightfall had penetrated the outer defences. About midnight a brilliant charge by the 6th KOSB carried the inner anti-tank ditch and reached the heart of the town. With the daylight came the tanks of 4th Grenadier Guards and the Crocodiles to help with the mopping-up of the German garrison. Simultaneously in the south the 51st Highland Division had burst into the town. Street fighting continued all day with the help of the Crocodiles. In the evening, the garrison commander surrendered.

Goch, the linchpin of the Siegfried Line east of the Reichswald, had fallen. With its southern supply route south of the forest thus opened, 1st Canadian Army could now bring its full weight to bear on the 1st Parachute Army. Horrocks, in all sincerity, could say in a personal message to his soldiers on 23 February:

You have now successfully completed the first part of your task. You have taken approximately 12,000 prisoners and killed large numbers of Germans. You have broken through the Siegfried Line and drawn on to yourselves the bulk of the German reserves in the West. A strong US offensive was launched over the Roer at 0330 hours this morning against positions, which, thanks to your efforts, are lightly held by the Germans. Our offensive has made the situation most favourable for our Allies and greatly increased their prospects of success. Thank you for what you have done so well. If we continue our efforts for a few more days, the German front is bound to crack.

13: 'BLOCKBUSTER'

It was mirk, mirk night, there was nae starlight,
  They waded thru' red blude to the knee;
For a' the blude that's shed on the earth
  Rins through the springs o' that countrie.

Thomas the Rhymer

The build-up of the 9th US Army on the Roer to a total of 10 divisions had proceeded with astonishing speed in vile weather. Whilst the 1st Canadian Army battled on towards the south, the Americans had awaited with impatience for the waters to subside. On 17 February it was decided to force the crossing of the flooded river, provided the break in the weather continued on the 23rd. The struggle for Goch and the thrust to the Hochwald layback had now forced Schlemm to denude his southern front. When, therefore, the 9th Army at 3.30 a.m. on the 23rd attacked across the river, they met comparatively little opposition. Simultaneously the 1st US Army assaulted astride Duren. Attacking as they did before the waters had sunk to their normal level, the Americans caught the enemy unawares. Casualties were very light — under 100 men killed in the four assaulting divisions of 9th Army. By last light on the 23rd, no less than 28 battalions were east of the Roer and by dawn next day, 11 bridges and a number of ferries and foot-bridges were carrying troops and equipment across the swollen river. By the 24th they had a bridgehead 20 miles wide and had taken 6,000 prisoners. The 15 divisions of Schlemm's Army thus faced a bleak future. Nonetheless, the position he now held in the Hochwald was immensely strong and the morale of his troops was unshaken.

Between Calcar and Udem a belt of relatively high ground shaped like the quarter of an orange runs due south. This Schlemm held with the 6th Parachute Division on the left and the 116th Panzer Division on the right, strengthened in manpower, tanks and guns recently arrived from the Eifel, both under von Lüttwitz's XLVII Parachute Corps. On the left the II Parachute Corps held the sector from Udem to Weeze, with one good and four weak divisions. LXXXV Corps and LXIII Corps prolonged the front to south of Roermond.

Three miles to the rear astride the two main roads leading to Xanten stood the Hochwald layback, the last prepared position on the left bank of the Rhine covering the bridgehead at Wesel. Between Marienbaum near the Rhine bank and the village of Sonsbeck six miles to the south stood a wooded ridge through the centre of which ran the railway from Goch to Xanten. North of the railway the Hochwald had excellent observation over the country to the west: south of the railway, in the Balbergerwald, the field of fire was more restricted and under observation from the heights near Udem. The southern end was less formidable. Three trench systems about 500 yards apart sited on the forward slopes straddled the whole position: there was some wire. Scattered wooden mines to which mine detectors would not react had been laid deep in large numbers. To strengthen the anti-tank defences, Schlemm had some 50 88-mm. guns, diverted from their normal anti-aircraft role. Thus the position between the Rhine and the road from Udem to Sonsbeck was deep, dominating and strongly fortified, and held by troops as good as any in the German Army under a commander of great experience and capacity.

Why Crerar elected to make his main effort with 11 Canadian Corps in the north where the enemy was strongest has never been satisfactorily explained. Whether the southern approach was ever considered is not known: the Canadian official history says nothing on the subject. Admittedly Crerar had to get the use of the roads leading from Calcar to Xanten and from Udem via Sonsbeck to Xanten. Both sides, partly owing to bad Anglo-Canadian security on the air (it was amusing for the listener to sort out from the chaos on the air, the broad Canadian voices from the Scottish, Welsh and public-school dialects) and partly to the surprising willingness of German prisoners to display their impressive knowledge of their commander's intentions and the layout of their own troops, were fully aware of their opponents' strength and whereabouts. The going on the axis of XXX Corps to the right was no worse than in the north. There was a tolerable road via Kevelaer, Winnekendonk to Kappeln. A main effort in this quarter might well have ended in outflanking the formidable Hochwald-Balbergerwald position.

It may well be that the fact that II Canadian Corps was already in the northern sector decided the issue. So far, most of the fighting by the 1st Canadian Army had been done by UK-based troops: it would be invidious, however, to suggest that the wish to ensure that the Canadian divisions got their share of glory influenced Crerar's decisions in any way.

Simonds' plan, never committed to writing, was Napoleonic — reminiscent in fact of the Emperor's later technique at Borodino — to blast a great hole with his massed batteries and then pour through it a huge mass of assaulting troops. 'Blockbuster', its title, aptly reveals its aims and the spirit which inspired it. In addition to the 2nd and 3rd Canadian Divisions, he now had under his command the 4th Canadian Armoured Division, the 11th Armoured Division and the 43rd Wessex Division. He proposed to launch a deliberate assault across the ridge from Calcar to Udem, to breach the Hochwald position and then exploit to Xanten and Wesel. Every available division would be employed simultaneously, each on a narrow front. Maintenance difficulties had slowed down the advance of XXX Corps in the early stages of 'Veritable': Simonds had no intention of being held up in this way. In the centre of his front ran the Goch-Xanten railway, on an embankment through the gap between the Hochwald and the Balbergerwald. As the battle progressed, Simonds' engineers would tear up the track and develop a road.

In more detail, Simonds' plan envisaged an attack by the two Canadian infantry divisions to carry the Calcar-Udem plateau. This done, the 4th Canadian Armoured Division was to thrust direct into the gap astride the railway between the Hochwald and the Balbergerwald. The 11th Armoured Division on the right would take Sonsbeck at the southern end of the whole position. Both would be closely followed up by the infantry divisions. In the final stages, the two armoured divisions would exploit the victory to Xanten and Wesel. The artillery backing provided was on a gigantic scale — 19 field, eight medium and three heavy regiments to blast in the infantry and subsequently to maintain the momentum of the assault. Superimposed on this avalanche of fire, all available aircraft were to bomb likely trouble spots in the path of the advance. In his approach to battle, Simonds had returned to the concepts of Haig in 1917.

The battle, which began two hours before dawn on the 26th was, despite the presence of innovations such as Kangaroos, in spirit reminiscent of the muddy fields of Passchendaele and the shell-torn slopes of Vimy Ridge, a struggle to the death between Canadians and Germans of equal valour, attack and counter-attack. Sergeant Aubrey Cousins' exploit which gained the Victoria Cross, described in the Canadian official history, epitomised the nature of the fighting. When his battalion, the Queen's Own Rifles of Canada, was checked,

He took command of the other survivors of his platoon, only four in number. Through the thick of the enemy fire which was sweeping the area from all sides he ran twenty five yards across an open space to a tank of the 1st Hussars which had now come up in support. Seating himself in front of the turret he calmly directed the Gunners' fire against German positions and then broke up a second counter-attack by plunging the tank into the midst of the startled paratroops. Next, taking the offensive, he reorganised his little group, and still crouched on top of the Sherman, ordered the driver to ram the first of the three buildings. While his men gave covering fire he went inside, killed several of the defenders and captured the rest. When he entered the second house, he found the enemy had not awaited his coming. Covered by the tanks' fire he then crossed the road alone to clear the third strongpoint — a two-storey building held by several Germans. 'We followed him from building to building gathering the prisoners', one of his comrades later reported. Having thus broken the hard core of resistance in Mooshof, Cousins gave orders for consolidating the position and set off to report to his Company Commander. On the way he was killed by a sniper's bullet … he had himself killed at least 20 of the enemy and captured as many more.

By dawn on the 27th, the plateau south of Calcar, littered with bogged-down and burnt-out tanks, Wasp flame-throwers and Canadian and German dead, and the fortified town of Udem, were firmly held. The thrust toward the main Hochwald position could now go forward.

About an hour before dawn on the 27th, 'Lion' Croup, consisting of the 29th Armoured Reconnaissance Regiment and the Algonquin Regiment under Lieutenant-Colonel R. A.

Bradburn, moved down the eastern slope of the Udem ridge, their route marked by Bofors, tracer and red marker shells, and headed for the gap between the woods. By dawn, leading companies had burst through the anti-tank ditch, minefields and knee-high wire in the mouth of the gap, and carried the final line of trenches on the railway line. Thus began the six-day struggle to pierce the centre of the Hochwald defences.

Every German gun and mortar within range from south, east and north, concentrated on the Algonquins. The volume of fire surpassed anything experienced by the Canadians in the whole campaign. Von Lüttwitz flung in a fresh battalion of the 24th Parachute Regiment to fight alongside the 116th Panzer Division in the gap. All attempts by the 10th Canadian and the 4th Armoured Brigade on the following day were brought to a standstill. On the flanks, although the 2nd Canadian Division were approaching the main Hochwald defences in the north and the 11th Armoured Division had carried the Goch Fortzberg ridge south-east of Udem, it seemed that a deadlock had been reached.

From the south, however, there was good news. It was now the sixth day of the US 9th Army's breakout. Three armoured divisions had broken loose and were surging north and north-east between the Maas and the Rhine. The right flank of the German 15th Army had been destroyed. Schlemm's Parachute Army was now in dire peril of encirclement. If the Americans could cut his only escape route through Wesel, his Army was doomed. He was caught between the jaws of a vice. He therefore now began to prepare to withdraw to a shorter perimeter extending from Xanten to the Bonninghardt forest and thence to the Rhine at Mors, opposite Duisburg, and to withdraw elements from the Canadian front to bolster up his wavering southern flank. Meanwhile, he was subjected to a spate of contradictory orders emanating from the Führer himself. He must hold the west bank of the Rhine at all costs, so as to ensure the safe passage of coal-boats from the Ruhr along the Rhine and the Lippe and Dortmund-Ems Canal to the North Sea ports. He was made personally responsible that none of the bridges to the east bank of the Rhine fell into enemy hands. As he said later to his interrogator, Major Milton Schulman: 'Since I had nine bridges in my sector, I could see my hopes for a long life rapidly dwindling.' Not a single man or a single piece of equipment was to be evacuated across the Rhine without special permission from the Führer himself. As a result, the shrinking bridgehead became cluttered up with damaged tanks, transport and guns and administrative troops of no fighting value from the supply services.

Although forced to weaken his left flank to meet the threat from the south, Schlemm showed no disposition to relinquish the struggle in the Hochwald — in fact he reinforced his front here with two fresh battalions. The violent artillery duel and man-to-man struggle continued night and day. In the gap, the 6th Canadian Brigade relieved the exhausted 10th Brigade. North of the gap, the 2nd Canadian Division, in face of bitter opposition, secured a foothold in the forest. It was here on 1 March that Major F. A. Tiltson of C Company the Essex Scottish earned the Victoria Cross. His company

> had to cross 500 yards of open ground and ten feet of barbed wire to reach the foremost trenches. That they succeeded in their task was largely due to the inspired leadership of their Commander. Although wounded in the head during the advance, Major Tiltson was the first into the enemy trenches, silencing with a grenade a machine-gun post that was holding up his platoons. As he pressed on with his main force to the second line of defences he was again severely wounded in the

thigh, but remained in command. In vicious hand to hand fighting the Essex cleared the trenches; but before there was time to consolidate the Germans launched a counter-attack, heavily supported by mortars and machine guns. Through this hail of fire, Tiltson calmly moved in the open among his depleted forces (now one quarter of their original strength), organising his defences platoon by platoon. Six times he crossed bullet-swept ground to carry grenades and ammunition to hard pressed men. Though hit a third time, he refused medical aid until, lying in a shell hole, he had ordered his one remaining officer to take over and briefed him concerning the absolute necessity of holding the position.

Major Tiltson's almost incredible courage cost him both legs.

On the same day, the British 3rd Division on the inter-corps boundary made a three-mile advance and, reaching the town of Kurvenheim, found it strongly held. Here the 2nd Battalion the King's Shropshire Light Infantry found themselves faced by a 70- yard gap swept by a hail of bullets. A white goat followed them into action.

The leading platoon was pinned down by intense fire. Whereupon Private Stokes, armed only with a rifle, dashed forward against a hail of bullets and although he was wounded captured single handed a small building and twelve prisoners. The platoon advanced, but again came under heavy fire. Once more Stokes dashed forward receiving more wounds, but again silencing the enemy. He refused to leave his comrades and later, while forming up to attack the final objective, the platoon was subjected to intense enemy fire. Although severely wounded and suffering from loss of blood, Stokes advanced again, firing from the hip, but 20 yards from the objective he was swept by a hail of bullets and fell mortally wounded. As his platoon dashed past him in the final charge, he raised his arm and shouted Goodbye!

On 2 March the fighting in the Hochwald and the ill-omened gap reached a crescendo with Tiger tanks and Shermans in flames along the whole front and the infantry at death grips. However on the Canadians' right XXX Corps was now gaining ground. The 11th Armoured Division was nearing Sonsbeck. On 2 March 3rd British Division captured Kurvenheim and by the 3rd had reached Kappeln. On their right on 2 March, 53rd Welsh Division took Weeze and with little resistance pushed on to Kevelaer. As night closed in it began to snow. Nevertheless, the 12th KRR, groping in the dark, found a way through the minefield and through this gap. 'A' Squadron 4th/7th Dragoon Guards moved at dawn and shot their way forward to the northern outskirts of Geldem. Here they were fired upon by what looked like American tanks. An officer therefore walked forward over 400 yards of open ground displaying a recognition panel. The tanks proved to be the Cavalry Reconnaissance Squadron of XVII US Corps. 'Veritable' and 'Grenade' had at last linked up.

In the more open country to the south, nothing could now stop the Americans pounding on. It was otherwise in the Hochwald. Here for two more days, the 24th Parachute Regiment and the Parachute Army Assault Battalion, backed by tanks and assault guns of the 116th Panzer Division, amongst the trees and mines, continued their bitter resistance against the Canadians; every advance was counter-attacked; company positions were infiltrated in the dark. Time and again Canadian attacks were brought to a standstill. Not until the night of 3/4 March were there any signs of a German withdrawal. Next day, although the enemy continued to pound the woods with mortar fire, it became apparent that Schlemm had now pulled back to his last defensive line, covering the

Wesel bridgehead. The woods presented an amazing spectacle of abandoned equipment, burnt-out tanks and German dead.

Schlemm's final defensive position west of the Rhine held by what remained of the 6th, 7th and 8th Parachute Divisions, the 116th Panzer Division, a battle group of the 346th Infantry Division and remnants of anti-tank and flak units, ran from Xanten on the Rhine to Veen, Bonninghardt and Alpen. An anti-tank ditch and vast craters on the Calcar-Xanten road combined with dense minefields and well-dug emplacements made it virtually tank-proof. Schlemm had already blown all the bridges over the Rhine except at Wesel. Here he had concentrated a formidable array of antiaircraft guns which continued to exact such a heavy toll of the aircraft of 84th Group that they had to reduce the number available for close support. On 6 March he received permission to evacuate the bridgehead by the 10th. Establishing his forward command post on the west bank, he proceeded to ensure that his men exacted the maximum possible price to the bitter end. An attack by 2nd Canadian Division on the 6th came to naught. A full-dress operation to take the town therefore had to be mounted on the 8th, with the 129th Brigade of the 43rd Wessex Division on the left and the 4th Canadian Brigade on the right, supported by seven field and four medium regiments. When it went in at dawn the bombardment was like 'all hell breaking loose'. On the left, the 4th Somerset Light Infantry, despite heavy losses, forced the parachutists back inch by inch, penetrated the northern end of the town and with the aid of Crocodiles, finally mopped up the remnants. Their Brigadier recalled:

> At the end of the battle I told my brigade staff to stand in respectful silence as the battle-weary German prisoners passed us. This was not approved of by the Press. After the battle I

walked all over the fields of Xanten and looked at the shell craters. The artillery bombardment had been so severe that the craters were almost touching each other. The German garrison of Xanten were very gallant men.

On their right, an equally bloody battle raged all day on the front of 2nd Canadian Division and it was not until long after darkness fell that 5th Brigade finally succeeded in breaking out through the town to reach the Alter Rhein. On their right 4th Canadian Armoured Division paid a heavy price for the capture of Veen which was not finally taken until the following day. They pressed on to Winnenthal, a mile and a half to the east. In this fighting 10th Infantry Brigade suffered the heaviest casualties they had ever had. At no time did the German Command lose control. As their bridgehead slowly shrank, the rearguards disputed every inch of the way. Further south around Bonninghardt, Guards Armoured Division described the battle as 'some of the toughest and most sustained fighting in which the division was ever engaged. The conditions too were certainly the most unpleasant under which we ever fought. For the Germans, they must have been infinitely worse, and the fact that the defence was skilfully conducted right to the end, once more served to remind us of their martial qualities even in defeat.'

Early on the morning of the 10th, quiet descended on the whole front. Then suddenly thunderous explosions announced that so far as Schlemm was concerned, the battle was over. He had withdrawn what remained of his army on schedule. At 10.40 a.m. an AOP pilot reported both Wesel bridges blown.

For over a month in abominable winter weather and a hurricane of fire, the 1st Parachute Army had fought as violent and terrible a battle as any in World War Two, with masterly skill and courage, and finally staged a model and well-disciplined withdrawal. They were finally overwhelmed by superior material might and equal courage. It had cost them 90,000 men and vast quantities of equipment, which could never be replaced. They were defeated but they were not humiliated. In the long term this can be considered a satisfactory end to 'Veritable' and 'Grenade'. Historically, alliances are impermanent. British and German troops had fought side by side in the wars against Louis XIV and Napoleon. For the future statesmen and civilian military pundits could at least note that there is much to be said for ensuring that British and German troops fight on the same side in any future war.

The price paid by 1st Canadian Army was severe. The majority of the casualties were British: 770 officers and 9,660 men. The Canadians lost 379 officers and 4,925 men, the majority in the later stages of the battle after 26 February. The 9th US Army's losses were just under 7,300.

Despite exposure 24 hours a day for over a month, to the almost incessant rain and sleet and intense and sustained enemy fire, the morale of the British troops as the battle progressed rose rather than declined to a higher level than at any other stage during the campaign. The numbers of evacuated sick, including psychiatric cases, were surprisingly low. These men, the majority of whom had been new to the horrors of the battlefield in Normandy, had now got into their stride. The idea that the only way to end the war was to kill the Germans in front of them had struck home. This they proceeded to do with ever-increasing skill and indifference. Hardship in fact proved a powerful stimulant: it taught them to shift for themselves. Montgomery's policy in this respect was reasonable and enlightened: anything, whether it was a pig, a chicken or the contents of a housewife's store cupboard, could be requisitioned provided it met a military need and an officer's permission was obtained. An officer who had been wounded in the earlier stages of the campaign and who returned in the later stages of the battle, described at the time his impressions on taking over his old company as follows:

> It was a tonic to find oneself again in the free air of good comradeship, cooperation and good humoured stoicism of the front line after months of jealousies and petty rivalries so rampant further back.... The Company looked a truly amazing sight as they marched into our area. They were loaded down with the usual impedimenta of ammunition, guns, picks and shovels; but then in addition, every man had some personal treasure; some had hurricane lamps, some oil house lamps, or an odd oil stove, others carried baskets and two whole sections arrived each with some joint of the pig we had killed the day before slung across their haversacks. They looked a motley crew in their camouflage jackets, scarves and weather-beaten faces.

To subsequent generations accustomed to soft beds, security and elaborate food, it may seem strange to describe Horrocks' Command in the Reichswald as a happy Corps. In fact a mess tin of hot stew washed down with tea with a tot of rum in it in darkness and rain gave many a hungry soldier greater pleasure than a banquet in later years. He slept more blissfully when he had the chance in the tail of a truck or on the stone floor of a cellar in his clothes than often later in a heated bedroom in a luxury hotel. Such is the perversity of man that the prospect of ceasing to be alive in the near future adds to the flavour of living at the moment. The good soldier who has stood the test of battle carries with him an unspoken feeling of moral superiority over those who lack his experience, which he retains for the rest of his life. Horrocks' own enthusiasm and lively sense of humour infected his whole command. He never forgot a face or a friend nor missed a chance to praise work well done or crack a joke. Every day found him somewhere in the forward area. Equally courteous whether addressing a general or a private soldier, it could be said of him, as Lord Chesterfield said of a greater British general: 'He could refuse more easily than others could grant and those who went from him most dissatisfied as to the substance of their business, were yet charmed by his manner and, as it were, comforted by it.'

Much capital has been made of Montgomery's alleged lack of tact in dealing with his allies. This cannot be said of his relations with Crerar in the Reichswald. Had he been dealing with a British as distinct from a Canadian Army commander, judging by his handling of the Alamein, Mareth and 'Goodwood' battles, he would have called off the struggle in the gap of the Hochwald the moment the initial surprise failed to show a dividend and staged a full-scale attack elsewhere. In leaving Crerar to fight his own battle in his own way, he avoided an Anglo-Canadian breach of confidence, the consequences of which might have been far-reaching. In any case, he knew that the Canadian soldier would win through no matter what orders reached him from above.

On 5 March, Simpson, Commander of the US 9th Army, suggested to him that he should bounce the Rhine at once, leaving the 1st Parachute Army in the Wesel bridgehead to be rounded up at leisure. The circumstances seemed propitious; the defences on the east bank were flimsy; the German reserves were virtually exhausted. At the time, however, all the administrative stocks needed to sustain a deep advance into Germany were on the wrong side of the Maas and could not be brought forward until the entire west bank of the Rhine was in

Allied hands. This was not the moment for giving subordinate generals the opportunity to advance their reputations by a display of technical expertise: nor were Eisenhower's Armies engaged in a race in which the laurels would go to the one who first crossed the river. Whatever the generals did now, from the narrow military point of view, the war was already virtually won. Montgomery rightly turned down a promising gamble for an absolute certainty in three weeks' time. His immediate aim was to inflict such destruction on the 1st Parachute Army, penned in the Wesel bridgehead, as would make it incapable of effective resistance when the time came to cross the river.

That he succeeded subsequent events were to show. The punishment inflicted on the hard-bitten parachutists was indeed grievous. It would have been greater still had not bad weather in the last seven days of the battle and the strong anti-aircraft defences prevented the RAF from exacting a heavier toll from the vast traffic jam around the Wesel bridge. The converging Allied advance apparently made it necessary to exercise greater care than had been apparent up to this time. There had been many occasions when the troops had wondered which side the airmen were on.

In deciding at the end of the Ardennes battle to protect his one remaining industrial area — the Ruhr — by fighting west of the Rhine, Hitler committed his third great error in the North-West Europe campaign: the other two were his decision to fight south of the Seine in Normandy and to launch the Ardennes offensive. Had he chosen instead to stand behind the formidable obstacle of the river itself and husbanded his resources, he might well have prolonged the war by several weeks. So far as 21st Army Group were concerned, an assault crossing of the Rhine in the face of the 1st Parachute Army would in all probability have been a bloody and protracted undertaking. Instead he chose to put what remained of the elite of his once great Armies through the mincer of the Reichswald. As a result, as Eisenhower wrote, 'the enemy was now in no condition to hold fast in the defended line to which he had been compelled to retreat'.

14: THE CROSSING OF THE RHINE

It had been observed that God was with him, and that affairs were blessed under his hand.

One of Cromwell's soldiers

Dramatically at the end of the second week of March, the weather suddenly changed to spring. The sun shone warm and sparkling over the devastation between the Maas and the Rhine. Crocuses and even a stray daffodil emerged amongst the bomb craters: in the evenings the setting sun turned the dust clouds raised by the never-ending traffic into red gold. Leaving the 3rd and 52nd Lowland Divisions and the US XIII Corps to hold the line of the Rhine, the rest of the assault troops of 21st Army Group pulled back to the ground over which they fought in the mud and sleet of winter. There were mines and wire everywhere; the very earth seemed to have gone sour. Not a single house had escaped utter ruin; all the doors had been removed to provide head cover for German dugouts; all the windows had been shattered; practically all were roofless and pitted with shrapnel. Dirty straw, broken ammunition boxes, empty tins, the garbage of two armies, fouled the ground like the rubbish tip of a great city. Nonetheless, a wave of high spirits surged through the Army: the spring had come, the end was in sight, one more battle and it would all be over. Overhead, formation after formation of aircraft headed for the heart of the Reich. Rooms were cleared, windows patched up: the smoke of burning rubbish filled the air. Where houses were beyond repair, men slept cheerfully under two-man bivouac sheets.

Under Montgomery, men had respites from action: they never rested — with good reason, Man anyhow has all Eternity to rest in. When not in one battle they trained for the next. They exercised with live ammunition over the dry heather country, often in shirt sleeves. Reinforcements arrived and were inoculated to the noises of battle, and taught the techniques which had brought success in the Reichswald. They practised crossing the Maas in assault boats, attended demonstrations of the use of the Wasp flame-thrower, empouched in Kangaroos, went for long runs across the heather and played football. Arms and equipment were overhauled. One brigade even sharpened its bayonets: this was quite unnecessary but showed they had got the right idea. The last leave parties departed for 48 hours in Brussels, ENSA troops arrived on an unprecedented scale. One lady of the variety stage, wearing a jerkin with almost all the formation signs of the Army and bearing letters signed by quite a number of senior officers authorising her to proceed without let or hindrance, added considerably to the traffic congestion.

Whilst the 1st Canadian Army had been fighting in the Reichswald, planning for the crossing of the Rhine had gone ahead at the headquarters of the 2nd Army on the assumption that some 58,000 German troops would be available, apart from the 1st Parachute Army, to defend the river line, and that Schlemm might succeed in withdrawing from the Reichswald with his forces more or less intact long before on orders from Hitler he actually pulled out the remnants. Provision had to be made not only for the actual crossing but for the advance in unlimited depth with which Montgomery intended to follow it. The engineer effort demanded was stupendous: nine bridges had to be built over the Maas and four across the Rhine itself on the front of XXX Corps alone. A great dump — there was

30,000 tons of it — of engineering material had to be built up which stretched for miles along the road north of Goch. Sixty thousand tons of ammunition, 28,000 tons of rations and stores, not only for the actual crossing but for the subsequent advance, had to be brought forward. The problem of firm parking places for vehicles and stores had to be solved: it was — by literally bulldozing the ruins of Kevelaer on to the fields. The troops taking part had to be regrouped: the components of 79th Armoured Division, itself twice as strong as a normal division, had to be 'married up' with the formations with whom they were to fight. All this demanded work round the clock for all the staffs. In World War One some of the staff lived a life of luxury in chateaux well behind the line, whilst the troops wallowed in the mud. The lot of the staff officer in Montgomery's Army was unenviable: most regular officers condemned to it prayed for the day when they could get back to their regiments. Their task now reached an intensity of exasperation unequalled throughout the campaign. Many junior staff officers worked through the night only to be told at dawn that their complex calculations had been based on assumptions no longer valid: many working in bad light and struggling with the complexities of light scales, raft and Buffalo loads, permanently damaged their eyesight, and laid the foundations of the duodenal and gastric ulcers which were to plague them later in life.

The technical problem of an assault crossing of the Rhine between the Lippe and Nijmegen had been the subject of intense study since the previous October. Much useful information was obtained from two captured German bargemasters and from the Dutch. The current varies from two to five and a half knots. In normal conditions it is about 1,000 feet wide, but in times of flood it can increase to as much as three miles. At the time it was 500 yards wide and the flood plain was still sodden from the heavy rains of February. The banks varied greatly in steepness and in many places were artificially built up and protected by groynes. The engineering difficulties to be surmounted taxed the ingenuity and professional skill of the Sappers to the limit. There was a need too to familiarise the assaulting troops with the arrangements made for the marshalling, loading and waiting areas, for traffic control and for dispersal on the far bank and to train them in embarking and disembarking in Buffaloes by night. To this end, two of the three Scottish divisions, the 51st Highland and 15th Scottish, had been withdrawn in the latter half of February from the Reichswald battle for training on the Maas south of Nijmegen. The rehearsal on the night of 14 March was not an unqualified success. The banks of the river were very steep, which made it difficult for the Buffaloes to take the water: also the steering arrangements for these strange craft left a good deal to be desired. Some made a complete circle and landed the troops near the point where they had embarked. The presence of unlocated mines blowing up in the area also enlivened the proceedings.

Whilst all these preparations were going forward in the south, Bradley's offensive had gone ahead with ever-increasing speed and spectacular results. On 5 March, the 1st US Army reached the left bank of the Rhine at Cologne. Two days later, the leading troops of the US 9th Armoured Division under Lieutenant Karl Timmerman, with a platoon of tanks and a company of infantry, emerging from the woods on the high ground overlooking the Ludendorff bridge at Remagen, dashed forward and carried it before it could be demolished. By the following morning Bradley had a strong bridgehead over the Rhine. Into this he poured with remarkable speed four divisions, against which piecemeal German counter-attacks evaporated. On 14 March Patton's 3rd Army burst over the Lower Moselle and with lightning speed struck south-east across the rear of the German 1st Army in the Palatinate and reached the Rhine from Mannheim to Mainz.

The 3rd and 7th US Armies had taken over 100,000 prisoners. On the night of 22/23 March, the US 5th Infantry Division slipped across the Rhine at Oppenheim, south of Mainz, six battalions at a cost of eight killed and 20 wounded. By the evening of the 23rd, Patton, to his own intense gratification, had a bridgehead six miles deep and seven miles wide and was already moving his armour across the river. German capacity to resist on this part of the front virtually collapsed.

On Montgomery's front, however, the enemy still showed no disposition to throw in the sponge. At the end of February Schlemm had withdrawn the headquarters of LXXXVI Corps under General Straube to organise the defences on the east bank. In the fortnight's lull between the end of 'Veritable' and 23 March, the 1st Parachute Army had been able to construct rifle and machine-gun pits at all the likely crossing places, and to supply Wesel and Rees with perimeter defences and an anti-tank ditch, II Parachute Corps — what remained of it at any rate — held the river bank between Emmerich and Xanten; on its left LXXXVI Corps defended Wesel; thence LVIII Corps held the river as far as Duisburg. The first-named had less than 100 field and medium guns and some 60 88-mm. anti-aircraft equipments which could be used in a ground role. All three were desperately under-strength, short of ammunition and in low spirits. However, the Army Group Reserve, XLVII Panzer Corps, still full of fight, despite the mauling they had in the Reichswald, were located on the northern flank with their headquarters at Silvorde, 10 miles north-east of Emmerich. They still had under command those formations, the 15th Panzer Grenadier Division and the 116th Panzer Division, which had made a permanent contribution to the history of the British and Canadian Armies. They were understrength and could muster only 53 tanks between them, but were still game. On 21 March, Allied aircraft scored a direct hit on Schlemm's headquarters and badly wounded him. His place was taken by General Gunther Blumentritt, who had been von Rundstedt's Chief of Staff in Normandy; no one was better qualified than he to preside over a debacle. Model still commanded Army Group B and Blaskowitz, Army Group H. In the purge which followed the disaster at Remagen, von Rundstedt had been dismissed for the last time and his place taken as Commander-in-Chief West by Kesselring, recalled from the Italian front. He is said to have announced to his staff on taking over his bankrupt estate: 'Well, gentlemen, I am the new V3!'

Montgomery's orders for the crossing issued on 9 March and passed down suitably modified to every man of the one and a quarter million troops under his command, lacked none of his normal lucidity and bite. The assault, by the 2nd Army on the left and the 9th US Army on the right, and its subsequent development would be delivered with the maximum possible weight and impetus with a view to the complete destruction of the enemy. The boundary between the two armies would be the River Lippe. The first phase envisaged the establishment of a bridgehead on an arc about 40 miles long and 10 miles deep at its widest point, between Duisburg at the easternmost tip of the Ruhr and Doetinchem, 10 miles east of Arnhem. The primary task of the 9th US Army was to secure the right flank south of Wesel: 2nd Army was to take Wesel, Xanten and Rees. On the extreme left 11 Canadian Corps was made responsible for expanding the bridgehead on the extreme north flank and for the capture of Emmerich.

The initial crossings were to be made by night. Assuming they were successful, XVIII US Airborne Corps, consisting of the British 6th and US 17th Airborne Divisions, were to land a mile or two east of the river in daylight on the following morning, help to disrupt the defences of Wesel and by seizing the crossings of the Issel help 2nd Army's advance. The experience gained at Arnhem had been taken to heart. In deciding to land the airborne troops *after* the assault across the river the advantages of a daylight drop were secured. Moreover, full use could be made of the artillery during the night assault. Furthermore the airborne troops were to be dropped close to their objectives within range of artillery support from the west bank. This time there would be no delay in the link-up between the ground forces and the airborne divisions.

1st Commando Brigade had the special task of taking Wesel after preliminary bombardment by the RAF. These tasks completed, 2nd Army would exploit initially to a depth of about 40 miles to Munster-Rheine and Hengelo, and 9th US Army would seal off the northern edge of the Ruhr. Simultaneously at this stage, a thrust due north by 1st Canadian Army was envisaged, to trap such German divisions as remained in Holland. Further operations deeper into Germany would then be developed 'quickly in any direction as may be ordered by Supreme Headquarters'. At this time, Montgomery as yet had no reason to doubt that Eisenhower's subsequent main effort would be in the north and the subsidiary effort south of the Ruhr on the line Frankfurt-Kassel, as had been assumed almost since the start of the campaign.

When Montgomery issued his orders the air aspect of the battle was already well on the way under Tedder's direction. This initially took the form of intensive attack on the Ruhr and its approaches to cut off movement of supplies and troops to the front. As early as 22 February, the vital viaduct at Bielefeld was hit, and it was finally destroyed on 14 March. Five days later the Arnsberg viaduct was wrecked. Altogether, between 21 February and 24 March, no less than 42 attacks were made on bridges and viaducts. As a result, by 'D-Day', 24 March, the enemy's rear communications by rail and road were virtually paralysed. For the actual crossing, Tedder prescribed all and even more support than the Army normally expects from the Air Arm. Firstly, the airmen were to sweep the enemy from the skies, especially at the crossings over the river and the landing zones of the airborne troops. They were to smash the anti-aircraft defences, protect the airborne landings, provide close support on call to the attacking corps and cut off reinforcements attempting to reach the area of the battle.

To blast the infantry forward, Montgomery proposed to concentrate some 2,000 field, medium and heavy guns — twice as many as at Alamein. To this avalanche of explosive he added the fire of a further 3,000 anti-tank, anti-aircraft and rocket projectors. He had more guns and more ammunition at his disposal than any British commander in history. He would now use them to cut down the cost in British and American life.

The move forward, without lights, on the night of 21 March from 30 miles back of the immense columns of assault equipment for the crossing — Buffaloes, armoured bulldozers, RAF winches to operate the rafts, armoured sledges, 6-ton Matador lorries, RASC 3-tonners, AVREs and 50-foot pontoon trailers — long remained in the memory of those who saw it. All this on arrival in the concentration area had to be made into sledge or trailer loads on the near bank of the river. By dawn on the 22nd it all stood ready skilfully camouflaged by an American camouflage platoon. On the next night, the din of the traffic drowned by the noise of fighters overhead, the great mass of artillery moved in. So skilfully were they hidden under their nets by dawn, that it was hard to believe that the fields and orchards concealed this gigantic mass of guns, waiting in silence for the evening zero hour.

It was fitting and in character that Churchill, unlike Hitler despatching orders for the mass suicide of his troops and countrymen from the mephitic atmosphere of his funk hole in Berlin, should have chosen this very moment to appear on the battlefield. Despite the gloomy forebodings of Alanbrooke and the evasions of de Guingand, Montgomery's Chief of Staff, for once unsuccessful in his role as the man with the oilcan greasing the creaking machinery of the Allied Higher Command, Churchill made it clear to all so far as the British were concerned where the power lay. At this supreme display of the armed might of his people, the eager, well-equipped and well-commanded troops, and the great air fleets overhead, he would be present in person in the front line. Almost five years back, his soldiers and airmen had been driven out of the Continent with little more than their small arms; besieged in their small island, without an ally, he and his people had stood alone, until German and Japanese blunders pushed the USSR and the United States into the war. In 1942 his soldiers had been humiliated in the Far East by the Japanese and driven back in Africa almost to the gates of Cairo. Now at Imphal in Burma, Mountbatten and Slim were on the point of inflicting decisive defeat on Hitler's Eastern allies. In Italy, Alexander stood ready finally to annihilate the German Armies in the valley of the Po. This was the moment which the greatest

Englishman of his day, with his sense of history and of theatre, rightly chose to appear at the centre of the stage.

He had often said to Alanbrooke that 'the way to die is to pass out fighting when your blood is up and you feel nothing'. If this should happen he would make a truly Roman exit.

On 23 March, accompanied by his valet, Alanbrooke and his ADC, he took off from Northolt about 3 p.m. and flying over Calais, Lille and Brussels, arrived at Venlo, Montgomery's headquarters, in time for tea.

Whilst Churchill was still airborne, Montgomery had given the order 'Over the Rhine, then, let us go. And good hunting to you on the other side.' It was a warm spring evening. At 7 p.m. as darkness fell, the vast array of guns concealed behind the river, from the 40-mm. Bofors spraying the far bank with their light shells to the 240-mm. heavies pounding the enemy's rear with shells weighing more than half a ton, opened up.

For the next three hours they saturated the far bank with a hurricane of intense and annihilating fire. It was a bright moonlit night. The bombardment now reached a crescendo: dense smoke covered the front of the assault. At 9 o'clock in the hazy darkness, the leading Buffaloes of the Northampton Yeomanry, carrying four battalions of the 51st Highland Division — the 7th Black Watch, the 7th Argylls, the 5th Black Watch and the 5th/7th Gordons — slid into the Rhine. Within a few minutes they were on the far bank. Colonel Jolly of the Royal Tank Corps planted the regimental flag. There was little resistance. At four minutes past nine precisely, Horrocks in his observation post overlooking the Rhine, received a message, in its way historic: 'The Black Watch has landed safely on the far bank.' At to o'clock 1st Commando Brigade, about two miles west of Wesel, slipped across the river and within half an hour were formed up on the outskirts of the town, already badly damaged as a result of a previous air attack during the afternoon. Two hundred and twelve Lancasters and Mosquitoes of 5th and 8th Groups now came out of the night sky and dropped over 1,000 tons on the doomed town. The results were shattering. Whole streets were blocked with debris and all roads and rail bridges to the west smashed. Fifteen minutes later the last bomber headed for home, 1st Commando Brigade burst into the ruins, closed with the dazed defenders and systematically despatched them either to Valhalla or Paradise, or the prisoners' cage, according to taste. The fighting here was still unfinished next morning when Churchill himself, having crossed the river, was only with great difficulty persuaded by his escort to refrain from thrusting himself into the heart of the fray.

The crossings of the 15th Scottish Division and the US 30th and 79th Divisions in the early hours of the morning were equally successful. Casualties were light. By dawn the infantry of 21st Army Group had three strong bridgeheads and were moving rapidly across. Only in Rees and Wesel was there obstinate resistance.

Saturday 24 March was a cloudless day. Just before 10 o'clock the great air Armada of XVIII US Airborne Corps appeared in the sky dead on time. Whilst England breakfasted, wave after wave of aircraft, Dakotas, Stirlings, Halifaxes, Lancasters, Fortresses and Liberators, with their attendant trains of gliders of the British 6th Airborne Division from the coast of Kent right round to Norfolk had headed out to sea towards the Rhine. A similar fleet bearing US 17th Airborne Division had set off from 12 airfields around Paris. Escorted by aircraft of Fighter Command and the British and American Fighter Air Forces, these gigantic fleets made rendezvous over the fields of Waterloo and turned in on parallel courses towards the Rhine. Churchill, at a viewpoint near Xanten, in the midst of the massed batteries supporting the attack firing at full blast, watched the most spectacular air operations of the war. The whole Army looked upwards and cheered wildly.

Over the river 900 fighters maintained an air umbrella: deeper in Germany, others kept the Luftwaffe away from the battle zone. For the next three hours relay after relay of aircraft delivered their loads and streamed back with doors open and parachute strings hanging under them. In all, 1,700 aircraft and 1,300 gliders landed some 14,000 troops. Within a matter of hours it was evident that the operation had been a success. The 6th Airborne Division captured Diersfordt and the crossings over the Issel, and 17th US Airborne Division Dinslaken. By nightfall, they had both secured all their objectives and linked up with the troops advancing inland from the Rhine. The cost to 6th Airborne was comparatively light — 347 killed and 731 wounded. Unquestionably their action greatly accelerated the development of the bridgehead which at last light along the whole front was on average 5,000 yards deep. Only on the extreme left at Speldrop and in Rees was there still cause for concern.

It took the Gordons and the Black Watch, in no mood to stomach opposition, to flush the parachutists of 11 Parachute Corps out of the ruins of Rees. Every house and street had to be methodically cleared. In the process Captain McNair and his crew of 454th Mountain Battery, in their first battle, won the admiration of their fellow-Scots. The 3.7 howitzers they used were familiar to the British public as a star turn at military displays in time of peace, competing teams taking the gun to pieces, clearing obstacles and, sweating at every pore, reassembling it. These gun teams, after hard training near Inverness, had been sent out specially for the Rhine crossing, since the guns could be carried in a Buffalo. Grant Peterkin pays tribute to them:

> This was McNair's first action and such enthusiasm for battle as he showed can seldom have been seen before — in fact, it was rather easy for some of our more battle-weary officers to be quite funny about it. For each situation in his street to street battle, McNair had some suggestion for using his gun. He hauled it over rubble, rushed it round corners, layed it on a house that was giving trouble, dodged back again, prepared his charges, and then back to fire again. He even took it to bits and mounted it in an upstairs room. 'Exactly which window is the sniper in?' he said and then, when the sniper fired at him, 'Oh! that one!' and layed his gun on it. It set houses on fire as well as any Crocodile, and the effect on the enemy was devastating. This very brave officer took incredible risks; finally he ran out into a street which was under fire and pulled in a wounded officer. He and his gun became the talk of the companies, and already in a few hours, he has become an almost legendary character.

It is not the modernity of the weapon which counts, but the man behind it.

It was at Rees that the Commander of the Highland Division, Major-General Thomas Rennie, was mortally wounded. The Highlander is temperamental. Under the leadership of a commander who has captured his imagination, and is of his own lineage, he can rise to magnificent heights. In Normandy the division had fallen below the great reputation it had gained in the desert and Italy. Rennie, brought in to command it in late July, had restored its fighting spirit to a new high level. One of his men said: 'Aye, he was a guid General. He wasna' a shouting kind of man. The men liked his style and they had great confidence in him.' No commander could ask for a better epitaph.

It took two days for the 51st Division, reinforced most appropriately by the Highland Light Infantry of Canada, to clear the village of Speldrop. Here men of the Black Watch were overrun but refused to surrender. The parachutists of II Parachute Corps fought with the utmost ferocity. 'Every house had to be cleared at the point of the bayonet; single Germans made suicidal attempts to break up our attacks.' The fortified houses could only be reduced by Wasp flame-throwers and concentrated artillery fire. 'It was necessary to push right through the town and drive the enemy into the open where they could be dealt with.'

On the extreme left, the 15th Panzer Grenadier Division had been brought in to hold the Alter Rhein bottleneck and the important road junction to Bienen. Here it was two days before they were overwhelmed by the 9th Canadian Brigade and the 43rd Wessex Division, neither in a mood to put up with obstinacy of this sort any longer. When the Panzer Grenadiers finally reeled back they left over 400 dead. The casualties of the 9th Canadian Brigade were severe.

By the evening of 28 March, the bridgehead was 35 miles wide and extended to an average depth of 20 miles. All opposition had virtually collapsed. During the day the American 17th US Airborne Division, carried on the tanks of the Guards 6th Armoured Brigade, had thrust forward up the valley of the River Lippe. On the morning of the 29th they were 35 miles beyond the Rhine. Poised ready to advance into the North German plain, Montgomery had 20 divisions and 1,000 tanks, all up to strength and eager to go, and backed by an administrative build-up capable of sustaining his forces all the way to Berlin, 275 miles ahead. The Battle of the Rhine was over and the way open to the Elbe and beyond.

The plan for the crossing of the Rhine had been made to cover the possibility that the Germans would withdraw from west of the Rhine in time to stage a full-scale battle on its banks and in the faith that thereafter the main Allied effort would be in the North German plain leading to Berlin — hence the vast assembly of troops and lavish-scale provision. Instead of exercising normal military common sense, the Germans on Hitler's orders had chosen to sacrifice the greater part of their effective troops west of the river in February and the first weeks of March. In actual fact, the crossing had been accomplished with surprising ease. Judged purely as a military operation, it is impossible to fault Montgomery's plan and its execution — the linking together of the land and air operations, the achievement of concentrated firepower both from the ground and the air, the foresight devoted to tactical and administrative planning and the exploitation to the full of the characteristics of the many components of the land and air forces. It was Montgomery's final masterpiece, executed in a manner soon to be outmoded, but nonetheless, like a Constable, a work of art.

On 28 March he issued his orders for the drive to the Elbe by 2nd and 9th Armies so as to gain quick possession of the plains of Northern Germany. The right of 9th US Army was directed on Magdeburg and the left of 2nd Army on Hamburg. In the course of its advance, the 9th Army was to seal the northern and eastern exits of the Ruhr and link up with 1st US Army about Paderborn. To this end 9th Army was given the sole use of the Wesel bridge. Meanwhile 1st Canadian Army would swing north, cut off the German forces remaining in Holland and clear the Frisian coast.

That night more than one of his commanders at their own order groups, held in pouring rain, dismissed their subordinates with the words 'Next stop — Berlin'.

15: THE ADVANCE TO THE ELBE

Promises and piecrust are made to be broken.

Dean Swift

In the history of World War Two and particularly of Western Europe, 28 March was a turning point. This was the situation on that day: 21st Army Group consisting of 1st Canadian Army, 2nd British Army and 9th United States Army held a bridgehead over the Rhine about 35 miles deep and 20 miles wide on either side of Wesel and were on the point of enveloping the north side of the Ruhr. 1st Canadian Army stood poised ready to strike north and liberate Holland. In the centre, 1st US Army had exploited their bridgehead at Remagen with amazing speed and were about to envelop the Ruhr from the south. To support it 3rd US Army which had crossed at Oppenheim, south of Mainz, on 22 March was now streaming across the river at Patton's normal speed in the face of comparatively little resistance. Prisoners taken since 8 February had reached the 300,000 mark. Model, with approximately a similar number of troops — the debris of three armies — faced inevitable encirclement in the Ruhr. In Italy, Alexander was on the point of launching his final offensive which was to end a few weeks later in the capitulation of Army Group C in the valley of the Po. On the Eastern front the Russians had a bridgehead over the Oder only 30 miles from Berlin but had made little progress since the first week in February. Nominally, Kesselring in the west commanded some 60 divisions: many of these however were little more than battle groups. Allied Intelligence estimated them as the equivalent of 26 divisions at most. It was now obvious to the whole world that the Germans were doomed.

Eisenhower's original directive for the campaign from the Combined Chiefs of Staff had been to undertake operations aimed at the heart of Germany and the destruction of her armed forces. The directive argued that, although Berlin was the ultimate goal, the Allied attack initially must be aimed at the Ruhr because this was the economic heart of Germany and therefore all German resources would be concentrated to defend it. The opportunity would thus be created for completely destroying the main German Armed Forces. This time had now come: the end of organised resistance in the Ruhr could now only be a matter of days. All, apart from Eisenhower's most intimate circle, still assumed that it would be followed by a concentrated and rapid thrust by Montgomery's Army Group on Berlin. Montgomery had always considered Berlin a priority objective and until late on 28 March had thought that Eisenhower shared his view.

The results of battles which are never actually fought must always be a matter of conjecture. There are however strong reasons for believing that, if the main Allied effort had been directed on Berlin under Montgomery after the encirclement of the Ruhr, he would have got there before the Russians, who did not in fact complete the capture of the city till 2 May. His Army Group was firmly established across the Rhine backed by an immense advanced base and ample transport. Beyond the river, roadheads had been pushed forward while behind these the railway bridges over the Maas were connected with the whole rail and canal network of France and the liberated parts of the Low Countries. To strengthen the logistic position still further, the railway bridge over the Rhine at Wesel would be open once more within a few days. Bridging material adequate to meet every foreseeable need all the way to Berlin was ready to hand. Vast reserves of ammunition were available and the means to move it forward. Allied command of the air was absolute: supply columns could move in daylight, if necessary and often inevitably, nose to tail without the slightest risk of attack from the air. Despite the losses in the fighting west of the Rhine, all units, British, Canadian and American, were virtually up to strength: the reinforcement camps were full. Deficiencies in equipment had been made good. Ahead lay country which with the improvement in the weather was rapidly drying out, much of it, unlike the Low Countries, well suited to the employment of armour. At long last it seemed that the Allies would be able to exploit their overwhelming numerical superiority in tanks.

The British Army in particular had reached a higher standard of training than at any other time in its history except possibly 1914. Before 1939 the cavalry, tanks, gunners, engineers and infantry had seen little of each other and opportunities for training together and for considering their tactical problems as one had been rare and fleeting. There was no agreed doctrine as to the part armour should play in the battle. Until the School of Infantry was opened in 1941 the training of this vital arm had often been unrealistic, uninspired and subject to the whims of subordinate commanders. The truth must be admitted that in the first years of the war the Germans of all ranks had proved themselves more highly professional than the British. Until the arrival of Montgomery in North Africa in 1942, Rommel had shown them how much they had to learn. It is ironic to record that the German Army created the instrument of its own final destruction. The British Infantry were now in no way their inferiors in advancing by night, in infiltration and in fighting in woods: in fact the boot was on the other foot.

Never before had the technical skill of the regimental officer — the real leader on the battlefield — been higher. The majority of the battalion commanders were under 33. If an infantry officer cannot command a battalion at the age of 30 he never will: this had been the experience in World War One and it was now confirmed in World War Two. Of the brigade, divisional and corps commanders it can at least be said that they were now as good as their opposite numbers in the German Army — with, in most cases, the added advantage of a sense of humour. At any rate they satisfied Montgomery — which is saying a lot. Like Mountbatten, Montgomery concentrated all press publicity upon himself and spared his subordinates from exposure to journalists. Eisenhower would have saved himself considerable embarrassment if he had been able to do the same.

Morally this Army was immensely strong. It had tasted success, than which there is no better stimulant to high morale. It was bound together by many loyalties: the mutual loyalty of men who had shared the same risks and hardships for a long time, the loyalty of the troops to their regimental officers, who knew their jobs and shared their dangers, the loyalty of the services to the front-line troops, the loyalty to the divisions whose very titles emphasised the vitality of the amalgam of national and provincial prejudices and traditions which constitute the psychological make-up of the British people. Berlin as an objective had captured their imagination. Above all they had a loyalty to Montgomery himself. He had never put them into a battle which he did not win: he would not do so now.

Similar considerations sustained the Canadian Army: the recently arrived conscripts had already shown themselves to be no less offensively minded than the veterans. The 9th US

Army had behind them a record of unbroken success; battle-hardened and brilliantly led, they were, with that gift for quick exploitation which is characteristically American, as formidable as the British and Canadian Armies. The majority of the British and Canadian commanders who were present at the time and who subsequently went forward to the Elbe and the Baltic were convinced that if the 9th Army had not been taken away from Montgomery he could have reached Berlin before the Russians. German military opinion has subsequently confirmed this view.

But it was not to be: on the evening of 28 March he heard that Eisenhower had changed his plans and that the 9th Army was to remain under his command only until the Ruhr was encircled (which actually occurred on 2 April); it would then revert to 12th Army Group, which thus raised to a strength of 48 divisions would constitute the Allied main effort under Bradley aimed not at Berlin but via Leipzig on Dresden. Here it would link up with the Red Army, thus cutting the remaining German forces in two. In this new plan Montgomery's role was reduced to covering Bradley's left flank and taking Hamburg and Bremen. Finally Devers' 6th Army Group was ordered to protect Bradley's right flank and be ready to move down the Danube to seize the 'National Redoubt' before the German could organise an effective defence there.

This plan Eisenhower sent direct to Moscow marked 'Personal for Marshal Stalin' with a copy 'For Information' to the Chiefs of Staff. In the eyes of the British he thus usurped the functions of Roosevelt and Churchill and their governments and violated the implied promise to make the main effort in the direction of Berlin. As Eisenhower's personal integrity was never in doubt, it is vital to understand the reasons which, according to his own account, at the time, induced him to make this dramatic and irrevocable change of plan. They were these: the national zones of occupation had already been agreed by the Allied political chiefs at Yalta. His orders from the Combined Chiefs of Staff for conducting the war had been to land in Europe and, proceeding to Germany, to destroy Hitler and all his forces. He argued therefore that his mission was not the capture of localities but the destruction of Hitler's armed might. No matter how deeply into Germany the Allied armies reached they were all under the obligation at the end of hostilities to withdraw immediately to within the agreed zones of occupation. Berlin was deep inside the Russian zone and 200 miles from the Ruhr. In any case, the Russians were only 30 miles from the German capital. The odds therefore on their getting there first were in his opinion overwhelming. Finally the cost of a thrust on Berlin seemed to him at the time likely to involve an unnecessary sacrifice of Allied life merely to gain what he described as a symbol.

There were, however, other reasons. Marshall was pressing him to end the war in Europe quickly so that all possible American resources could be switched to the Pacific. At the same time his Intelligence staff were telling him that the Germans would never surrender whilst Hitler lived. This led Eisenhower to believe that he was likely to be faced with a prolonged campaign in the National Redoubt which it was alleged was being constructed in the Bavarian Alps. His Intelligence staff too took seriously the possible military effects of the Werewulf movement which the Nazis were rumoured to have organised amongst their fanatical young supporters — 'As if,' as General Westphal said later, 'what the Wehrmacht had failed to do could be accomplished by a rabble of Boy Scouts.'

At this late stage of the campaign Eisenhower undoubtedly considered that, as the area around Dresden and Leipzig contained what little remained of the heavy industries of the Reich, its occupation was more important than the capture of Berlin.

The reaction of Churchill and the British Chiefs of Staff to this unilateral abandonment of the plans jointly agreed upon was vehement and unequivocal. They were angered at the high-handed way in which in their view Eisenhower had exceeded his authority in communicating direct with Stalin over their heads. The war was virtually won; their armies faced little more than a gigantic mopping-up operation. What mattered now was the postwar balance of power in Europe. Quite apart from the immense prestige advantage which the Russians stood to win by capturing Berlin, there was the additional danger that, Montgomery having been deprived of the 9th Army, they would reach the North German ports first and thus gain an outlet to the North Sea and the Atlantic. To ensure that they did not had been an object of British policy since the days of Peter the Great. They pointed out that at Yalta the Russians had signed the 'Declaration on Liberated Europe' undertaking to hold free elections in all the countries they liberated. In Rumania and Poland however they had torn up this declaration. Therefore the British argued the Western Allies should reply by tearing up the arrangements regarding the zones of occupation and tell their forces to advance as far east and south-east as possible and stay there.

The American leaders unfortunately were incapable of seeing the situation in this light. Roosevelt was dying and, although it was not generally known, had been incapable of concentrated work for some time. He therefore had passed responsibility for a decision to Marshall the Chief of Staff. In principle this was a glaring error: soldiers should not be called upon to solve political problems. As Disraeli said, the qualities of the soldier and the statesman are as the poles apart. Able strategist and great organiser of victory though he was, Marshall was out of his depth. He backed Eisenhower to the hilt, stating that 'such psychological and political advantages as would arise from the capture of Berlin should not override the imperative military consideration which is the destruction and dismemberment of the German military forces'. It was thus brought home to the British, although they were slow to realise it, that they were now very much the minor partner in the alliance and in American eyes on their way out as a world power. It seemed more important from the American point of view at this time to keep on good terms with the Russians whose aid was required in the Pacific than with the British. It was never realistic on the part of the British to imagine that American public opinion and Eisenhower's subordinate generals would ever have allowed the palm of victory to go to a mainly British Army under, of all persons, Montgomery, with his incorrigible habit of emphasising unpalatable truths and of cutting all concerned down to size.

Accordingly the vast mechanised mass of the Allied Armies surged eastwards as Eisenhower wished. Late on 1 April the 1st and 9th Armies with 6th Guards Armoured Brigade under command met at Lippstadt, thus completing the encirclement of what remained of Model's Army Group in the Ruhr. The diversion of 18 American divisions to mop up this vast industrial complex in no way prevented the rest of Eisenhower's forces from continuing their remorseless drive towards the Elbe. Kesselring's front was now wide open: only on the flanks could he put up even the semblance of serious resistance.

The British 2nd Army advanced on a front of three Corps, VIII Corps on the right directed on Osnabruck, Celle and Uelzen, XII Corps in the centre on Rheine, Nienberg and Luneburg and XXX Corps on the left on Enschede, Bremen and Hamburg. Resistance was lightest on the VIII Corps front: elsewhere it was sporadic, except on the front of XXX Corps where the utter hopelessness of the situation had not penetrated the minds of the survivors of 1st Parachute Army, which still retained some of its artillery. Opposition when encountered generally came from hastily formed battle groups, some of which fought with considerable skill until swamped by Allied tanks, blasted out of existence by Allied guns or enveloped by Allied infantry working round their flanks.

Despite the disintegration of the supply and command systems the Germans had lost none of their normal skill in using demolitions and laying mines and seldom failed to exploit the delaying power of the many waterways, especially the Dortmund-Ems and Ems-Weser Canals. The fight put up by the 1st Parachute Army at Lingen gained the admiration of Guards Armoured Division. The strain on 2nd Army's engineer resources was considerable. Altogether some 500 bridges had to be constructed in the course of the advance. On XXX Corps' front Lieutenant-General Erdmann conducted the withdrawal with greater professional skill than consideration for the suffering of his own countrywomen and children. Travelling in a captured jeep, he raked together, time and time again, the remnants of many formations and forced them to fight until annihilated. At Ahlhorn, for example, one of these battle groups, some 300 strong, caught the full blast of the whole artillery of XXX Corps. For days ammunition had been coming forward and demands for it had been few: the RASC were begging the gunners to take it off their hands.

After the battle — if battle it was — old men and women emerged from the neighbouring woods to carry away their dead lying in the fields outside the village. They were mostly boys of 14 or 15 and old men who had been hurriedly pressed into uniform.

The British troops found themselves ill-prepared for their reception by the German civil population once fighting had died down. A pamphlet emanating from the Higher Intelligence Staff in Paris, and widely circulated when the advance started, read:

> Your attitude towards women is wrong in Germany. Do you know German women have been trained to seduce you? Is it worth a knife in the back? A weapon can be concealed by women on the chest, between the breasts, on the abdomen, on the upper leg, under the buttocks, in a muff, in a handbag, in a hood or coat.... How can you search women? The answer to that one is difficult. It may be your life at stake. You may find a weapon by forcing them to pull their dress tight against their bodies here and there. If it is a small object you are hunting for, you must have another woman to do the searching and to do it thoroughly in a private room.

The reading aloud of this illuminating document enlivened many a bivouac. This and other literary efforts of the Higher Intelligence Staffs illustrates their isolation in a humourless world of their own, remote from the hearty common sense of the front line. Fraternisation of any kind was forbidden.

In the event, the civil population showed every disposition to cooperate with their invaders and even to be friendly. Military Government staffs and detachments, hot on the heels of the fighting troops, generally found the burgomasters, police and civil officials more than eager to cooperate in restoring order, electricity, water and sewerage services. Just before the advance started Montgomery had appointed Major-General Templet Director of Civil Affairs. Had it not been for the fundamental humanity, organising ability and dynamic drive of this British general many Germans leading prosperous lives 20 years later would have perished of starvation and disease. The unwisdom of the official policy of non-fraternisation soon became apparent. An unknown but significant number of Germans had hated the Nazi tyranny and had lived in the hope that one day it would be overthrown. To find themselves treated as outcasts, as something less than human, was the last straw. Fortunately it proved impossible to stop British soldiers giving their sweet ration to children, casting an approving eye on a well-developed blonde or helping an old woman refugee. But the mentality of many Germans was an enigma to the British both then and for many years to come. In the woods they found deer sacrificed, presumably to Wotan, on strange altars and in the houses evidence in the form of expensively produced literature devoted to the cult of the old pre-Christian gods. The horrors revealed at Belsen, when liberated on 16 April, Fallingbostel and other satellite camps are well known: suffice it to say that they were effectively to prejudice the British, rightly or wrongly, against the whole German people for a generation.

The morale of the British prisoners of war when released varied considerably. Fallingbostel presented the greatest surprise. The squadron of 8th Hussars sent there to liberate them found on their arrival that the British prisoners of war had already taken over and that the main gate was guarded by sentries of the 1st Airborne Division, immaculate in scrubbed belts and gaiters and well-creased battle dress. Inside were 10,000 British and American prisoners, commanded by Regimental Sergeant Major Lord of the 1st Airborne Division, who was busily engaged in his office in giving orders as in peacetime to his orderly warrant officers. If leadership, comradeship, discipline and self-respect are the basis of high morale then all were present here.

There is an element of high tragedy in these last weeks of the war in the West when the political destinies of the peoples of Europe lay in the hands of American generals. British warnings of the danger of advancing simultaneously on three fronts at the expense of delay in the north were ignored. In consequence, Eisenhower was compelled on 14 April to inform the Chiefs of Staff that he was outrunning his supplies and must, after all, withhold his centre on the Elbe whilst he cleaned up his flanks. This intention he revealed frankly and openly to the Russians who naturally were quick to accelerate their own advance on Berlin.

Roosevelt's death on 12 April accentuated the paralysis of political purpose among the Western Allies. Truman, through no fault of his own, had no experience of international affairs. Roosevelt had never taken kindly to the idea that his Vice-President should share in the conduct of the war and had done little to keep him informed of the greater issues. Overnight American political direction of the war ceased to exist.

At this time, at a point between Wittenberge and Brunswick, the 9th Army had a small bridgehead over the Elbe roughly the same distance from Berlin as the Russians. 21st Army Group was within striking distance of Hamburg and thus reasonably certain of reaching the Schleswig-Holstein peninsula before the Russians. In the south, Patton's 3rd Army was well placed, and more than eager if required, to liberate Prague.

Assured by Marshall that he could safely disregard political considerations, Eisenhower proceeded to disclose his intentions to the Russians where in his opinion this was necessary on military grounds. At their request he refrained from sending the 3rd Army into Czechoslovakia until 4 May; Patton could, in fact, have reached Prague without difficulty at any time during the previous fortnight and changed the course of history. Fortunately, however, Eisenhower did authorise Montgomery to push into Schleswig-Holstein and to seize the Kiel Canal and the North-West German ports. In fairness to Eisenhower, it is only just to reiterate that the reasons behind these decisions *at the time* were threefold: the belief fostered by his Intelligence advisers that the Germans would make a last-ditch stand in the National Redoubt, the need to ensure that the approaching armies did not clash with each other and his own desire to get all Armies within the agreed zones as soon as possible.

As Disraeli said, 'finality is not the language of politics', but a generation later the military and political situation in Europe shows how in 1945 the Americans failed to grasp the fact that 'war is nothing more than the continuation of politics by other means'. Stalin on the other hand never lost sight of this truth. Appropriately the grave of Clausewitz is behind the Iron Curtain.

16: CLIMAX ON THE ELBE

My sword I leave to him that shall succeed me in my pilgrimage and my courage and skill to him that can get it.

Bunyan, 'The Pilgrim's Progress'

The situation on the whole Allied front was now changing from hour to hour. In the Ruhr, Model and the commanders of the remnants of Army Group B and a mass of rear services struggled to retain some sort of order in the face of ever-increasing demoralisation. Hourly the position became more hopeless as news came through of continuing Allied advances to the east. Model's Chief of Staff is said to have pressed him to surrender in order to spare the soldiers and the civil population further pointless sacrifice of life. He refused. By 15 April ammunition and supplies had virtually come to an end: the troops in ever-increasing numbers were laying down their arms. By the next day the rush to surrender had become a stampede. By the 18th, resistance was all but over.

Altogether the Americans had taken 317,000 prisoners including 30 generals — more than the Russians had captured at Stalingrad. This was the largest mass surrender of the war up to this date. Model, despite the efforts of Major-General Ridgway to persuade him to surrender himself and his entire command, refused to give himself up. He had, in fact, in publicly criticising Paulus for surrendering at Stalingrad, put himself into a quandary. Field-Marshals, he had said, never surrender. Accordingly on 21 April he walked into a dense part of the forest near Dusseldorf and shot himself. He thus by British standards spoilt what was in fact a magnificent fighting

251

record on both the Eastern and Western fronts. The manner in which in August and September he had eventually stabilised a front which had collapsed, thwarted the British at Arnhem and in November brought Bradley's offensive to near standstill, showed competence of a high order. Had he been given a free hand by Hitler he might well have humiliated both the British and Americans and prolonged the war. All that was necessary now at this final hour was to form his own battle group, if necessary of one man only, and fight on. There were plenty of Allied soldiers only too ready to ensure him a more dignified exit from a stage on which he had played a distinguished if somewhat sinister part.

On the extreme left of the Allied front similar signs of German disintegration had become increasingly apparent. Here 1st Canadian Army, now augmented by the arrival of I Canadian Corps from Italy, had struck north and north-east from Emmerich and Nijmegen. The Dutch behind the German lines in Western Holland were known to be near the limit of starvation. Accordingly when feelers from Seyss-Inquart, the Reichskommissar in Holland, suggested something in the nature of a deal, Supreme Headquarters found it possible to reconcile the requirements of strategy, and indeed common sense, with humanity. Lieutenant-General Foulkes with only two divisions and an armoured brigade available had little to gain from attacking Blaskowitz's 25th Army, 120,000 strong. Accordingly on 22 April Montgomery ordered 1 Canadian Corps to halt about Amersfort: a truce on this part of the front followed on 28 April. Next day aircraft of Bomber Command and 8th US Air Force dropped 510 tons of supplies for the starving Dutch within what were still the German lines. Thereafter 1,000 tons a day followed by road. Meanwhile on the front in North-East Holland and North-West Germany II

Canadian Corps fought on till 5 May: the cost at 5,515 killed wounded and missing from the clearing of the bank of the Rhine to the final surrender was not light. The gratitude of the Dutch to their Canadian liberators was spontaneous, sincere and lasting: in Holland a quarter of a century later the memory of those big, brave and generous soldiers in their distinctive battledress was still green.

Concurrently with these operations XXX Corps had drawn near to the outer defences of Bremen. These they found to be defended with greater courage than tactical skill by sailors and low-category troops. Some of the posts were sited facing in the wrong direction. Before the war Bremen had been the next largest port in Germany after Hamburg. Behind it stretched a long history going back to the Middle Ages when the Hanseatic League here and at Hamburg and Lubeck had built up a vast trade in which the English shared. The merchants of Bremen in the past had played a conspicuous part in the development of the modern world and their lovely old houses and public buildings in the Altstadt east of the river formed part of the heritage of Europe as well as Germany. The city had expanded into the Neustadt west of the Weser. Here were sited the U-boat pens, the Focke-Wulf aircraft factory, the Atlas Works and many other large industrial undertakings. The Norddeutscher Lloyd had operated from the huge docks. Into this city the remnants of part of the 1st Parachute Army had withdrawn and reinforced the considerable garrison, XXX Corps now approached the city on each side of the Weser. From mid-April onwards the leading troops could raise the civil telephone and receive the reply 'Hier 1st Bremen'.

With the vast armament of his own Corps and the striking force of the RAF at his command, Horrocks was in no inordinate hurry to complete the capture of the city. To throw away British and German civilian life unnecessarily at this stage of the war merely to score a dramatic triumph would have been out of character. Accordingly on 20 April he fired 4,000 shells containing leaflets into the city. They read:

> The choice is yours. The British Army is lying outside Bremen, supported by the RAF, and is about to capture the city. There are two ways in which this can take place. Either by the employment of all the means at the disposal of the Army and RAF or by the occupation of the town after unconditional surrender. The choice is yours as to the course to be followed. Yours is the responsibility for the unnecessary bloodshed which will result if you choose the first way. Otherwise you must send an envoy under the protection of a white flag over to the British lines. You have 24 hours in which to decide.

The same information was conveyed to the German Commander by telephone. But there was no German in the city of sufficient moral stature to face the inevitable. Responsibility for the sufferings of the civil population in Bremen during the next six days rests on German shoulders.

Bremen finally fell on 27 April to assault by the 43rd Wessex and 52nd Lowland Divisions north of the Weser and the 3rd Division attacking from the south.

In the falling rain the city presented a sense of sordid horror. Great piles of rubble blocked the streets, the twisted lamp standards silhouetted grotesquely against the sky, the stench of buildings still burning offended the nostrils and the open sewers stank to heaven. The people were broken-spirited and listless — many of them were literally green in colour for the ventilation in the big air-raid bunkers had broken down and the sanitary arrangements inside had collapsed. They were docile, bewildered and hopeless. By early afternoon, a Military

Government Detachment had established itself in each of the four police areas with a headquarters in the Polizei Presidium. The fighting had released thousands of slave labourers from Eastern Europe and the USSR who broke loose and fell without restraint on the large stores of wines and spirits in the city. Some even drank the commercial spirit in the docks. Fighting, rape and murder broke out and the troops had to intervene to protect the civil population. None of them were sorry, when they had restored order, to move out from this charnel-house which had once been a gracious city into the clean air of the Cuxhaven peninsula.

To enable 21st Army Group to advance to the Baltic and thus cut off Schleswig-Holstein and Denmark and seize the Kiel Canal and the North-West German ports, Eisenhower gave Montgomery the assistance of XVIII Airborne Corps of three divisions. Montgomery accordingly ordered them to protect the right flank of 2nd Army beyond the Elbe as far as Wismar on the Baltic, VIII Corps was given the task of establishing a bridgehead across the Elbe about Lauenburg and then breaking out north to seize Lubeck: XII Corps following on their tail was to pass through the bridgehead and swing west to mask Hamburg preparatory to an assault on the city. Accordingly at 2 o'clock on the morning of 29 April 15th Scottish Division and 1st Commando Brigade under cover of a formidable bombardment crossed the river in amphibians supported by dd tanks. It was their third crossing of a major river in the campaign. German resistance was perfunctory and feeble. During the day the RAF shot down 13 enemy aircraft. Next morning further south 82nd Airborne Division forced the crossing in assault boats at Bleckede with little loss. On 1 and 2 May both Corps made rapid progress. On the left 11th Armoured Division with 5th Division on its right covered the distance to Lubeck in two days. On the afternoon of 2 May, the 2nd Fife and Forfar Yeomanry carrying the 1st Cheshire Regiment entered the town without opposition. On the same day, the British 6th Airborne Division of XVIII Airborne Corps, unhindered by opposition, reached Wismar on the Baltic coast, thus severing Army Group Vistula's line of escape from the advancing Russians. A few hours later Russian tanks appeared and made contact with our troops.

Meanwhile part of XII Corps had passed through VIII Corps' bridgehead at Lauenburg directed on Hamburg. Fortunately for all concerned actual attack as at Bremen proved unnecessary. On 29 April a deputation from Major-General Wolz, the German Commander in Hamburg, arrived in the lines of 7th Armoured Division with a request that the hospital at Hamburg should be spared artillery fire. These negotiations developed into proposals for the surrender of the city itself — a course which the civilian member of the deputation, the Manager of the Phoenix Rubber Works, had the moral courage to support. He undertook to take a message to Major-General Wolz. It read:

TO: Major-General Wolz,
Kampfkommandant, Hamburg

Herr General,

1. The Reichsführer SS has already made an offer of unconditional surrender to the Western Powers. This offer was made through Count Bernadotte in Stockholm.

2. Before attacking Bremen we demanded the surrender of the City. As this offer was refused, we had no alternative but to attack.

with artillery and air support. Bremen fell in 24 hours but not without much unnecessary bloodshed.

3. In the name of humanity, Herr General, we demand the surrender of Hamburg. For you as a soldier there can be no

dishonour in following the example of famous generals such as Gen. D.Pz. Josef Harpe, GOC Fifth Panzer Army, Gen. Fritz Bayerlein, GOC LIII Corps and many others who have surrendered themselves and their comrades. From the political point of view, there can surely be no reflection on you if you follow the example of the Reichsführer SS.

4. We therefore ask you, Herr General, to send into our lines an officer empowered to negotiate the surrender. Our forward troops have been warned to expect his arrival and not to shoot at him. He will be treated according to the Geneva Convention, and returned after the parley to his own lines.

5. The population of Hamburg will not easily forget its first large-scale raid by over one thousand heavy bombers. We now dispose of a bomber force five to ten times greater numerically and operating from nearby airfields. After the war, the German people must be fed: the more Hamburg's dock installations are damaged, the greater are the chances of famine in Germany.

6. If this offer is refused, we shall have no alternative but to attack Hamburg with all the forces at our disposal.

On the evening of 1 May Hamburg Radio announced the death of Hitler and the accession of Admiral Dönitz to the solemn setting of music from Wagner and Bruckner's Seventh Symphony. News of the fall of Berlin to the Russians followed. That same night Major-General Wolz sent his reply:

Major-General L. O. Lyne,
Commander of the Allied Troops, Hamburg
1 May 1945

Herr General:

The thoughts for which you have found so lucid an expression in your letter of 29 April 1945, have been considered by myself and by countless other responsible

Commanders; not unnaturally, considering the present military and political situation.

The eventual surrender of Hamburg would have far-reaching military and political consequences for the whole of that part of Northern Germany that is not yet occupied and for Denmark. For this reason, the orders given to me to hold Hamburg to the last man can be seen to have a clear justification. But in spite of this I am prepared, together with an authorised representative of Reichsstatthalter and Gauleiter Kaufmann, to discuss with a representative empowered by GOC Second British Army to make decisions on military and political matters, the eventual surrender of Hamburg and the far-reaching consequences arising therefrom.

May I ask you to inform the GOC Second British Army of these proposals and to request that a time and place for discussion be fixed.

Wolz,
Major-General

For once the Germans in their opening paragraph equalled the British in the art of understatement. It is refreshing to record the survival of at least an element of the courtesy customary between opposing generals in similar circumstances in the more civilised atmosphere of the eighteenth century before the French Revolution. The staff officer bringing this message was informed that the General Officer Commanding the British 7th Armoured Division would see General Wolz the following night if he came to offer unconditional surrender. According to the history of the 7th Armoured Division the German staff officer on his way back to his own lines asked if he might speak to Brigadier Spurling alone. 'As soldier to soldier', he said, 'I ask your advice whether I and the staff ought to commit suicide on our return.' The Brigadier replied: 'That's entirely up to you.' A colonel pointed to the scarf covering the interpreter's eyes. 'Isn't that a Brasenose scarf?' 'No, Christ Church', replied the captain, 'I was there studying the House of Lords.'

Late on the night of 2 May, Major-General Wolz arrived in person. His opening words were: 'The principal point is the actual time General Lyne wishes to enter Hamburg.'

Agreement was speedily reached to hand over the city on the afternoon of 3 May. Furthermore it was now ascertained that Wolz had far wider powers, no less than to facilitate the onward move of a delegation from Admiral Dönitz under Admiral von Friedburg to Field-Marshal Montgomery's headquarters to negotiate the surrender of all North Germany and to press for special consideration for refugees and troops in flight from the Russians. This delegation passed through *en route* to Luneburg Heath on the morning of 3 May. The occupation of Hamburg itself by 7th Armoured Division and the 53rd Welsh Division duly proceeded in an atmosphere of military efficiency and rectitude on the part of all concerned. The Hamburg Police lined the route as far ahead as the eye could see as the British troops entered. They stood at regular intervals about 100 yards apart — erect and white-coated, silhouetted against the neatly stacked piles of rubble which marked all the Allied bombing had left of a large part of the city. As the leading vehicle of a column drew level each policeman came smartly to attention and remained at the salute until the whole of the column had passed towards the city centre.

What happened on Luneburg Heath is well known. At 1830 hours on 4 May all German armed forces in Holland and in North-West Germany, including all islands, surrendered to Montgomery with effect from 0800 hours British Summer Time on Saturday 5 May — unconditionally. Para. 3 of the

Instrument of Surrender contained a characteristic phrase not unfamiliar to his own soldiers: 'The German Command to carry out at once, *without argument or comment* all further orders that will be issued by the Allied Commanders on any subject.' As in all Montgomery's transactions all concerned were left in no doubt as to what was expected of them.

No inkling of the negotiations for surrender had reached the forward troops during the morning and afternoon of 4 May. It is true that they had heard from the BBC of the fall of Hamburg and Berlin and the capitulation of two German Armies in Italy. At 8.40 p.m. the BBC beat the Corps Commanders to the post by announcing the surrender. Official confirmation followed soon afterwards: 'Germans surrendered unconditionally at 1820 hours. Hostilities on all Second Army Fronts will cease at 0800 hrs tomorrow 5 May. No repeat No advance beyond present front line without further orders from me.'

The strain and fatigue of 11 months' almost ceaseless fighting had been such that the news when it came was almost an anti-climax. It had been the same in the front line in the falling rain on the morning of 11 November 1918. The history of the Guards Armoured Division merely records that the event did not pass unnoticed. The 4th/7th Royal Dragoon Guards found the news when received in black and white hard to believe. The 4th and 7th Somerset Light Infantry noted no visible excitement. In 1st Canadian Army the unit diaries make it clear that there were no cheers and few signs of emotion. The truth is that at this turning point in their lives the infantry, tanks, engineers and artillery were conscious of the cost. The infantry casualties since D-Day, although light in comparison with those of World War One, had reached a total of between one-and-a-half and twice the official strength of battalions — in other words between 150 and 200 per cent.

Once authorised by higher authority in both opposing armies the arrangements made for surrender went through with military precision. The 7th Parachute Division in the Cuxhaven peninsula refused to capitulate to any troops other than Guards Armoured Division with whom they had been continuously in action in the Reichswald and all the way from the Rhine. The actual surrender was carried out meticulously and with good discipline and mutual respect on both sides. 15th Panzer Grenadier Division, truculent to the last, stressed their long and honourable record in war with the British Army, especially 51st Highland Division, since the days of Alamein. They pressed their claim to surrender as a formation distinct from the miscellaneous troops of Corps Ems in the area whom they regarded with justification as a lower form of military life than themselves and for their officers to be allowed to retain their revolvers. They also volunteered their services within Germany on police duties. Here it was found possible to come to an arrangement whereby they were disarmed last of all. Anyhow they had virtually qualified if not for some form of affiliation with the British Army at least for some form of association in view of their considerable contribution to its history. Thus was settled in an atmosphere of frigid professional respect a score dating from 23 October 1942.

Immediately after the surrender Montgomery, as Caesar had been wont to do, toured his Army and addressed his victorious troops. The Western Allies, he said, had won for four main reasons: the enemy's mistakes, Allied air dominance, Anglo-American cooperation and the fighting qualities of the British, Canadian and American soldiers. These are still valid.

Although it can now be seen in the late sixties that Hitler, having miscalculated the military strength of the USSR, was probably doomed from the moment the United States entered the war, his errors in the last six months of the campaign in North-West Europe were those to be expected from the greatest of all barrack-room lawyers of all time. He had ignored the advice of what remained of the Great General Staff and concentrated control of operations in his own incompetent hands. In the Ardennes, he had expended more of Germany's strength than she could afford — hence the disasters of January on the Eastern front. In the Reichswald he had hung on too long, with an excessively high proportion of his forces, with the result that he not only created the opportunity for 1st and 3rd United States Armies to break through to the Rhine, and then cross at Remagen and Oppenheim, but also found himself incapable of defending the line of the river in the vital northern sector. Throughout he had perpetrated the classical errors of over-dispersion and inflexible defence virtually to the point of insanity.

The more popular section of the press at the time, both British and American, tended to portray the Allied statesmen as if they were the leading actors in some gigantic play and the generals like jockeys engaged in a nightmare international steeplechase. Montgomery with his flair for personal publicity, his gift of concise and acid expression and built-in conviction that he had been selected by the Almighty to destroy Hitler and all he stood for, was the answer to the journalists' proverbial prayer. In consequence, Anglo-American clashes of opinion and personality during the campaign were exaggerated then and have been since. Eisenhower may not have been a strategist of genius; nonetheless he will go down to history as one of the most diplomatic and personally likeable commanders of all time. In the last resort, command in an alliance has to be by consent. Eisenhower did achieve Allied unity of action: only he of the American commanders available could have stood up to the blandishments of Churchill and the arguments of Alanbrooke and Montgomery and at the same time have retained the respect and affection of the British. Above all Eisenhower had common sense and charm. It is impossible to imagine any other great general devoting two pages of his last book to his own recipe for vegetable soup: 'The things I like to put into my soup are about as follows: 1 quart canned tomatoes, ½ cup peas or cut green beans, 2 potatoes diced, 3 branches celery, 1 large sliced onion, 3 large carrots diced, 1 turnip diced, ½ cup canned corn, 1 handful raw cabbage chopped.' No wonder the citizens of London in particular took him to their hearts and gave him the greatest honour within their power to confer — the Freedom of the City whose courage and constancy in the dark days of 1940 had saved the Western World from tyranny.

In this book the spotlight of personal recollection and subsequent study has been turned on one corner only of the vast canvas of the cataclysm which in the Spring of 1945 engulfed the German armies. If the British and Canadian effort is to be seen in true historical perspective it must be borne in mind that, at the time of the final surrender, Eisenhower had under his command 61 American divisions (that is, over three million men), the largest army ever entrusted to a single general in the whole history of the United States as against the combined British and Canadian contribution of 18 divisions. Practically the whole of the French army in the south and to some extent the British was dependent for supplies on American aid. In these operations weapon development had reached a stage in which troops in carefully prepared defences had an immense advantage over their exposed opponents. From late September onwards most of the Siegfried Line and certainly the toughest part of it, faced the Americans alone: it was in fact as formidable as the Barrier Fortresses of Marlborough's day and the Lines of Torres Vedras had been in their time — a system designed with great tactical engineering skill embodying artfully laid and elaborate minefields, deep anti-tank ditches, hidden concrete pillboxes and machine-gun nests exploiting every available natural obstacle to the full, often several miles in depth and linked together by a superb system of communications. Even when held by second-class defenders it presented terrifying and baffling problems to the attackers. That this Devil's Garden should have been penetrated and its garrisons destroyed is evidence enough of the American achievement in the last six months of the war in Europe.

Within the scope of this book it has not been possible to deal in any detail with the vicious fighting by 1st United States Army in October 1944 leading to the fall of Aachen, with Patton's Homeric struggle for Metz and with Devers' battles in the Vosges ending in the restoration of Strasbourg to France. The exploits of 1st and 3rd United States Armies in the Ardennes are the subject of many books. Bradley's triumphant advance to the Rhine and crossing at Remagen in early March and the concurrent destruction of the German 7th and 1st Armies by Patton and Patch west of the Rhine were outstanding achievements. Each of these large-scale operations merits a book on its own: fortunately the American official histories now available satisfy every standard of military scholarship and human appeal except portability. When Jodl signed the instrument of surrender at Eisenhower's headquarters at Rheims at 2.41 p.m. on 7 May the American

Army alone presented the most powerful military machine ever assembled in Europe.

The final Russian operations started on 16 April on the Oder and the Neisse were on an equally gigantic scale. For the capture of Berlin Stalin concentrated in Zhukov's and Konev's Army Groups no less than two and a half million men, 41,000 guns, 6,000 tanks and self-propelled guns against Heinrici's Army Group Vistula, estimated at one million strong. On the actual fronts of attack the Russians enjoyed a superiority of between 3 to 1 and 5 to 1 in men, tanks and guns. In the initial break-in they are said to have used one gun to every 13 feet of front. Berlin itself was finally encircled by concentric attacks by the two Army Groups on 25 April: all German resistance was finally stamped out in a stupendous and macabre mopping-up operation ending on 2 May. It is with these American and Russian achievements that the British effort must stand comparison: nevertheless it can do so without loss of prestige or pride bearing in mind the fact that the British were simultaneously maintaining Alexander's Army Group in Italy and Slim's in Burma and that American and Russian resources in manpower were in each case five times as great as theirs.

This is no place to enter into the complexities of strategic thought and discuss how far the strategic air offensive fitted into the grand strategy of the war, whether the Air Marshals got out of political control, whether air support on a greater scale should have been given to the other two Services, especially the Navy, and whether area bombing was ever morally justified. After Arnhem however it does seem that there might have been a greater concentration on destroying the German oil resources in the last four months of 1944. The bombing of Dresden to help the Russians was repugnant to many professional soldiers after they had witnessed the havoc wrought by the Allied Air Forces in Bremen and Hamburg. In the event, the bombing of Cleve hampered rather than aided the advance of 1st Canadian Army. A high proportion of the forward troops suffered at one time or another from the attentions of their own Typhoons: divisional and brigade order groups seem to have been favourite targets. In both Services sheer ignorance of each other's characteristics and limitations was abysmal: a good deal of time which the soldiers could ill afford was taken up in explaining to RAF officers sent forward with wireless sets the difference between an infantry division and an infantry section and similar elementary facts of Army life. The Army-Air bureaucracy, intervening between the front-line soldier and the pilot, was at times frustrating — notably in the Walcheren operations. More generous bomber support here would have reduced the cost in Canadian and British life. Nonetheless the virtually complete command of the air achieved by the courage and skill of the Allied bomber and fighter pilots was a decisive factor in the Allied victory. Above all it gave the Armies freedom to move and fight virtually immune from air attack both on the ground and in the air. Although the Air Arm on the battlefield itself had little effect on the German soldier's determination to fight on, the attacks on his oil resources and his transportation system reduced the German Higher Command and its supply system to impotence.

Had this book been written immediately after the war, it would have been sufficient to mention Montgomery's final factor, the fighting qualities of the British, Canadian and American soldier, and leave it at that. The Allies had a better cause, a better command system, complete command of the air and sea on a scale never likely to be achieved again, and vastly superior material resources to the Germans. Nevertheless to ensure victory it was still necessary for the infantry and tanks to close with the German Armies and fight it out to a finish. There is some truth in the statement that he who has not fought the Germans does not know what war is. They remained formidable until driven back across the Rhine. During the winter battles many of their formations displayed much of the skill, drive, flexibility and endurance which had taken their armies to the gates of Moscow and Leningrad, to the Crimea and to Alamein. In the end, in a world remote from the higher headquarters, they were outfought on the Western front by troops, British, Canadian and American, as well-trained, as well-led and as tough as themselves. It is still true, and likely to remain true, that without aggressive and skilled assault troops, firmly disciplined and ready if necessary to sacrifice their lives for a cause in which they profoundly believe, indifferent to hardship and danger, there can be no decisive victory.

APPENDIX: OUTLINE ORGANISATION OF BRITISH AND GERMAN DIVISIONS

British

Armoured Divisions

One armoured brigade of three armoured regiments and one infantry battalion

One infantry brigade of three battalions

Two field regiments RA

One anti-tank regiment

   Plus Royal Engineers, Signals and Services

Tanks were either Shermans (30 tons), Churchills (40 tons) or Comets

The armoured divisions were: Guards; 7th, 11th, 79th, 4th Canadian; and 1st Polish

Infantry Divisions

Three infantry brigades of three battalions each

One reconnaissance regiment

One machine-gun battalion

Three field regiments RA

One anti-tank regiment RA

One light aa regiment RA

   Plus Royal Engineers, Signals and Services

Total vehicles — about 3,100

The infantry divisions were: 1st Airborne; 3rd, 5th, 6th Airborne; 15th Scottish; 43rd Wessex; 49th West Riding; 50th Northumbrian; 51st Highland; 52nd Lowland; 53rd Welsh; 1st, 2nd and 3rd Canadian

Specialised Allied Equipment of 79th Armoured Division

DD tanks — amphibious tanks

AVREs — specialised vehicles for dealing with various types of defences, including flame-throwers called Crocodiles

Crabs for exploding minefields

CDL armoured searchlights — for blinding the defence

Buffaloes — tracked amphibians

Flails — mine-clearing devices

German

Infantry Divisions

Three infantry regiments of two battalions each — approximately 10,000 to 12,000

Panzer Grenadier Divisions

Two motorised infantry regiments of two battalions each

One motorised artillery regiment — approximately 14,000

Panzer Divisions

Two Panzergrenadier regiments

One tank regiment

One Panzer artillery regiment

   Plus supporting troops — approximately 14,000

Parachute Divisions (Air Force)

   As for infantry divisions with an authorised strength of 16,000 and a larger allotment of automatic weapons

Volksgrenadier divisions

   Formations of about 10,000 organised in September 1944 and strong in automatic weapons

There was a sharp distinction between the ordinary Army formations (Wehrmacht) and the Schutzstaffel formations which bore the prefix SS. These were originally restricted to

Nazi Party members and were considerably stronger in numbers and firepower than the Wehrmacht formations

Weapons

The outstanding weapons were:

Tanks: Tiger 1st Series — 58 tons

　　Tiger 2nd Series — 70 tons. With 88-mm. gun

　　Panther — 45 tons. With 75-mm. gun

Mortars — Nebelwerfer (six-barrelled)

Spandau — general purpose machine-gun

Schmeizer — sub-machine-gun

Artillery — 88-mm. gun, general purpose field, anti-tank and light AA

BIBLIOGRAPHY

Ahrenfeldt, R. H., *Psychiatry in the British Army in the Second World War*, Routledge and Kegan Paul, 1958

A Short History of the 7th Armoured Division, Privately, 1946

Barclay, C. N., *The History of the Duke of Wellingtons Regiment*, Clowes, 1953

Barclay, C. N., *History of the 53rd (Welsh) Division in the Second World War*, Clowes, 1956

Blake, G., *Mountain and Flood*, Jackson, Son and Co., 1950

Bryant, Sir A., *Triumph in the West*, Collins, 1959

Cole, H. M., *The Ardennes Battle of the Bulge*, Department of the Army, Washington DC, 1965

Collier, B., *A Short History of the Second World War*, Collins, 1967

De Guingand, Sir F., *Operation Victory*, Hodder and Stoughton, 1947

Donnison, E. S. V., *Civil Affairs and Military Government in North West Europe 1944-45*, HMSO, 1961

Eisenhower, D. D., *Crusade in Europe*, Heinemann, 1948

Eisenhower, D. D., *At Ease*, Hale, 1968

Esposito, V. J., *The West Point Atlas of American Wars*, Vol. 2, Praeger, 1959

Essame, H., *The 43rd Wessex Division at War*, Clowes, 1952

Essame, H., and Belfield, E. M. G., *The North West Europe Campaign 1944-45*, Gale and Polden, 1962

Fergusson, B., *The Watery Maze*, Collins, 1961

Fuller, J. F. C., *Decisive Battles of the Western World*, Vol. 3, Eyre and Spottiswoode, 1956

Gill, R., and Groves, J., *Club Route in Europe*, Privately, 1945

Godfrey, E. G. *History of the Duke of Cornwall's Light Infantry, 1939-45*, Privately, 1966

Greenfield, K. R., *Command Decisions*, Methuen, 1960

Hanson, B., *Battles Lost and Won*, Hodder and Stoughton, 1966

History of the East Lancashire Regiment 1939-45, Rawson and Co. Ltd., 1953

History of the 4th Battalion Somerset Light Infantry, Privately, 1946

Horrocks, Sir B., *A Full Life*, Collins, 1960

Incidents with the 7th Battalion Somerset Light Infantry, Privately, 1945

Liddell-Hart, Sir B., *Strategy: The Indirect Approach*, Faber and Faber, 1967

Macdonald, C. B., *The Siegfried Line Campaign*, Department of the Army, Washington dc, 1963

Meredith, J. L. J., *The Story of the 7th Battalion Somerset Light Infantry*, Privately, 1945

Minott, R. C., *The Fortress that Never Was*, Longmans, 1965

Montgomery, Viscount, *Normandy to the Baltic*, Hutchinson, 1946

Montgomery, Viscount, *Memoirs*, Collins, 1958

Montgomery, Viscount, *A History of Warfare*, Collins, 1968

Nobecourt, J., *Hitler's Last Gamble*, Chatto and Windus, 1967

North, J. W., *North West Europe 1944-45*, HMSO, 1953

Parham, H. J., and Belfield, E. M. G., *Unarmed into Battle*, Warren and Sons, 1956

Record of a Reconnaissance Regiment, White Swan Press, Bristol, 1949

Rosse, Captain the Earl of, and Hill, E. R., *The Story of the Guards Armoured Division 1941-45*, Bles, 1956

Stacey, C. P., *The Canadian Army 1939-45*, Department of Defence, Ottawa, 1948

Stacey, C. P., *The Victory Campaign*, The Queen's Printer, Ottawa, 1960

Salmond, J. B., *The History of the 51st Highland Division*, Blackwood, 1953

Saunders, H. St G., *The Red Beret*, Joseph, 1950

Saunders, H. St G., *The Royal Air Force 1939-45*, Vol. 3, HMSO, 1961

Stirling, J. D. P., *The First and the Last*, Art and Educational Publishers, 1946

Tedder, Lord, *With Prejudice*, Cassell, 1966

Vandeleur, J. O. E., *A Soldier's Story*, Gale and Polden, 1967

Wellard, J., *The Man in the Helmet*, Eyre and Spottiswoode, 1947

Westphal, S., *The Fatal Decisions*, Joseph, 1956

Wilmot, C., *The Struggle for Europe*, Collins, 1952

ACKNOWLEDGMENT

The author and publishers wish to acknowledge their debt to the sources from which passages have been reproduced, notably Rosse and Hill, *The Story of the Guards Armoured Division, 1941-45*; the US Official History, *The Siegfried Line Campaign*; Godfrey, *The History of the* DCLI, *1941-45*; Grant Peterkin, *So Few Got Through*; and K. S. Giniger of New York for permission to reproduce part of an article by Major-General Strong which appeared in the *Sunday Telegraph* on 17 December 1967.

A NOTE TO THE READER

If you have enjoyed this book enough to leave a review on **Amazon** and **Goodreads**, then we would be truly grateful.
Sapere Books

Sapere Books is an exciting new publisher of brilliant fiction and popular history.

To find out more about our latest releases and our monthly bargain books visit our website:
saperebooks.com

Printed in Great Britain
by Amazon

49243904R00155